Medicine:

In *Search of a Soul*

The Healing Prescription

Pamela J. Maraldo, PhD

BALBOA.
PRESS

A DIVISION OF HAY HOUSE

Balboa Press books may be ordered through booksellers or by contacting:

Balboa Press
A Division of Hay House
1663 Liberty Drive
Bloomington, IN 47403
www.balboapress.com
1 (877) 407-4847

Print information available on the last page.

Library of Congress Control Number: 2016914801

ISBN: 978-1-5043-6582-6 (sc)
ISBN: 978-1-5043-6583-3 (hc)
ISBN: 978-1-5043-6606-9 (e)

Balboa Press rev. date: 08/16/2017

TABLE OF CONTENTS

ACKNOWLEDGMENTS

A famous philosopher once said, "In life, do that which you cannot, not do." That's what this book was for me. Many people gave incredibly helpful insights and i would like to thank them. Most of all, my friend Elaine Garzarelli, who took extraordinary care in reviewing the manuscript, and giving constant insights, feedback and encouragement.

Also extremely helpful were my sister, Donna, Scott Erikson, Dianne Osgood, and Sue Schoenberg.

Thank you all from the bottom of my heart, and last but not least, my deepest gratitude to Bill Bauman, without whom I would never have had the awareness or the inspiration a work like this entails.

Pam Maraldo

MASTERY

PART ONE

Learning the pathways to healing: how mastering your thoughts, emotions and beliefs will allow higher frequency healing energies to flow through you; listening to your soul's direction and how it speaks to you through illness.

I

MEETING THE MASTER

The sturdy fair-haired man stood on the red mountains looking over the valley. *The soul of this is taking shape*, he thought. He didn't move. He was deep in thought. Then he heard the bell ring. *Ding ... ding ... ding ...* It was time to get started. "All here?" he bellowed.

"We're ready to go," his assistant called out. Inside, everybody was buzzing. An array of people were perched in their seats—many highly educated with mystical leanings—from unexpected places like the State Department, Health and Human Services, the FDA, and other branches of government, in addition to leadership positions in the ranks of corporate America. Some were doctors. Some were nurses.

The gathering was on mastery. *Human* mastery. The participants had one thing in common: they wanted help in fulfilling their highest destinies. Anxiously awaiting their first foray into the depths of the energy this man was radiating, they sat in anticipation. Spiritual masters radiate energy. When they enter the room, the room shifts to a higher place. The presence of the Master draws out darkness and almost immediately opens the way to spontaneous feelings of joy. This is a powerful, powerful person.

In this age of high-minded science and technology, we have been so convinced of the importance of the intellect and the supremacy of reason that any talk of the soul or any power that lies beyond the mind seems borderline crazy—until you experience it. Nobody in the group could've anticipated the lightness, the joy, the absolute giddiness that they were now feeling. Destiny had ordained their meeting with this man.

More and more highly educated prominent scientists are telling about similar experiences. They dare to stand out in a world of scientific conformity. As beyond the mind experiences transformed them, their lives would never be the same again. Among them are the following: Edgar Mitchell, PhD, Apollo astronaut, and the sixth man ever to walk on the moon; David Hawkins, MD, PhD, a psychiatrist and prolific author who became enlightened through a near-death experience; Herbert Benson, MD, founder of the Harvard Mind-Body Institute; Eben Alexander, MD, the neurologist who wrote about his near-death experience in *Proof of Heaven*; Greg Bradden, PhD, an engineer who worked as a scientist and an engineer at Martin Marietta and Cisco Systems and authored *The Divine Matrix*; Bruce Lipton, PhD, cellular biologist and former professor of medicine at Stanford and author of *The Biology of Belief*; my own teacher, psychologist Bill Bauman, PhD, author of *Soul Vision*.

Then there are physicists such as Amit Gotswami, PhD, who wrote *The Self Aware Universe: How Consciousness Creates the Material World*; and physicist Lester Levinson, who wrote *No Attachments, No Aversions*. Lester was sent home after a near-fatal heart attack, on the verge of suicide because of the severe restrictions his illness placed on his life— no stairs, no lifting groceries, no sex—yet he was completely healed.

These scientists and many others sparked a new pinnacle of understanding the secrets of the universe and realms beyond the mind. Their stories enthrall us. The best part? They speak from personal experience. Their experiences have opened up new territory that science has dared not tread in the past. Scientific discoveries leap from their expansions in consciousness, from the spiritual realms beyond the mind.

I was a member of the Mastery Group. Mastery meant a series of seminars designed to lift us up; to teach us to master the human experience by getting to know our true nature, our souls. That includes healing, the province of the soul. I myself would have laughed hysterically had someone told me ten years ago that I would not only experience that realm but also write a book about it. Yet I did have many peak experiences. One in particular, a healing experience, led me on a search to find the underlying cause of what was happening. That experience led to writing this book.

Everything is purposeful. My mind, steeped in the social sciences, became like a big searchlight looking for answers everywhere. I needed to make sense of what had happened. The amazing thing: repeatedly, I saw that science is headed in the direction of a world once reserved for mystics—people who are *otherworldly*. But let me step back for a moment and tell the story of how it all began.

One Saturday night I climbed into the bed of my Manhattan apartment after coming home late from dinner and a show. As I lay awake taking inventory of my day, I began to feel a strange sensation in my head—first a pressure on the top-right side and then a soft tingling energy burst into my awareness. Oozing over me, starting at my head and working its way down, it eventually cradled me. Like many, I was in the habit of reviewing the day's events before I drifted off to sleep. Mentally ticking things off, my to-do list started to take shape for the next day.

But of all the niggling things that would have normally created waves of fear and anxiety—a deadline coming up, a project I didn't have time to get to, a phone call I forgot to make—none of it fazed me. The oozy energy lifted me above those mundane worries. In the wake of my usual fretting, a warm blanket of energy settled in like a presence, enveloping me and making me feel blissful, protected, and at peace.

My thoughts flashed back to a conversation with my younger sister earlier in the week. "Pammie, Jodi and I are going to Baltimore this coming weekend to see a man that they say is a guru. But he's not Indian. He's American and has a PhD. Do you want to come with us?"

Donna mentioned the PhD knowing I would be skeptical of anybody referred to as a "guru." But I had plans for the weekend. "Thanks anyway, Sissy," as I called her. "I would love to, but I'll be out of town."

To which she quickly offered, "It's okay. We'll *invite you in.*"

Invite me in? Was she kidding? Was this a joke or had my sister gone off the deep end? Meanwhile, back in my bed, afraid the blanket of delicious energy would leave, I filed the conversation away, settled in to enjoy my dreamy state, and drifted off to sleep.

Late Monday afternoon she called me. "The weekend was amazing. His [Bill's] energy is so powerful that a lot of people just fall asleep. But most feel elated, incredibly happy and full of zest. Kind of like you have a new lease on life." She went on and on, with more and more enthusiasm. The weekend sounded off the charts. She loved this new guru. Bill Bauman was his name. She described a variety of participants in whom transformations had taken place. "Bill is the real deal," she concluded, meaning she could tell that he was enlightened.[1]

When she finished, I told her about my Saturday night experience with the energy. I reluctantly posed my question: "Do you think there might be any connection to your weekend with the guru?"

"I'm quite sure there is," she shot back confidently, emphatically. Clearly sensing my ongoing skepticism, she added, "Don't take my word for it. He's going to be in New York in a few weeks. See for yourself."

"Maybe I will," I muttered halfheartedly. I had been a "seeker," someone looking for answers to all the big questions in life, and I was quite proud of my own intellectual abilities at the time. I had a PhD myself, and I did a lot of public speaking on the mind-body-spirit connection, so I wasn't highly motivated to go hear someone else speak on subjects I thought I knew about.

I was in for the surprise of a lifetime. As things transpired, on the weekend of Bill Bauman's seminar in New York City, I had absolutely no plans. I was completely free. This in itself was highly unusual, and I wondered if the universe might be orchestrating this whole thing. So I went.

The weekend was transformative. I saw for myself that Bill Bauman seemed to be authentic, indeed, the "real deal," as my sister had said. How could I tell? He emits an energy that is palpable and has a kind of magical effect. It's the way you feel when you're floating on nitrous oxide at the dentist, only you're not! All weekend, in this man's presence, I felt the same energy I felt that Saturday night pouring into me, through me. Even though I didn't understand what was happening, I felt giddy, happy, and alive, as well as confident and enthusiastic about everything. Answers to questions that had been gnawing at me came spontaneously.

I immediately made a decision to study with Bill. I wanted more. I wanted to bathe in this energy, this *juice*, as we playfully referred to it,

---

[1]   Enlightenment is a state of felt oneness with all that is.

permanently. I wanted to learn more about the energy, the light, that this very kind, gentle, and loving man was emitting. Being in the presence of this awakened man felt fabulous—a feeling bordering on ecstasy. But then when you go back to your own day-to-day surroundings, the helium escapes from the balloon. Gradually, the breezy, happy feelings give way to punctuated periods of all-too-familiar annoyances and anxieties coming to the surface to be released. It is a time of expansion and contraction as you grow and then shrink back to face the core issues that are still unresolved and holding you back. Your higher self designs your circumstances so that you can face them and finally be completely free of them.

One summer for the Mastery Class, Bill held a weekend retreat in Dallas, Texas. Huge evergreens, spacious grounds, and sprawling buildings at the University of Texas created a welcoming enough space for us, but the steamy heat hanging from the trees dampened my enthusiasm. Besides feeling as if I were in a sauna, I was limping. Nursing a painful knee injury from slipping in the New York subway on a rainy day, combined with July heat and humidity, really put a damper on the whole thing.

However, I felt obligated. I had made a commitment to attend. Before long, it became clear to me that I made the right decision. Bill was, as usual, spectacular. As an enlightened soul, the energy that streamed out of him was particularly radiant that weekend. Determined to have its way with us, the energy traveled through each participant in different ways. It was overwhelming for some, and they nodded off to sleep as if they had taken a sedative. It ripped through the mentally resistant energy centers of others. Visceral reactions, like gastrointestinal upsets or backaches, often resulted. As the energy charged through their systems, aiming to dissolve any areas of resistance, their bodies reacted.

Eventually, everybody went through a "dark night of the soul." To achieve mastery, you have to confront your demons: the demons that created the energetic blockages in the first place.

The goal: clearing the unconscious. Clearing cellular debris that accumulates over a long time paves the way for higher energy frequencies to flow through. Old debris is loosened and released—an apparent prerequisite to becoming "lighter" and relieved of the energies of old repressed emotions. The extremely high frequency light he emitted accomplished all of this. Sometimes Bill referred to himself as a "light technician" and what he does as "surgery," metaphors that were somewhat tongue in cheek. However, in less material ways, on an energetic level, these terms were quite apropos, as we would come to learn.

On the first day of the Dallas seminar, limping into Bill's opening session, I sat a few rows from the front of the room. He talked about things he usually talked about, ranging from the nature of the light that we are all made of to some of the recent discoveries in quantum physics. One of his favorite things to talk about was that we are mostly composed of empty space (sort of—it's really not empty but teeming with energy you can't see). We are free to shape the space as we choose.

As I was listening intently to Bill continue speaking about our being interconnected in that space, like lattices of subatomic particles that reach across unlimited distances, something magical was happening. When I got up from my chair at the end of the session to walk out, I immediately noticed that there was no more pain in my knee. No pain at all. No limp. My knee felt completely normal. *It was healed.*

Healed on the spot! *How in the world did it happen?* It left a powerful impression on me. I was driven to understand it and find out what had happened. Educated as a nurse with a PhD and *very* familiar with all the procedures and paraphernalia that would normally be required to heal my knee, I wanted to understand the science behind what seemed to be a miracle. I hadn't prayed to be healed. I hadn't asked Bill to heal me. In fact, having my knee healed was the furthest thing from my mind when I entered the session. Yet I knew what I knew. When I walked in, I was limping. When I walked out, I wasn't. I was walking straight, and my knee no longer hurt. As I reflected on what happened, I remembered hearing—though I hadn't paid much attention to it at the time—that Bill had healed others. Now I wanted to know all the details. Exactly how did he do it?

THE LIGHT THAT HEALS

It didn't take long to discover the source of the healing. A power we all have in the form of high-frequency energies—light, really—does the healing. Everything is light. But way more light than usual, high-frequency light that we can feel but cannot see, emanated from Bill. Yet he kept telling us that it was something present in every one of us. Eastern teachings say that the light of our souls becomes more and more pronounced, even visible to some, as we are cleansed of old energetic layers of fears, anger, doubt, and guilt. Through light, purification and healing can be achieved. When we repress emotions we don't want to feel, they weigh our cells down with their heaviness. The more we stuff them, the more they eclipse the light. If we don't release them, they weigh us down more and more. They gradually diminish our light. They can also create illness.

As these layers are shed, more and more light seeps in and more healing occurs. Many have written about their healing as they release repressed negative emotions. Physicist Lester Levinson's autobiographical account *No Attachments, No Aversions* is an extraordinary story of healing. Sent home by his physician after a severe heart attack, he verbally attacked the physician for saving his life. Facing life as a cardiac cripple, he thought, *I would rather be dead.* On the verge of suicide, he decided to take inventory of his life before he killed himself. Why not take a little time to think about what it all means, what happiness is all about?

First he poured over all the books an educated man like himself had accumulated. One by one, he tossed them aside, realizing they had no light whatsoever to shed on what makes someone happy. He spent several months taking inventory of when he was happiest. As he thought about past love relationships, successes, and failures, he experienced all the emotions he had repressed over a lifetime and allowed himself to *feel* pent up-painful emotions from those past events. Tears poured out of him. *Feel and release. Feel and release.* After he felt them, crying and feeling the anguish, he would release them, just letting the painful feelings go, over and over again, off into the sunset.

At the end of a period of a few weeks, he felt light and full of energy. A happiness he had never thought possible permeated his life. And there was an unanticipated benefit: *he was completely healed.* Besides being healed, continually releasing the negative emotion buried inside him produced a profound awakening experience, described in his book and in many other accounts. He went on to become the founder of the Sedona Method, a systematic methodic of releasing negative emotion. Lester's mantra: if you want to badly enough, anybody can be healed. He had a powerful motive—staying alive—but the approach is the same for anyone who *wants* to heal.

DO YOU WANT TO BE HEALED?

There is one caveat. It must be said at the outset that healing *must be something that a person desires*, something you really want. Many people *say* they want to heal, but they have split intentions, split energy about it. I have a friend that says she really wants to lose weight, but she orders ravioli as an appetizer. A part of her wants to lose it, but if she were serious, she would forgo the ravioli. It's the same with healing. You can say you want to heal and then spend a lot of your time doing things that work against you, like complaining and rehearsing everything that's wrong or binging on Twinkies or potato chips.

Some are here for a soul purpose that may not include physical healing. Consider Stephen Hawking, one of the world's most brilliant theoretical physicists. His mind is obviously of paramount importance to his work. Who's to say that if his body was healed, the focus of his mind's energy wouldn't be diluted or dispersed in a way that wasn't as conducive to his genius—that is, to the energy devoted to his mind? He may well have created a lifetime through which his purpose was achieved through the use of such a physical challenge, and to live this lifetime in a wheelchair with ALS, amyotrophic lateral sclerosis.[2]

Less famous examples include situations where a person may choose a short life span for reasons that may be helpful to others. A child, for instance, who dies at an early age of a rare disease may be the catalyst for a family's emotional reunion and reconciliation.[3] What looks bad may, from the soul's perspective, be just what was called for to heal an even bigger set of circumstances. In other situations, a person—like my dear friend Amber, who recently passed away—may feel as though her time here is finished. Then physical healing is obviously not a primary aim.

One evening while I was there for dinner, Amber said something that I didn't want to accept. It revealed her feeling of having concluded her time here. It came up when we were discussing her physician. Unhappy with her current cardiologist, a woman I had recommended, she lamented, "I think my doctor is losing interest. She doesn't seem to be paying attention anymore." She was a capable cardiologist, and Amber had seemed pleased with her for a long time. But now she required more medical attention and a different expertise.

I quickly offered to find a new physician. "I'll get you a new cardiologist," I offered. "Maybe she's really busy or doesn't know what to do. It's easy enough to get a new physician. I know someone who is excellent. I'll call him for you on Monday."

Amber immediately railed against my suggestion. She was incredibly resistant to going to anyone else. "She knows me. I don't want to have to get used to anyone new. They'll ask the same questions, and there's nothing they can do anyway." She went on with more and

---

[2]   It is not unusual to hear from people who have had near-death experiences that during their experience, they learned how they chose various aspects of their lives to be predestined before they were born.

[3]   People report having chosen their birth parents, their missions and purposes in life, and how they will die. In addition, reincarnation is a concept found in many cultures and religions; even Christians at one time gave credence to the concept of reincarnation. It was phased out due to opposing sentiments by various church authorities.

more objections. Her resistant attitude reminded me of her husband's, who had died twenty years earlier.

"You sound like Dean did," I protested. He had been misdiagnosed by a prominent specialist who was the chief of the thoracic surgery department at a major medical center in New York. Dean had lung cancer, and his specialist missed it completely.

Dean was still in his fifties. When we found out he had a lung tumor, we were shocked. In no time, he was having trouble breathing. When I heard the news, I immediately offered to find a new specialist, thinking Dean would jump at the chance to see someone new, someone more thorough. After all, his specialist had just made a grave mistake. Instead, he got angry and indignant and refused. Hitting a brick wall, I dropped it. Dean died six months later.

When I mentioned to Amber that she was acting like her husband, I expected she would see the error of her thinking and consent to seeing a new specialist. But she didn't. Instead, she said with chilling clarity, "I understand how he felt. He wanted to die." My friend passed away soon afterward. You often see similar behavior in many who are seriously ill; they resist any suggestions that might be helpful in healing, only to succumb to the illness. Often it's a sign that they are ready to die.

> In the final analysis, healing is a journey of the soul and the soul must be willing to take it.

Every time Bill held a seminar, he would ask the person who had requested his attention to whatever problem or distress or disease, "Do you *want* this to be taken away? Do you want to be healed?" I always thought it seemed somewhat gratuitous. My mind reasoned, *If these people didn't want to be healed, why in the world would they have come to the seminar? Why would they raise their hands to ask for help? Of course they wanted to be healed.*

However, I eventually realized it's an important thing to ask. It's important because it calls people's attention to a *focus* on healing so they don't simply respond mentally. The act of posing the question "Do you want this," calls upon a person to focus their full intention on responding emotionally, deeply, and authentically as well as mentally. In this way, they can begin to make their choice to heal a very conscious one, and with that choice, they can begin to bring into their consciousness all that may be standing in the way. Because healing usually requires new attitudes and behaviors, it's important to be aware of what choices are helping and which are hurting. In the final analysis, healing is a journey of the soul, and the soul must be willing to take it. Taking the journey will inevitably mean change: changes in beliefs, attitudes and patterns of behavior, as well as lifestyle—maybe even a change in a job or a relationship.

For most of us, healing is a desirable thing. As I've delved into the science and the spiritual sides of healing, and experimented with it more and more on my own since my experience in Dallas several years ago, I have seen that we have much more power within us to heal than we know. We especially have more power to heal than we have been taught to believe. If the desire is there and is great enough, *anything can be healed.* Further, healing is effective not because we have used one specific method or another but because the method we use allows the higher laws of nature to come into play.

If you are interested in healing, this book is intended for you. Mastering the art of unleashing the healer within will hopefully become a reality for you as I share my own experiences and those of the trailblazers and real scientific geniuses who have laid the energetic blueprint for an exciting new path to healing.

II

THE HEALTH-CARE DILEMMA:
IT'S THE MODEL, STUPID!

We've been trying to get the medical profession for the last thirty years to look beyond the chemical model of treating the body and peddling pills and to look at the electromagnetic, the quantum ... and what we would normally call complementary or alternative medicine.

—Apollo astronaut Dr. Edgar Mitchell
(Quantum Hologram and ESP lecture)[4]

People are too much of an afterthought in hospitals these days. Medical machines and procedures take priority. Exhausted from struggling with pain? Up all night because of the beeps and burps and loud pagers? Patients hear this feeble apology: "We're so sorry to have to get you up this early. The only thing they had available on the MRI schedule was at six a.m."

On the upside, medical breakthroughs defy the imagination. They can work magic. A man in New York badly marred by a fire just had a successful face transplant—an amazing triumph of modern medicine. But too often these new discoveries take on a life of their own and the patient is left out of the loop. Time for discharge. "Oops, nobody mentioned it? Well, sorry about that. It's four in the afternoon. It's time to go. Medicare stops paying tonight at midnight."

---

[4]   Edgar Mitchell lecture. "The Quantum Hologram and ESP." March 29, 2005. Disclose TV.

If you've had the misfortune of spending time in the medical system, you know firsthand that insurers, tests, and procedures rule. Soaring numbers of people using complementary therapies like yoga and meditation, herbs and acupuncture, are taking matters into their own hands. Unless the problem is truly acute, people opt for an alternative. Visits to alternative providers surpassed conventional physician office visits about a decade ago.[5]

Health care is always on our minds because it's costing us too much or we're afraid because we constantly hear stories of poor quality in the headlines. High rates of medical mistakes persist. Incidents like operating on the wrong body part, or giving someone the wrong medication, or acquiring an infection in the hospital when you're supposed to be in there to rest and recover happen all too frequently.[6] So frequently that the front covers of the *Atlantic* and *Time* magazines have featured leading stories like "How American Health Care Killed My Father"[7] and "Bitter Pill: Why Medical Bills Are Killing Us."[8]

Maybe we're asking the wrong questions. As the Sufi legend goes, a man loses his keys. A fellow comes along and asks him where he lost them. The man says, "Over there," pointing to a bush several feet away.

"Then why are you looking over here?" the fellow asks.

"Because that's where the light is," he retorts.

We too seem to be looking for the proverbial keys under the lamppost because that's where the light is.

A key question leaps out: has medicine's disease-based focus—one that treats humans like a mechanical system, mostly treating symptoms

---

[5] *Complementary and Alternative Medicine in the United States.* Institute of Medicine US Committee on the Use of Complementary and Alternative Medicine by the American Public. Washington DC National Academies Press, 2005.

[6] Marty Makary, MD. *Unaccountable: What Hospitals Won't Tell You and How Transparency Can Revolutionize Heallthcare.* Marty Mackary, MD, 2012.

[7] David Goldhill. "How American Health Care Killed My Father." *The Atlantic.* September 1, 2009.

[8] Steven Brill. "Bitter Pill: Why Medical Bills Are Killing Us." *Time.* February 20, 2013.

with drugs and surgery, reached its limits? Many factors point in that direction. A whirlwind of scientific findings reveal some serious fallacies in the way medicine is practiced, calling the holy grail of scientific medicine into question. For one, we now know that our genes do not determine our destiny as we have always thought they did.[9] Recent discoveries show us that we are the masters of our genes, not the other way around. Another is that what we've thought of as "the mind" is not just in the head but also in every cell in the body.[10]

> For one, we now know that our genes do not determine our destinies as we have always thought they did. Recent discoveries show us that we are the masters of our genes, not the other way around.

Another: the space between us and around us isn't empty space as science thought it was. There is an energetic matrix or an endless field of energy from which all else emanates,[11] and it is the underlying connection of all living and non-living things. These findings have profound implications for healing, leading to an inside-out approach rather than looking outside ourselves for someone or something to fix us. Healing is an "inside job."

Even though the latest scientific pearls of wisdom are shining a light on a new and different path to healing, change in medicine comes very slowly. New ideas have a long history of being rejected by the scientific community in control.[12] Because new approaches often run counter to the established organizational and professional cultures, they reject them. A good case in point is the well-known story of poor Dr. Semmelweis, who tried to tell his physician colleagues that not washing their hands was

9   Bruce Lipton. *The Biology of Belief*. Hay House, www.hayhouse.com. June 2013.

10   Candace Pert. "Neuropeptides and Their Receptors. A Psychosomatic Network." *Journal of Immunology*. 1985, 135:820–826.

11   Max Planck. "Das wesen der Materie. [The Nature of Matter]." Speech in Florence, Italy, 1944, from archive zer Geschichte der Max Planck Gesellschaft, Abt. Va., Rep. 11 Planck, Nr. 1797.

12   Thomas Kuhn. *The Structure of Scientific Revolutions*. University of Chicago Press, 1962.

causing deaths. An early pioneer of antiseptic procedures, Semmelweis ended up in an insane asylum because his pleas for hand washing fell on the deaf ears of his colleagues. They ostracized and jeered at him:

> During the mid-1800s, in Ignaz Philipp Semmelweis's time, germs and infections hadn't been discovered, and prevailing experts believed diseases were caused by an imbalance of bodily fluids—blood, phlegm, yellow bile, black bile. They assumed women got "childbed fever" when they gave birth because the mother had an imbalance of these fluids.
>
> Semmelweis, a Hungarian doctor working in the maternity clinics at Vienna General Hospital, observed that about 15 percent of pregnant women would die after childbirth due to "childbed fever." But Semmelweis noticed that one clinic had a much lower mortality rate than the other. He also noticed that women who gave birth at home had a low incidence of childbirth fever. Semmelweis was determined to find out why.
>
> One day Semmelweis's friend Jakob died after accidently cutting himself while doing an autopsy. Semmelweis couldn't help but notice that his friend's symptoms were strikingly similar to the mothers with "childbed fever." He reasoned that the fever could be caused by something being transmitted by the physician to the bloodstream of the mother.
>
> To test his theory, Semmelweis asked everyone to wash their hands in a solution of chlorine before performing childbirth. Immediately mortality rates dropped down to 1 percent, even going to 0 percent for some months.

Presented with the data, the medical community completely rejected Semmelweis's ideas. The idea that physicians themselves were responsible for the deaths was completely unacceptable to them. Further, the idea that diseases could be carried through invisible particles on the hand was rejected as preposterous![13]

Doctors only had to try washing their hands in chlorine for a month to see the effects for themselves, but they refused. Semmelweis went crazy trying to convince them. Admitted to an insane asylum by force, he died soon after. A short twenty years after his death, the germ theory validated all his convictions.[14]

Semmelweis experienced the well-known closed-mindedness of the powers that be to change. His is a dramatic example, but there are many, many others. Some of the most notable will be discussed in the next chapter. As for the germ theory that preoccupied Semmelweis and was to become the cornerstone of medicine after his death, it has helped us make giant leaps in medicine.

THE LIMITS OF THE GERM THEORY

There's a lot it hasn't done, however. A narrow focus on the germ theory has led the scientific community to think in terms of fighting outside invaders instead, perhaps, of restoring balance or alleviating stress. Until fairly recently, because it couldn't be seen under a microscope, medical experts didn't believe that such a thing as stress existed. An NIH scientist recalls a time, not long ago, when she didn't even want admit that she knew Hans Selye, who discovered stress, for fear she would be marginalized and berated.[15]

---

[13] Semmelweis Society International. Semmelweis.org/

[14] Ibid.

[15] Ester Sternberg, MD, interview "The Science of Healing Places." *On Being* with Krista Tippet. Onbeing.org/program/the-science-of-healing-places/4856

A narrow focus on the germ theory has led the scientific community to think in terms of material outside invaders. Until fairly recently, because it couldn't be seen under a microscope, medical experts didn't believe that such a thing as stress existed.

It seems like I always knew, even as a child, that stressful emotions created "dis-ease" and that the mind and the body were connected in some fundamental way. I'm not so unique in this respect. Most of us intuitively get the connection. We sense that chronically repressed negative thoughts and emotions create dis-ease[16]. As I explained these views one evening over dinner with a group from graduate school, I remember a prominent dean of a nursing school saying to me, "Then I guess you don't believe in the germ theory?" I actually didn't then and don't believe now that it tells the whole story. So many other factors are involved; the germ theory seems much too simplistic.

For instance, consider studies done on babies who were taken out of the blitz of WWII and placed in a safe, clean environment. Properly bathed, fed, and clothed on a consistent basis, they failed to thrive. The babies weren't gaining weight or developing normally. They were lethargic and didn't cry or respond normally. Then they assigned some nannies to hold the babies, cuddle them lovingly, and play with them regularly. It made all the difference in the world. Magically the babies began to grow and thrive in leaps and bounds.[17]

Love made the difference.

Consider a more recent study done on three groups of men who had knee injuries that were so bad they had trouble walking. They were all told they had knee surgery by a very prominent surgeon at the nearby medical center. Only one of the groups, however, really had the surgery.

---

[16]   Dis-ease means a lack of ease in the flow of energy—the life force—though the energy centers and cells throughout the body.

[17]   Daniel Goleman. "The Experience of Touch." NYT, Archives, February 2, 1988.

The other two were just told they had had it; the surgeon made a simple incision in their knees. Several months later, all three groups of men were hopping, skipping, and dancing like men in their twenties! The fellows who had the fake surgeries were just as well off as the fellows who had the real thing.[18]

Belief made the difference.

The wisdom of our bodies is always making decisions about what illnesses we will succumb to and which ones we won't. Most of the time it's not a conscious process. Our beliefs—often unconscious—are the drivers of our health or illness. In fact, the same can be said for everything in our lives: our habitual thoughts and patterns of behavior created it.[19] Our consistent patterns create our experiences, even though we may not be conscious of it. Therefore, by changing our thoughts and behavior patterns, we can change our experiences. And we can learn to heal.

Germs are everywhere. Why are some of us affected by them and not others? Because our ability to resist them differs tremendously. Something different is happening in our levels of awareness. That's why some patients respond better to treatment than others. Because we all have different belief systems and different attitudes. As a result, something different is happening in our immune systems.

> Germs are everywhere. Why are some of us affected by them and others are not?

The latest research shows that our bodies register every thought, word, and feeling that we have—immediately. A friend of mine recently came down with a very bad cold with flu-like

---

18 Bruce Lipton. *The Biology of Belief.* Hay House, www.hayhouse.com, June, 2013, 109–110.

19 For most of us, these basic healing principles are adequate to heal us. For others, when an illness persists, there is a particular message the illness offers. In these situations, the purpose is to bring greater awareness to something that still needs to be learned. Some illnesses have a strong karmic propensity and the illness may be serving a particular purpose, such as Stephen Hawken's condition, mentioned in the introduction.

symptoms. When I asked her how she caught it, her response was revealing. She said, "I know *just* when it happened. I was standing near a man on the subway who was sneezing and coughing all over the place, and I was right in the line of fire! I thought to myself, *His germs are making a beeline straight for me!*"

Actually, the germs didn't cause my friend's cold; her *belief* that they would did. In almost all situations having to do with poor health—mental or physical—there is a strong tinge of fear, repression, and/or denial. Emotional upset is a key factor in the creation of a disease process. Even when someone is injured in an "accident," it is often a very specific part of the body that is affected, and often it is the same part that has had problems before. So is it really an "accident" or is there an underlying pattern and a reason for the way events occur in our lives?

> In almost all situations having to do with poor health—mental or physical—there is a strong tinge of fear, repression, and/or denial.

Medicine, as it is currently practiced, is grounded in a narrow subset of science, focused on the physical. This approach reduces us to patients with separate body parts that can be fixed in the same way that a mechanic fixes a car. How many times have we heard stories of woe about a health-care system that is overspecialized?

"The cath showed everything is fine with her heart," announced the cardiologist to my dear friend Doreen about her mother, "so it's probably the lungs that are causing the hypertension. You should talk to the pulmonologist [lung specialist] from now on."

"*Really?*" my friend challenged. "Don't you talk to each other?" She'd entrusted her mother's care to the cardiologist. Now he was exiting stage right. "The heart and lungs work together, don't they?" she protested. "I thought it was a heart problem that brought her in here." My friend was right. Poor perfusion caused her hypertension and fluid buildup in the tissues as well as the lungs. Nonetheless, his part of the puzzle had been solved. Off he went.

You hear it often: a person goes to see a specialist for a heart problem and dies of lung cancer because the heart specialist didn't look at his lungs. *Not his purview.* Much of the time, our system's highly specialized approach fails to take into account that the person has feelings and fears and a need for support in other areas after one "part" has been fixed. These fears and beliefs can be self-limiting and in fact interfere with a person's healing.

> **A new story that appreciates our emotions and thought patterns and the underlying biochemistry affecting our energy patterns and immune systems is badly needed.**

Dubbed "medicine's spiritual crisis" because we are always looking to external interventions—namely drugs and surgery—for solutions, Herb Benson, the director of the Mind-Body Institute at Harvard, realized medicine's limitations. Benson saw that his "patients' progress and recovery often seemed to hinge upon their spirit and their will to live." The spiritual side of medicine, however, is still absent, for the most part, in theory as well as practice.[20]

Early in his career, Benson, one of the founders of mind-body medicine, admits, "I could not shake the sense I had that the human mind—and the beliefs we so often associate with the human soul—had physical manifestations." While Benson tells the story of how he wanted to believe so much in the power of medical science, he confides that during his years of practice he "had a nagging feeling that medicine was missing a critical point."[21]

The critical point is indeed, as Benson put it, that we continue to worship a "god" of Newtonian science—based on the discoveries of Isaac Newton, who lived in the seventeenth century and explained the physical world in terms of separate parts that were related mathematically. Even though science has shown us repeatedly that there is much more than what the five senses and their access to the physical world reveal,

---

[20]   Herbert Benson, MD, with Marg Stark. *Timeless Healing.* Schreibner, 1997.
[21]   Ibid.

Newton's version of science, reductionism, as scientists call it, can be observed in medicine as it is still practiced today. *Reductionism* is shorthand for reducing the world to its separate parts.

Since science has revealed the connections between the mind, body, and spirit, the old Newtonian story of a single germ that causes the problem seems overly simplistic and needs to be reconsidered. We need a new story that appreciates our emotions, thought patterns, and the underlying biochemistry affecting our energy patterns and immune systems. A new story is called for to examine what causes a gene to "express itself," or turn into an illness. Just because you have the gene for a particular illness doesn't mean you'll get sick.

Many of the diseases and conditions that plague us don't respond to the methods of scientific medicine as we know them. More and more, that's the case. In the early days of the twentieth century, diseases were simpler. It was medicine's task to devise an appropriate and specific cure, and huge progress was made in eradicating infectious diseases like polio, syphilis, typhus, and smallpox.

But in many ways, we seem to be running in place nowadays. We're not making the progress we expected to make. This is especially the case in curing cancer. Because there *is* no outside invader, the germ theory doesn't apply. As renowned oncologist David Agus points out, "The disease is self-generated in the sense that it's our own cells that have gone awry." Agus tells the story of how he blurted out, before a gathering of distinguished colleagues at an American Association of Cancer Research in Denver, "We've made a mistake." Explaining how we've grown accustomed to a certain mode of thinking based on scientific discoveries made a long time ago, Agus tells how he heard a disheartening chorus of hissing in the audience as he was speaking. Agus was referring to the limits of the germ theory.[22]

---

[22] David Agus MD, with Kristin Loberg. *The End of Illness*. Free Press, A Division of Simon and Shuster, 2011.

TIME FOR A NEW MODEL, A NEW STORY

Like Dr. Agus, many believe that our medical mind-set is wrongheaded. Primarily mechanical and structured in silos, our bodies are viewed as exceedingly complex machines. Illness, as a malfunctioning of that machine, is brought about by infections, trauma, inherited defects, degeneration, and of course cancer.[23]

Emotions play a key role in illness,[24] yet modern medicine continues to ignore them. Why? Because emotions don't fit into the *model* of medicine as we know it: germ A causes disease B and is treated by drugs and surgery C. They aren't mechanical and cannot be seen under a microscope, so there is no place for them in the germ theory. Pioneers in mind-body medicine have fought an uphill battle with colleagues who were trained to make a sharp division between emotions and things of the mind and things of the body. They have a great deal more comfort dealing with the body, barely taking a person's frame of mind or emotional state into account.

Lest some be tempted to say that *used* to be the case but isn't any longer, I want to share a story with you. I accompanied Bettina, a dear friend, to a visit to her cardiologist recently. She was having shortness of breath symptoms. At the time, she was caring for her husband, Peter, who was ninety-seven years old, with some dementia and increasing mobility problems. Since Bettina had asked me to come into the consult room when the physical exam was over, in a spirit of trying to be helpful, I offered my observations to her cardiologist: "Bettina has been struggling with caring for her husband. It has put a great deal of emotional strain on her. I think the shortness of breath may be anxiety related, but we wanted to see what you think."

Dr. Gordon blurted back, lighthearted and unapologetically, "I'm not one for all the emotional, psychological stuff. I focus on the

---

23   John Sarno. *Healing Back Pain: The Mind-Body Connection.* Warner Books, A Time Warner Company, New York. 1991.

24   Carolyn Myss, PhD, and Norman Shealy, MD, PhD. *The Creation of Health.* Three Rivers Press, Random House, New York, 1997, xiv.

physical. Actually, I almost became a mechanic. I love working on cars. Let's get an echocardiogram so we can see what's going on." *End of story!* He is in his early fifties and has a thriving practice. He *is* very good with the mechanical; a hefty segment of his business comes from doing echocardiograms. He has a reputation for being good at these procedures. But that's not nearly enough. Healing is not just about the physical. What happened to talking to a patient and trying to find out what's going on in her life to help with the problem—maybe even *before* it shows up on an echocardiogram?

Many trailblazers in mind-body medicine are trying to change things. Recognizing that there is a lot of science that doesn't actually fit into the traditional biomedical model, they disagree with the approach that sees disease as physical only and reduces us to body parts. They disagree with seeing diseases as invading organisms or germs that can be fought with a specific drug or surgical procedure.[25] They bemoan the fact that medicine has not adopted the new understandings of physics.[26]

Astronaut Edgar Mitchell—who holds a PhD in aeronautics from MIT, was the sixth man to walk on the moon, and describes himself as having been "about as left-brained as you can get"—is among these pioneers. Says Mitchell, "We've been trying to get the medical profession for the last thirty years to look beneath the chemical model of treating the body and peddling pills and to look at the electromagnetic, the quantum, and what we would normally call complementary or alternative medicine … and I am very much convinced that those techniques are rooted right in the level we're talking about."[27]

"So getting beneath that chemical model that we've used and had almost for a century now is key; because the quantum hologram is likely responsible for most of these subtle energies, these numinous

---

[25] Bernard Lown, MD. "Power to the People: Patient in Command." Blog Essay 32, November 3, 2012.

[26] Bruce Lipton. *The Biology of Belief.* Hay House, www.hayhouse.com, June 2013.

[27] Edgar Mitchell Lecture. "The Quantum Hologram and ESP." March 29, 2005. Disclose TV.

effects that we know happen in humans, that we just don't have a good explanation for."[28]

"We haven't discovered those energies, the ch'i or the zero point field, but the first place we ought to look is within the quantum effects and the interaction of the electromagnetic and the quantum with the macro scale quantum … getting beneath that chemical model that we've used [in medicine] and had almost for a century now."[29]

The roots of an illness cannot be explained in a simple cause and effect way. Illness is more complicated and personalized. Actually, you could say that the illnesses we succumb to are tailor-made for us, just what we ordered for our next phase of growth and development. External experts using drugs and surgery can help with an illness, help with the pain, but not its root cause. Only we ourselves—alone—can erase the roots of the dis-ease.

> Actually, you could say the illnesses we succumb to are tailor-made for us.

Proponents of a new story of medicine take an enlightened view of illness: every situation we encounter—even if it looks awful from the outside—is exactly what we need to learn to progress beyond the things that are holding us back. In fact, we created it or attracted it—not consciously, perhaps—for that very reason.

Illness makes its appearance to help us, and it *can* actually serve us. Everything that comes happens for a reason and has our imprints, growth, and best interests at heart, and it comes because we created it.[30] The model of medicine that is practiced today is based on averages and standards. Until recently, the standards for health and disease were

---

[28] Ibid. Mitchel is referring to a fundamental energy that flows through all and everything, an energy that forms every living thing. The zero point energy field is similarly a fundamental energy. A concept developed by Einstein, it is the lowest possible energy that a quantum physical system can have, the energy of the ground state.

[29] Ibid.

[30] Carolyn Myss, PhD, and Norman Shealy, MD, PhD. *The Creation of Health.* Three Rivers, Random House, 1997, 154–192.

based on research done on predominantly thirty-something males. Now gender-based science tells us that women's bodies are different. Research on the elderly shows us that bodies of the elderly are different as well; and the situation is the same with children, different races, and ethnic groups. When we progress a little further, we will likely learn that each individual is so different that a standard approach to treatment for anyone is a nonstarter.

START THE NEW STORY WITH HEALTH, NOT ILLNESS

Ultimately, we need to evolve to a system of self-care and self-healing. We're trained like obedient soldiers to reach for the drug or surgery that will fix whatever it is that ails us, yet drugs and surgery, while all well and good, have their limits. Overmedication is a problem. We're becoming resistant to certain antibiotics because they're overprescribed. Seniors complain, "How can this be good for me? I'm taking twenty pills a day, and all I do is plan for my next doctor's appointment." The average number of prescriptions filled a year for every senior citizen is 28.5.[31]

As we learn to activate the healers within us, we can begin to use drugs and surgery more sparingly. To get there, we need retraining. With new answers and a new story, health-related questions lead to a very different worldview from the current one focused on disease: People wonder, *Where does health come from? What can I do to stay healthy? Why do some centenarians defy all the rules of diet and exercise and live to a ripe old age? What can I do to heal?*

A new worldview would reassure us that our bodies are on our side. It would reassure us that the placebo effect, which science tosses aside as an annoyance that must be controlled, is actually our brain's built-in

---

[31]   Arvind Modawal. MD, MPH. "Prescription Medication in the Elderly." NetWellness.org

healing system! [32] We should be empowered to realize that we can change what's happening in our bodies, even in our DNA. We need a story with a new and different focus on how we see ourselves, one that begins with the understanding that *we have the power to heal within us.*

If your problem is acute, our medical system is outstanding. (If you get hit by a truck, yoga is not the answer!) However, it will only take you so far. If your problem is chronic, which most are these days, conventional medicine doesn't have much to offer. Healing is what you need, especially your ability to activate the healer within. Our own internal healing mechanisms can play the starring role in making headway against chronic illness. Ironically, medicine's success in reducing infectious diseases, in eradicating many fatal prognoses, has left us with chronic disease, the eight-hundred-pound gorilla in the room. Chronic disease, by definition, will not succumb to a cure.

Medicine boasts a whirlwind age of magic bullets: drugs that lower blood pressure, decrease cholesterol, alleviate depression, treat pneumonia. There are targeted therapies, like insulin for diabetes. Intricate surgeries can be counted on to repair complex heart problems, complicated bowel resections, tumor removals, and the effective replacement of many, if not most, joints and body parts.

Nevertheless, if we want to learn what keeps people healthy, why not study the habits of healthy people? Examine their psyches and their thought patterns. What are their emotional lives like? How do they cope with problems? What are their eating habits?

THE ROSETO EFFECT

Dr. Stewart Wolf did just that. He studied people that lived in a simple, quiet town called Roseto, Pennsylvania, after its namesake, Roseto, Italy. Hundreds of Italians from the little town in the foothills of the Apennines immigrated there to make a better life. They replicated their

---

[32]   Herbert Benson, MD, with Marg Stark. *Timeless Healing.* Schreibner, 1997.

little Italian village in Pennsylvania, building butcher shops, bakeries, and flower shops, even erecting a little church modeled after Our Lady of Mount Carmel back home.[33]

It just so happened that Dr. Wolf, then head of medicine at the University of Oklahoma, was in town to give a talk to the local medical society. After his talk, a local Roseto doctor invited Wolf to join him for a drink. Over a couple of beers, he told Wolf about something striking he'd noticed: a stark absence of heart disease in Roseto. In men under sixty-five, there was virtually none; in men over sixty-five, the rate of heart disease was one-half the United States rate. People there essentially died from old age. "What in the world is going on here?" Wolf wanted to know. So he asked a colleague to help him explore the reasons for the exquisitely healthy state of the people of Roseto.[34]

Medical students and sociology students went door-to-door interviewing Rosetans to help Wolf figure out what was happening. Was it diet? Hardly. Rosetans feasted on high-fat diets with abandon: heaping daily platters of salami, meatballs, and sausages fried in lard with all sorts of cheeses, high in fat. A substantial portion of Rosetans were overweight, maybe even obese.

Did they have rewarding, fulfilling work? Not really. The men labored in slate quarries filled with gases and dust. Roseto also had no crime and very few applications for public assistance. To add insult to injury, they smoked unfiltered stogies and drank wine liberally!

> The secret of healthy living turned out to be intimate emotional connections and the deep sense of belonging that knitted the little town together.

What was their secret? How did Rosetans manage to stay healthy and ignore so many key principles of healthy living that science has taught us to obey? The secret turned out to be intimate emotional connections and the deep sense of belonging

---

[33] Malcolm Gladwell. *Outliers: The Story of Success*. Little Brown and Company, 2008.

[34] Ibid.

that knitted the little town together. Vegetable plots and grape arbors, well cared for, adjoined their modest houses. On front porches, chairs lined up, ready for the same evening's passeggiata (leisurely stroll) the townspeople took every evening in the Old Country. Church bells from Our Lady of Mount Carmel Church accompanied the procession. Frequently stopping to share the latest gossip and catch up on the latest happenings was the highlight of the day for the extended Italian-American families who lived there.[35]

"You go down the street and everybody says, 'Hello, hello,'" said Anita Renna, forty-three. "You feel like you're the mayor."

When Wolf and his sociologist coauthor John G. Bruhn published their findings in the Journal of the American Medical Association in 1966, Roseto's cardiac mortality rate defied the imagination. Nationally, cardiac mortality rates rise with age. But for Roseto, it dropped to near zero for men fifty-five to sixty-four, an age group usually at high risk. For men over sixty-five, the local death rate was ten per one thousand, half the national average, and uniquely, there were more widowers in town than widows.[36]

"The community," Wolf says, "was very cohesive. There was no keeping up with the Joneses. Houses were very close together, and everyone lived more or less alike." Elders were revered and included in every aspect of community life. Homemakers were respected, and fathers headed the families.[37]

Not so fast. Going back to these golden oldie customs from the Old Country is probably not going to happen in the United States, not here, not now. For starters, many more Americans, 27 percent, are living

---

[35]   Malcolm Gladwell. *Outliers: The Story of Success.* Little Brown and Company, 2008.

[36]   Ibid.

[37]   Ibid.

alone, and more families than ever before are headed by single women.[38] For the first time, married couples are no longer the majority.[39]

Yet we can learn a lot from the lessons of Roseto. What are the "takeaways"? The sense of belonging the Rosetans had. The feeling that who you are and what you do matters to others. Emotional support was there when you needed it. The rich bonds and connections you can count on were sacred. Maybe most important: the deep and abiding sense of purpose sparked by community for something greater than yourself.

Actually, these principals haven't disappeared from American life. Shape-shifting trends reveal that they are showing up in our lives in new ways. Technology offers us an exciting new brand of connectivity, of community. Intimate connections are only a text away. Countering trends toward doing our own thing and more of us living alone, Facebook, Twitter, Instagram, and other brands of social media bring lightning speed connection. Yoga clubs have sprung up throughout the United States. New affinities are created during yoga classes and hot yoga clinics, where millions, some estimates say nearly twenty-five million, Americans congregate.[40] Nearly as many practice meditation.[41]

An experiment tested a theory called the Maharishi Effect in Merseyside, England. A large number—over 1 percent of the population—meditated together every day from 1988 to 1991. The results were astonishing: The crime rate dropped so much that Merseyside went from third highest to the lowest-ranked city in England during the time of the study. Meanwhile, it was a controlled study, meaning a town of non-meditators was used as a basis of comparison. The crime rate

---

38 By Jonathan Vespa, Jamie M. Lewis, and Rose M. Kreider. America's Families and Living Arrangements: 2012. Population Characteristics. https://www.census.gov/prod/2013pubs/p20-570.pdf

39 Sabrina Tavernise. Married Couples are No Longer a Majority, Census Finds. *New York Times.* May 26, 2011.

40 The Statistics Portal. Statista.com

41 National Center for Complementary and Integrative Health. Nationwide survey reveals widespread use of mind and body practices, press release, February, 10, 2015.

for the town of non-meditators remained the same. Meditation was the only factor that made the difference; as the scientists took into account other factors like police practices, local economics, and demographics, all remained the same for both groups.

In the forefront of jump-starting the new story of focusing on health, not illness, more and more people are seeking all kinds of complementary and alternative practices. A study cited in the *Journal of the American Medical Association* found that the majority of alternative medicine users seem to be doing so because "they find these health-care alternatives to be more in line with their own values, beliefs, and philosophical orientations toward health and life." In particular, subjects reported a holistic orientation to health, a transformational experience that changed their worldview.[42]

Those of us who use alternative therapies rose from 33 percent in 1990 to 42 percent in 1997, and some estimate that the number of people in the United States using alternative therapies may be as high as 70 percent today. The trend began over twenty years ago, when Americans spent more than twenty-seven billion dollars on these therapies, exceeding out-of-pocket spending for all US hospitalizations, and the number of patient visits to alternative providers exceeded those to conventional practitioners for the first time that year.[43]

The top twenty-five reasons people seek medical care have to do with symptoms related to chronic conditions. By definition, *chronic* is something that medical experts believe can't be cured. Most common are hypertension (high blood pressure), hyperlipidemia (high cholesterol), mental disorders, asthma, and osteoarthritis,[44] with diabetes, back

---

[42] J.A Astin. "Why Patients Use Alternative Medicine: Results of a National Study." *Journal of the American Medical Association.* 1998 May 20; 279 (19):1548–53.

[43] David M. Eisenberg et al. "Trends in Alternative Medicine Use in the United States." *Journal of the American Medical Association.* 1998 Nov 11;280 (18) : 1569–75.

[44] Agency for Healthcare Research and Quality. "Medical Expenditures Panel Survey. 2012." http://meps.ahrq.gov/mepsweb/data_files/publications/st382/stat382.pdf.

pain, and obesity close behind.[45] Patients in these categories form the backbone of most general medical practices; and these patients report that they're not happy with the way they're being treated.[46] In an international survey, Americans said they were dissatisfied with how little time their physicians spend with them.[47] Chronic illnesses can be cured and have been cured, just not with the standard medical approach.

We actually *have* become better and better at living longer. Since 1950, death from heart disease has declined sixty to seventy percent, a great achievement. But was it because of new drugs and surgeries, newer and better diagnostics, or a new understanding of how much lifestyle matters?[48] Some believe our greatest leaps in lowering heart disease and stroke had more to do with lifestyle changes than it did with cardiovascular drugs and surgeries.[49]

MEDICAL PROGRESS STALLED?

Progress in medicine does seem to be stalled in many ways. Between 1953 and 2001, while the Human Genome Project was under way, people started pulling away from conventional medical doctors. It was during this period that many began to explore alternative approaches in record numbers. In the summer of 2000, Dr. Francis Crick, cofounder of the double helix and lead scientist on the genome project, announced that

---

[45]   www.KevinMD.com/blog/2012/patients-flock-alternative-medicine/providers.html.

[46]   Survey Sampling and The Research Intelligence Group. "Patients Around The World Are Not Happy with Their Physicians, Feeling Disrespected, Hurried Through Visits, and Shut out of Treatment Decisions." http://www.prnewswire.com/news-releases/patients-around-the-world-are-not-happy-with-their-physicians-feeling-disrespected-hurried-through-visits-and-shut-out-of-treatment-decisions-125559353.html

[47]   http://www.kevinmd.com/blog/2014/05/10-minutes-doctor.html

[48]   Agus, 22.

[49]   Joseph Califano. *America's Health Care Revolution: Who Lives, Who Dies, Who Pays,* Random House, 1986.

the project would reveal the keys to treating diseases like Alzheimer's in just ten to fifteen years.[50] Something went wrong.

Great medical leaps were promised, but what really materialized? A *Scientific American* headlined opined, "Revolution Postponed: Why the Genome Project Has Been Disappointing." As this insightful article explains, research springing from the genome project has failed to deliver on the promises that many researchers in medicine made a decade ago.[51] Tumor biologist Robert A. Weinberg of the Whitehead Institute for Biomedical Research in Cambridge, Massachusetts, says the returns on cancer genomics "have been relatively modest—very modest compared to the resources invested." Harold E. Varmus, former director of the National Institutes of Health, wrote in the *New England Journal of Medicine*: "Only a handful of major changes ... have entered routine medical practice"—most of them, he added, the result of "discoveries that preceded the unveiling of the human genome."[52]

What happened? Could the failure to find genetic variations that have much of an impact on disease mean the "common variant" hypothesis is wrong? Finding certain common DNA variants prevalent in people with illnesses like diabetes or atherosclerosis (hardening of the arteries) was supposed to lead to understanding how a susceptibility to those diseases gets passed down from one generation to the next. If someone had DNA variants prevalent in type 2 diabetes or atherosclerosis, would the person's offspring be susceptible to these diseases? Would they be passed down to their children?

The answer is that we still don't know. In 2008, David Goldstein, a geneticist from Duke, told the *New York Times*, "It's an astounding thing that we have cracked open the human genome and can look at the entire complement of common genetic variants, and what do we find?

---

[50]   Sarah Kate Kramer. "The Human Genome Project: 10 Years Later, Progress but still a Puzzle." WNYC News, July 31, 2010.

[51]   Stephen S. Hall. "Revolution Postponed: Why the Genome Project Has Been Disappointing." Scientific American, October, 2010, Nature Publishing Group, New York.

[52]   Harold Varmus, M.D. "Ten Years On—The Human Genome and Medicine." *NEJM* 362; 21. May 27, 2010.

Almost nothing. That is absolutely beyond belief." Goldstein has begun to be more optimistic recently with the discovery by a research team in Seattle that was able to make the first direct estimate of changes in DNA that will be passed down from parent to child.

Walter Bodmer, among the first to propose the genome project in the 1980s and a pioneer of studies that have dominated recent genomics, announced that searching for common gene variants is a biological dead end. "It is almost impossible to find what the biological effects of these variant genes are, and that's absolutely key," he says. "The vast majority of [common] variants have shed no light on the biology of diseases."[53] More recent studies have been somewhat more promising[54], but the initial approach was very disappointing and based on a faulty premise.

ABOVE THE TREES, UP TO THE FOREST

As it turns out, DNA is only half of the story. The epigenome, or the network of environmental factors that determine *which* genes will be activated, is where the real revolution most likely lies. Many factors are involved in understanding a particular disease process. And those that modify the DNA in a way that tells it what to do are being referred to as "epigenetic," or *above* the gene—meaning in a person's environment.

Epigenetic factors can influence gene expression and can be modified by environmental variables such as lifestyle, stressful behaviors, and so forth. In other words, something causes the gene to "express itself."[55] Just because you have the gene for heart disease doesn't mean you'll get it. In this way, the epigenome serves as a bridge between our genes and our environment. Your behaviors and the way you live your life determine whether the gene becomes active or not.

---

[53] Stephen S. Hall. Ibid.
[54] Nicholas Wade. "Disease Cause is Pinpointed with Genome." *New York Times*. Research. March 10, 2010.
[55] When a gene "expresses itself," it becomes activated.

The epigenome network is flexible and adjusts specific genes in our genetic landscape *in response to* factors such as stress, beliefs, diet, and exercise.[56] "A few brave voices are telling us that our biology runs a little deeper than a focus on DNA sequences and proteins alone can account for.

The current view of disease and the idea that the key to disease can be found in variants in the DNA code is probably too narrow a view. Many have introduced the idea that human disease is complex and a large collection of individually rare, personal conditions.[57]

Insights of this nature show that "the experts" aren't always right. We are beginning to see that the behaviors we choose, the way we lead our lives, and our self-healing strategies have much more power and potential than we know. A radical synthesis of new scientific discoveries combined with the personal experience of many forward-thinking physicians, nurses, and scientists is creating a sea change in the way we understand and confront disease, revealing the power we have to heal.

TIME FOR DECENTRALIZED MEDICINE?

Now is a good time to create a new blueprint for healing. It would be in step with the great movement toward decentralization taking place in other sectors of our lives. Whether it's trading your own investment account online, building your own new kitchen using Home Depot's do-it-yourself tools and materials, or learning the presentation of self in everyday life through Facebook, more and more *we're* the experts, the masters of our own destinies. The next radical phase of self-healing is for all of us to see that the answers do indeed lie within.

The radical idea is that the clinician does not have all the knowledge and power. As individuals, we can be shown how to access this power ourselves. Holistic practitioners assist us in activating our innate

---

[56] Bruce Lipton. *The Biology of Belief.* Hay House. www.hayhouse.com, June, 2013.

[57] John McClellan and Mary Clare King. "Genetic Heterogeneity in Human Disease." *Cell.* April 2010.

self-healing. Healing and holistic models of care fit nicely into a decentralized context. The basic premise of these approaches is that we have the power to bring about our own health and healing.[58] Holistic strategies flip the current approach on its head.

In its simplest form, the path to self-healing is about *aligning with the power of who we really are*. "Health is more than the absence of disease," claims the World Health Organization. Yet the usual approach in medicine is to look for a single cause in a single part of the body. We aim to find that single germ that causes the single illness, the plaque that caused the heart attack. We are beginning to see that this approach, while highly successful in some circumstances, is reaching its limits. It is misleading in that it does not tell the whole story. The whole story lies with you, the patient, the consumer, the person, the healer within, the powerhouse of human potential.

---

[58]   Complementary Medicine, NIH website, www.nih.com

III

THE EXPERTS: OFTEN WRONG, NEVER IN DOUBT

Power Step: Be open to believing you can heal, no matter what the experts say. Listen to your own soul's wisdom.

My friend Jonathan was diagnosed with late-stage prostate cancer. The diagnosis came from a top-notch specialist at one of the finest teaching hospitals in the country. He pronounced, "You only have months to live. There is nothing more we can do." But Jonathan, a confident, maybe even cocky, successful businessman describes his reaction to his prognosis: "I'm the guy who gets knocked down in the ring. The referee counts to three and the bell rings to tell him, 'You're out!' But he doesn't hear the bell. He totally ignores the bell and gets back up to keep fighting. Eventually, he wins the fight."

So it was with Jonathan. He ignored the expert's predictions that his life was over. Eventually, he was completely healed. He says he never *really* believed the reports. As he tells it, "I was determined to keep on living my life—laughing, doing what I liked, having a good time." Twelve years later and cancer-free, Jonathan volunteers to help people who have cancer. He says, "I am living proof to them that they too can be healed."

Like Jonathan, many defy medicine's holy grail. They have learned the hard way that the "experts" are often wrong, if never in doubt. Untold numbers of people are healed every day. Unraveling the reasons *why* seems to reside in the ineffable, in places that can't be easily described or measured. One thing is for sure: the reasons some people heal often lie outside of the realms of medicine and science as we know them. Let's look at why that may be.

MEDICINE'S SPECTACULAR PATH

> Robotic surgeries, ushering in another incredible arena of discovery, use tiny metal hands carefully to manipulate sutures deep inside a patient's body like something out of a science fiction movie.

To be fair, medicine's discoveries have been nothing short of spectacular. Scientific breakthroughs continue to raise our standard of living to incredible new heights. We can live with tiny artificial hearts and get new livers, lungs, and limbs. The story of a woman who suffered brutal burns, disfiguring her face, is in the news. Specialists came up with a brilliant solution: let's do a facial transplant. Taking the face off a young woman who'd just died, they transplanted the face onto the injured woman. She has a new lease on life because of the miracles of modern medicine.

Medicine is on the verge of even greater breakthroughs. The clinical advances of stem cell research have been amazing. Recently, European researchers genetically manipulated bone marrow cells taken from two seven-year-old boys and then transplanted the altered cells back into the boys and apparently arrested the progress of a fatal brain disease. Robotic surgeries, ushering in another incredible arena of discovery, use tiny metal hands carefully to manipulate sutures deep inside a patient's body, like something out of a science fiction movie. Robotic surgery is performed daily in a growing number of centers across the country. Soon traditional surgeries done by cutting the patient open will be completely outdated.

Medical progress in the past century has been astounding. In the process, an enormous economic enterprise has been created. Perhaps for that reason, over the years, medicine has been reluctant to embrace change that veered away from conventional cause and effect approaches. Yet it is obvious that what the experts believe changes continually; what the experts consider "healthy" and "what's good for you" changes dramatically from one decade to the next. Experts who swear by a certain treatment one day, often tell us soon afterward that it's not as good as they thought.

THE SHIFTING SANDS OF EXPERT MEDICAL OPINION

We discover that medical treatments we swear by one day aren't as effective as we thought and they're gone the next. For years, hormone replacement therapy (HRT) was thought to prevent heart disease in women. Then one day we hear that the Women's Health Study came to an abrupt halt when it was discovered that the women on HRT were experiencing heart disease at a greater rate than the control group. For many years, physicians prescribed HRT because research showed that HRT would likely *reduce* the risk of heart disease in women. Come to find out that the reason the studies showed women on HRT had less heart disease was probably due to the healthier lifestyles of women who take HRT rather than the medical benefits of HRT itself.

More recent studies of women, such as the Heart and Estrogen/progestin Replacement Study (HERS) and the Women's Health Initiative (WHI) showed that there is an *increased* risk of heart disease in older women who started HRT many years after menopause. So not only doesn't HRT prevent heart disease, but it may also even help to create it.

Another example of the shifting sands of expert opinion is the case of mastectomy as a treatment for breast cancer. For a long time, a mastectomy was the treatment of choice for breast cancer, until it was discovered that it did not prolong life any more than a lumpectomy. Even so, the rate of *double* mastectomies—removing the healthy breast as well—has doubled in the past ten years, despite the fact that there is no evidence that it prevents a recurrence.[59]

Depression has only fairly recently been recognized by the American Heart Association as a major risk factor for heart disease. Before that, it wasn't even on experts' radar screens. The prevailing wisdom was that emotions had nothing to do with disease. If you couldn't see it, it didn't exist. Now it's well established as a major risk factor for heart disease.

Well-meaning experts disagree on droves of issues. Take vitamin D, for instance. Dr. Cooper, from the University of Birmingham—who noted the huge sector in the scientific community that is "evangelical" in its pro–vitamin-D stance—warned that physicians have been here before. Many nutrients like vitamin D, tested on large populations, turned out to have no effect at all or were even found to be harmful. In fact, there is already evidence of risk with supplements of vitamin D from randomized clinical trials, with no evidence of benefit, Cooper argues. "Vitamin D—we all need more? Most of us don't, and more could actually do more harm than good."

The lack of effectiveness of back surgery is well known. At best, results are mixed. Yet many well-meaning surgeons perform back surgeries on nearly one million patients every year. Many times, they want to help and don't know what else to do. Nearly everyone experiences back pain at one time or another. A report by the National Center for Health Statistics found that more than a quarter of adults had low back pain in the past three months. It's the second most common neurological ailment in the United States, trailing only headaches, according to the National Institute of Neurological Disorders and Stroke.[60] Back pain alone costs Americans eighty-six billion dollars a year for surgeries, injections, pain pills, and other treatments. More complex procedures such as spinal fusions—in which vertebrae are

---

[59]   Agus, Ibid.

[60]   www.ninds.nih.gov

permanently bonded—have nearly doubled, from 203,000 in 1997 to 381,000 in 2007, according to the group.[61]

Nevertheless, evidence is mounting that for many patients, surgery is no better at relieving back pain than physical therapy and anti-inflammatory medicines. Some patients, like my friend Lulu, are even worse off after surgery, leading many to coin the term "failed back surgery syndrome."

As Dr. David Agus put it, "As they did in the past and still do to this day, drug companies and marketers and hawkers of all things 'good for you' tend to get it all wrong, and they do it in the name of profit, rather than an interest in what's actually good for us."[62]

Patients, and those close to them, see something vastly different from a huge economic enterprise when they think about health care. They see, or hope to see, encounters that assume an intimate position in our lives. The endlessly standardized medical tests and procedures—divorced from compassionate clinicians who have limited time and attention—have led to increasing unhappiness on the part of the people they are meant to help. Too often medical treatments leave out our emotions and the day-to-day things that may be affecting our health, like job worries, relationship problems, or financial concerns. For medical encounters to be effective, they should assume a rich intrapersonal or even a spiritual or soulful tone between the person and the clinician.

If the treatments of choice in medical science are constantly changing, instead of blindly following expert's opinions, we need to become our own experts and learn to translate the signs and signals that our minds and bodies, in addition to our souls, are sending us. Modern medicine doesn't often reach into our minds and emotions, let alone our souls. Until very recently, for many experts, the mind was not taken

---

[61]   B.I. Martin et al. "Expenditures and Health Status Among Adults with Back and Neck Problems." *JAMA.* 2008, 299 (6): 656–664.

[62]   Agus, Ibid.

seriously in medicine's scientific circles. It was considered an aspect of the brain's chemistry.[63] Consciousness is considered a brain function.

Candice Pert, PhD, former head of molecular biology at the National Institutes of Health, described a good example of this thinking. Trailblazer in mind-body medicine and author of *Molecules of Emotion*, Pert discovered that emotions play a powerful role in the psychobiology of health and wellness. With tongue in cheek, Pert commented, "For quite a few years now, I have watched with some amusement as neuroscientists, using the tools of brain imaging, have published their pictures showing the loci of various emotions, like fear, anger, and even spiritual consciousness, as residing in, or having generative origin in, rather specific brain areas.

"Their conclusions derive from enhanced metabolic activity, blood flow, or glucose utilization associated with these regions. Reminds me of the claim that Peter Jennings exists inside the TV tube, or circuit board, or transistor, or electron—let's just keep following this reductionist path."[64] In other words, Pert was saying that looking for consciousness in the brain is like looking for the announcer inside the TV set.

Reductionism in medicine is far from soulful. It means reducing the body to understanding each of its parts and thinking that this approach will eventually lead you to know all there is to know about what can go wrong and how to fix it. As Harvard physicians Bernard Lown and Thomas Grayboys put it, "We believe the modern medical model has become increasingly reductionistic ... Human beings are seen as malfunctioning organs in need of repair."[65]

In our Western medical culture, an increasing number of people are seeing this mechanistic approach to medicine, with its greatest investments in specialized drugs and surgery, as an underlying reason

---

[63] Mario Beauregard. *The Spiritual Brain: A Neuroscientist's Case for The Existence of the Soul.* Harper Collins, New York, 2007, www.harpercollins.com

[64] Candace Pert blog

[65] "Long-Suffering Patients." *The New Yorker.* May 11, 1999.

for the problems and dissatisfaction with our current system, its high error rates, and fragmented services.[66]

WE ARE STARDUST: A SAMADHI EXPERIENCE

One distinguished scientist who believes we're misguided in our current approach to science is Edgar Mitchell (as mentioned in the last chapter, an Apollo 14 astronaut and the sixth man to walk on the moon). Dr. Mitchell founded the Institute of Noetic Sciences to advance the study of consciousness. After he had an experience of samadhi, a higher level of consciousness where the body, mind, and intellect are transcended, on the way back from his lunar voyage, he was convinced there is more to this life than meets the eye.

Mitchell tells the story of his journey back to Earth: "Since we were not inside the screen set up by our atmosphere, the stars were ten times as bright, ten times more numerous than anything you can see on earth from the tallest mountain … so it was a powerful 'wow' experience."

"I had done my studying in astronomy at MIT and Harvard, and I knew that matter in our universe is created in star systems, and I suddenly realized that the material of my body and my partner's body and the spacecraft that we were in was either prototyped or manufactured in an ancient generation of stars. *We're stardust, as it were.* This was a 'wow' experience accompanied by a sense of ecstasy and overwhelming unity that we're all one. It's all the same stuff. And the unity and the ecstasy that goes with it was something I never quite experienced before, and I began to realize that perhaps the story told to us by our science is incomplete and perhaps flawed."

Not knowing what he had experienced, Mitchell plowed through the scientific literature for answers, only to find none there. So he turned to a few anthropologist colleagues at Rice University. "It sounds like you

---

[66]   David E. Newman-Toker, MD, PhD. "BMJ Quality and Safety." *Johns Hopkins Study of Diagnostic Error in Medicine.* October 2013. vol. 22, Suppl. 2.

had a samadhi experience,"[67] they told him. And that experience taught Mitchell that there was more to science than meets the eye.

Mitchell went on to immerse himself in a world that used to be just for the mystical. He is now among a long list of esteemed scientifically minded "believers" leading the charge to explain these spiritual heights through new quantum scientific discoveries. Mitchell is a living testimony to the new story of science. Healed of prostate cancer and later of kidney cancer with the help of spiritual healers on the board of the Institute for Noetic Sciences, and the well-known Canadian healer, nicknamed Adam, the Dreamhealer,[68] Mitchell is in the forefront of leading the new paradigm shift to healing.

Mitchell's samadhi experience told him there's more to healing than conventional medicine has to offer. Intuitively, many of us see the same limitations of drugs and surgery in our own experiences. In the early part of the twentieth century, we enjoyed great success with this approach—the model of cause and effect: germ A causes disease B and is treated by drugs and surgery C. But the world was simpler then. Our family doctors knew all the members of the family and the details of their lives by heart. As medicine became more highly specialized, it created greater and greater complexity, and its basic premises began losing power.

SAMADHI AND THE SOUL'S POWER IN ILLNESS

We all have the healer within us, but we have to learn how to access it. Each of us has had experiences that we knew were coming from our depths. Moments of courage and daring, profound love or deep inner peace touch us deeply. These experiences of the soul strike chords of

---

[67] Samadhi, in Hinduism, Buddhism or yogic schools, is a non-dualistic state of consciousness in which the consciousness of the person becomes one with the experienced object, and in which the mind becomes still, one-pointed, or concentrated, while the person remains conscious.

[68] www.dreamhealer.com/about

response in our deepest essence, our innermost self, who we truly are at the core. When we do what we believe in—even if it's not necessarily popular, like Ghandi, a small Indian man who brought the British Empire to its knees; or Rosa Parks, who refused to give up her seat on a bus—the experience often comes from the depths of the soul.

We're not as quick to recognize illness as a soulful experience. But it's one of the more dramatic ways that the soul demands our attention. During an illness, our souls speak to us from our depths. Our symptoms serve as a wake-up call, pleading for our attention, asking us to listen more clearly to what our souls are trying to tell us. Paradoxically, the soul, the seat of our deepest emotions, actually aims for us to benefit greatly from our illness.

Soul power emerges from illness if we listen carefully to its messages. In fact, illness can be our soul's ticket to profound journeys of self-actualization. It can even lead us to our true calling, to our destiny. But first we have to learn the soul's language. We have to turn within and learn to listen to the "still small voice" to find out precisely what it is our souls are seeking. In order to tap the soul's power, learning to listen within is key.

Yet listening is a scarce commodity in modern medicine. Harvey Fineberg, MD, one of medicine's powerhouses, former Dean at Yale and president of the prestigious Institute of Medicine, echoed this view. Delivering a keynote address to an audience largely comprised of physicians, he stressed the vital importance of listening to patients. He lamented, "For years in practice with my own patients, I pretended to listen and they pretended to understand."

Patients these days are feeling the frustration of clinicians who pretend to listen. In national surveys, one of five patients said that they did not spend enough time with their physician,[69] and more and more physicians said that they cannot spend enough time with patients to deliver quality care.[70]

---

[69] Roni Caryn Rabin. "Burnt Out Primary Care Docs Are Voting with Their Feet." *Kaiser Health News,* April 2014. Kaiserhealthnews.org

[70] Ibid.

In medical encounters, if a person' s innermost fears and desires are listened to and acknowledged at all, it is considered secondary, something to deal with after the important business of medicine is taken care of. When we see that the experts don't listen and often dismiss what we have to say, it squelches any tendency we might have to listen to our own inner messages and promptings as a path to healing. If the experts in medicine don't give our thoughts and feelings any importance, why should *we*?

Science has taught us to mistrust our own instincts and intuitions about our health. Instilled in us is a sense of powerlessness. The power of medicine resides in tests and procedures rather than in us as individuals. Yet our thought processes and emotions have great power and play a vital role in healing.

Anything can be healed. But before healing can happen, the soul's healing power must be accessed. Your alignment with your soul, having a sense of what your soul is saying to you, is key. Many have defied the odds and found their way to healing. Let's look at a few of these stories so that we can see what they did that worked.

IV

SOUL STORIES: REDEFINING ILLNESS AS THE WAKE-UP CALL

Power Step: Listen to you inner guide like a wise friend trying to help you … Your body is on your side.

Each patient has his or her own physician inside her. She comes to us not knowing that truth. Our job is to recognize that practitioner inside and heed her advice.

—Albert Schweitzer

As a young nurse at Sloan Kettering Cancer Center, I always wondered why some patients who were just as sick as others were got better. I wondered why the others didn't. As I thought about why, I saw that time and again, the patients who were willing to listen to what their bodies were trying to tell them—listen to what their souls "speaking" through their bodies were trying to say— got better.

> When you feel helpless to change your circumstances—as if your lot in life is to remain in situations where you're mistreated or not valued for who you are—you are creating situations where illness may be your only way out.

The ones who experienced recovery were the patients who were able to hear what their soul—through their illness—was trying to tell them. Illness appears when there is a loss of personal power, a loss of the ability to be who you are, a loss of personal spark, of inner essence, a loss of

46

connection to your soul. What kinds of circumstances would cause you to lose the connection to your soul? It could be losing heart because you've failed at something repeatedly; situations where you experience mistreatment or abuse that traumatize the soul; situations where people humiliate you and treat you with a lack of respect repeatedly, chipping away at your soul connection. You sever your soul connection if you do certain things just to "belong," whether it's belonging to your family or a peer group that demands that you do certain things in a certain way: dress a certain way, behave a certain way, choose a certain job or career path, or marry a certain way. "It was good enough for us, and it better be good enough for you" is a message that creates a big black cloud over the soul.

You might rationalize the situation by telling yourself that those who are mistreating you mean well and know better than you do about what's good for you. You lie to yourself or repress painful feelings. When you feel alienated from your inner essence, your sense of who you really are, for long enough, you will create mental or physical illness.

ILLNESS REDEFINED

As I observed patients who were diagnosed with serious, even supposedly terminal, illnesses, this seemed to hold true: *Those who managed to see their illness as something helpful, or as a "wake-up call" signaling that something major in their lives needed to change, were the ones who recovered.* We sometimes hear people in these situations say, "My illness was the best thing that ever happened to me. My unhappiness in my work (or marriage, or financial situation, or career, or whatever you wish to substitute) was making me sick, and my illness *forced* me to make a change." Those who saw no need to change succumbed to the illness.

Illness can be a *good* thing. It's a way of getting your attention, and, like your very own built-in GPS, it's telling you, "Please proceed to the highlighted route." What if we are getting the wake-up call message? Where do we begin? How can we make behavior changes of this magnitude happen?

We have to find a way to acknowledge painful feelings and situations and then release them. It can be with the help of another. It can be through faith. Traumatic circumstances like sexual abuse, the physical or emotional trauma of divorce, and loss of a loved one, often require the help of a counselor or therapist who provides care and emotional support. If you're feeling overwhelmed, that's a good place to start.

When we decide not to heed the wake-up call and to ignore our soul's important messages, we pay dearly. Pursuing a path in life that is not our own calling, a path designed to please others or maybe just to avoid being alone, is destined to create pain and illness. Whether it's a choice about who you marry or the work you do, or where you live or your political persuasion, these decisions are yours to make. They shape who you are. Everybody can seek guidance, but ultimately we each have to do our own choosing. Assuming the burdens and responsibilities others are meant to assume for themselves, even if they're dear loved ones, is also bound to create pain.

Each of us has our own path; each of us has our own particular brand of lesson to be learned. When we intervene on behalf of another—sparing a child unpleasant punishment for something he did wrong, keeping bad financial news from a spouse, doing a colleague's work because he doesn't want to or can't do it himself—we are actually depriving that person of the unique soul experiences designed to help him, to ease his way later on. When you spare someone from a difficult life experience, you also deprive his soul of learning its own lessons. The sense of confidence and self-respect that comes from learning to avoid self-defeating behaviors and repeating the same mistakes has to be developed on your own.

The longer we deprive our souls (or those of others) of what they yearn for, the more we pay a price. The price can range from mild depression, to sleeplessness or addictions and anxiety disorders, to chronic pain or heart disease or cancer. We neglect our inner guidance, the voices of our souls, at our peril. Medical crises in our lives often stem from the fact that our souls are begging us to listen to them.

Mona Lisa Schultz, MD, PhD, describes how she almost died because she ignored her soul's persistent doubts. She worked very hard to be a successful neurologist to fulfill her parents' dreams. "I was very right-brained, being forced to assume a left-brained path to please my parents."

She feverishly pursued her medical studies, and eventually, in her residency, her doctors told her she wasn't going to make it. Becoming nearly fatally ill, she recounts, "I was diagnosed with a malignant brain tumor and given only a few months to live. At an early age, I was extremely intuitive. I had premonitions and flashes of insight that always turned out to be stunningly accurate. But I denied that I had them, even to myself, because they scared me."

As she tells her story in *Awakening Intuition*, a close friend rescued her. "She came to see me every day, and our long conversations slowly helped me get to the bottom of my feelings. Deep down, I began to realize that I had to face up to the fact that the life I was leading was a far cry from what my soul was calling me to do."

Mona Lisa finally saw the light, and she began to listen within. She knew if she were to recover, she would have to forget her parents' dreams for her and follow her own soul's calling. As she did, with the help of close friends who supported her, she struggled to get hold of her deepest feelings and intuition about herself and her illness, to understand the meaning behind it.

"When something significant happens to us in our lives, the emotionally charged experience gets encoded in the brain. We may not even know the true significance of this experience, yet it, and other emotionally charged memories, will affect everything we do in the future, from who we choose for companionship to what we do for a living."[71] By examining our unconscious feelings, we can learn to know ourselves and heal, reclaiming our power from stored memories of things we repressed because they were unpleasant. This is especially true when you feel bad about bringing them up and releasing them.

---

[71] Mona Lisa Shultz, MD, PhD. *Awakening Intuition*. Three Rivers Press, New York, 1998.

"I wish I could say that I learned the connection between memories, dreams, intuition, and healing in a college course or, better yet, through divine inspiration. As fate would have it, however, I had to reach an understanding of this connection the way I believe many, if not most, people do—through illness."

Hers is a story with a happy ending. Mona Lisa heeded the wake-up call. Currently practicing as a well-known, highly sought-after medical intuitive, someone who can see intuitively and diagnose what is happening in the human body, she is on the path she knows her soul has called her to. I have referred several people, friends, and acquaintances to her. Many have similar stories. They learned to listen to their souls' calling the same way that she did, through illness.

A STORY CLOSER TO HOME

Another story comes from my own family. When I was about twelve years old, my younger cousin Stacey repeatedly lost consciousness. During these episodes, her eyes would stay open. After a couple of "fainting spells," as we called them, her mother took her to a highly respected neurologist at a major medical center. His diagnosis: Stacey had grand mal epilepsy.

> True self-knowledge is indispensable for health and vitality.

He put her on an appropriate medication regime, which worked fairly well during college. However, as her stress level increased with her first job in management, her neurologist increased her medication. My cousin complained that she was feeling drowsy all day, to the point where she was unable to function effectively. She knew that the increase in medication was causing the problem. She told her neurologist that her medication needed to be cut back. He was intransigent. "Look, I'm the doctor here," he told her firmly. "You have to take this medicine as it's prescribed. EEGs don't lie. We know that this amount is necessary to prevent a seizure from occurring."

> Healing depends on the ability to listen to the soul, to heed the deep inner wisdom of the voice inside us.

To Stacey, who refused to live her life in a medication stupor, this was completely unacceptable. She vividly recalls a voice inside that kept saying, "I know that this condition is not me. It hasn't always been there, and it doesn't have to stay. It will go the way it came." Listening to these constant echoes of her soul's truth inside—*that her illness was not who she really was*—she embarked on her own program to pay careful attention to her emotions and internal rhythms. She listened to her feelings and what her body was trying to say to her. As Stacey tells the story, "I experimented and learned to be sensitive to what I was feeling, what was upsetting me, when I needed rest, when and what I wanted to eat, and what people and situations were stressful and draining for me."

She noticed that some people and situations energized her, while others seemed to suck the life out of her. She saw that when she allowed herself to be around too many people and circumstances that drained her, she received a "warning": she would become light-headed. She would always receive the same warning before the "fainting spell" occurred—before she lost consciousness.

As Stacey heeded the wake-up call, she gradually learned to become conscious of the things she did that would trigger symptoms. She would say to herself, "When I push myself, I feel off balance. When I don't get enough sleep, I feel off balance. When I don't exercise enough, I feel off balance." She learned to be more attuned to her inner guidance, to the still small voice within.

She refused to put herself in situations that drained her emotionally. She learned to say no to people and places that were too stressful or unpleasant. She learned to say no to social invitations if she needed sleep, even if they were from the people closest to her. She learned how much exercise she needed to keep her stress level down. She altered her diet and kept strict watch over what she ate—becoming conscious of foods that created discomfort.

My cousin gradually decreased her medication on her own. As she grew more and more comfortable and confident about her new approach to life, she stopped taking it completely. She has not had to take medication for over twenty years. As Stacey predicted, the condition left, just as it came. She completely healed herself.

An incredulous neurologist now treating another younger cousin for the same disorder (it likely has a hereditary component), recently asked to interview Stacey to see exactly how she had accomplished her healing.

HEALING: KEY TO THE SOUL'S JOURNEY

In both cases, Mona Lisa's and Stacey's, their illnesses resulted from *some deep inner essence blocked from becoming its authentic self.* Both stories show what research into healing has shown: healing depends on the ability to listen to the soul, to heed the deep inner wisdom of the voice inside us.[72] The mind and the body are the soul's instruments. As you come to know what your inner guidance, the voice of your soul, is saying, you'll become clearer and clearer about who you are, your desires, your likes and dislikes. It is reflected in your thoughts and your feelings. When aligned with your soul, you become happier, more positive, more joyful. Your thoughts, feelings, and actions start to get in sync with one another.

As you allow yourself to be around people and in circumstances that cause you continuing discomfort, situations that do not support your being who you are—that are not "you," so to speak—your emotions, like a built-in radar system, will send you signals. If you ignore them or suppress them because of a need to please others, or because of some misguided idea of what others consider important, the negative feelings don't disappear; they get worse.

---

[72] Larry Dossey, MD. *Healing Words.* Harper Collins, New York, 1995.

Stacey is convinced that the neurological problem she had was created because she internalized all her feelings and anxieties. The firestorm of emotions she held inside created in effect, an internal explosion, like a detonating bomb that goes off when the fuse is lit.

Her "fuses" were the onset of puberty and hormonal shifts, coupled with personal anxieties, the added stresses of her work life. Never complaining or expressing her emotions outwardly created a troubled, highly charged internal environment.

Our souls are the keepers of our inner guidance and our uniqueness. Our individualities arise from our depths. Our personal power comes from assuming that special self, that original self that is brimming over with our signature emotional patterns and idiosyncrasies. When we stifle our uniqueness in order to be something we are not or to do something we're not meant to do, our souls fight back. Often they fight back through illness.

> We heal ourselves with our thoughts, our minds, our beliefs, our consciousness.

Like Mona Lisa or my cousin Stacey, we all get soul messages. Then we make decisions about what illnesses we will succumb to and which ones we won't. Most times, however, we don't make these decisions on a conscious level. The key to making these decisions in a way that is healthy for you is *knowing what you are feeling*. If you don't know what you are feeling and how to interpret your feelings to deal with conflicts and the tough life challenges, your unconscious dis-ease may create an illness to get your attention or to serve as a way out of the difficulty you may be facing. A clue to listening within: *If your thoughts are telling you one thing and your emotions another, listen to your emotions—that will be closer to the truth.*

We differ in our ability to listen inside and heed the soul's advice. Because of beliefs ingrained in us from early childhood, many times we ignore our soul's deepest urgings. Like Mona Lisa and Stacey, we often ignore the call many times. Stuck in the seventeenth-century science of Newton and Descartes, when it comes to our health, we tend to focus on different body parts and what we can physically see. If a person's inner voice is acknowledged, it is considered an afterthought, something to attend to once the more important scientific medical considerations have been addressed.

Yet there is a tipping point inside each of us, where we learn to create situations and relationships that make us feel good and help us be the best we can be. We must find this tipping point if we want to heal. The causal line of thinking in medicine—this germ is the cause of that disease—really doesn't have bearing on healing at this level, a level science has just begun to reach. Many studies, for example, have shown how yoga and meditation can bring us to the state where healing can occur. These practices connect us with the pure positive energy, often referred to as divine or universal, that resides deep within every one of us.

Once again, healing is an inside job. We heal ourselves with our thoughts, our minds, our beliefs, our souls. Creating ways to incorporate the soul's experience during illness would not only humanize medicine; it would bring new breakthroughs. In fact, many bold and courageous scientists have begun to chart this course. Thomas Moore, soul doctor and author of *Care of the Soul*, gives advice along these lines to a hospital administrator who took pride in his novel approach. Encouraging patients to read their own charts and understand their medications and vital signs, giving them pamphlets describing the biological aspects of their disease, the administrator was proud to be in the vanguard.

However, Moore's advice was more radical: he advised that patients ought to be encouraged to keep track of their impressions and their emotions during the course of their hospitalization and to note their dreams every day. Moore also recommends a time and place where patients can tell stories about their illnesses, not with an expert who would reinforce the medical format, but someone who would know the importance of letting the soul speak and find its messages. Radical indeed.

Healing can take place instantly when there's a recognition of what has created the illness. Illness seeks to teach us, sending a message from the soul. When you learn the lesson, the illness gets its cue to leave. It is our confusion—trying to be someone we're not—manifesting physically so that we will become aware of the problem.

When an illness is accepted for what it is, a lesson and a warning, and deeply looked into and heeded, it eventually dissolves. Pain speaks to us when we're ready to learn from it. When we accept it as helpful, instead of resisting it, it disappears. Emotional pain says one thing; physical says another. Even its location in the body is meaningful; nothing happens haphazardly. That's a hard thing to hear when you're in pain. Illness exists first in the energetic realm. It always has to do with emotional confusion or mental upset; it's never primarily physical. The inner state is projecting itself outwardly. You can use this information to your own benefit and make the changes you need in order to heal, just as Mona Lisa and Stacey did.

WHEN SOUL BECKONS THROUGH ILLNESS

The organs weep the tears the eyes refuse to shed.

—Wilhelm Reich

If the soul is so vital to healing, what is it all about and how do you listen to it? I remember the first time my teacher told me to "listen to my soul." I thought, *What in the hell is he talking about?*

When we talk about listening to the soul, self-examination is the starting point.

Perhaps Mathew Richard, molecular biologist turned monk, said it best: "Very often we look outside ourselves for well-being and healing. We think if we could gather up all the conditions for well-being, for healing, in the outer world, we can get there."[73] But if we do, we're headed in the wrong direction. Trying to "fix" things from the outside will help for a while. External remedies can be very helpful. They can jump-start the healing process. But it's the inside that really matters.

---

[73] Mathew Richard. TED Talk on "Happiness."

Like the calm of the ocean at its depths, even when storms are raging on its surface, we can develop an inner calm, an internal happiness, and an internal peace that heals.

> Like the calm of the ocean at its depths, even when storms are raging on its surface, we can develop an inner calm, an internal happiness, and an inner peace that heals.

We begin by listening to our souls. How do we listen? With simple observation: What are we thinking and feeling at the heart of every moment? What are the themes? What thought patterns are dominant in our minds? Are they optimistic or fear based? What speaks to us and energizes us? What depletes us? What inspires us? What is the still small voice inside trying to tell us? That voice is the voice of your infallible guide. If you learn to listen to what it's saying, it won't mislead you. It's the voice of your soul and the key to your healing. As you'll see in the following chapters, clearing your emotions and observing your mind's patterns will pave the way to tapping your soul's healing power.

A friend of mine who is a very successful Wall Street hedge fund manager was asking questions about healing and happiness recently. "You seem happy all the time. How do you get there?" he asked.

I wasn't quite sure how to answer, so I simply said, "It's a process, but you start by looking within." He looked at me incredulously and then burst out laughing! By now, I was laughing too because I knew his laughter was a sign of how absurd he thought my comment was. But I persisted. I wanted to hear what he would say, so still grinning, I asked, "What's so funny?"

He answered, "I've spent my whole life on Wall Street riveted on the market's every move and now I'm going to look within?"

"Exactly," I said, still laughing.

V

ANYTHING CAN BE HEALED

Power Step: We are born with a built-in self-healing system … with the power inside us to heal anything. Get to know this power, and learn to access it.

> *If someone wishes for good health, one must first ask oneself if he is ready to do away with the reasons for his illness. Only then is it possible to help him.*

—Hippocrates

Turning within is the key. If we trace happiness to its source, we see that every bit of happiness comes from within. The deeper we go within, the higher, the happier, the greater the feeling of well-being. The greater the healing power we tap into. A mega healing power exists within every one of us. It's like a sphinx's riddle: we've been taught to look for healing in the externals, when actually it's an inside job. An example is when we get sick, we search for the best specialists, the best medicine money can buy. Yet medical treatments, while all well and good in their own right, do not get to the most important aspect. If you want to discover the wellspring of healing power, you have to look within.

"Am I strong enough to heal?" you ask yourself. Actually, healing can be as simple as breathing, as long as we stay out of the way. "Staying out of the way" means letting go of the second-guessing, the doubts, the what-ifs that erect mental barriers and create an energetic ceiling on your healing path. When you cooperate with your basic nature, healing takes place.

What if we all *knew for sure* that as human beings, each of us inherited a powerful potential to heal, and that even though we have been taught to give away that power to external experts, we can reclaim it? It's true. We *do* have the potential to heal anything within us. We have all grown up learning that scientific medicine is the first line of attack against illness. Yet when you recover after treatment with drugs or surgery, it doesn't necessarily mean that you are healed, but that the physical *symptoms* have disappeared. Healing would mean that you got to the root of the problem, that you also understood the source of it and took steps to address it.

Healing actually takes place on three levels: the level of the symptoms (or the physical), the mental level, and the energetic level.[74] It is important to realize that healing begins on the energetic level. A willingness to adopt new beliefs and behaviors is needed to reach the "tipping point" where the healing process begins. Here are a few guiding principles:

(1) **The X factor: Embrace the belief that you can heal.** *This is the first important step: you have to open your mind and believe you can be healed.* We can call it the X factor because it is so vital to your

> Healing takes place on three levels: the level of the symptoms, the mental level, and the energetic level.

healing process. Without believing that you can be healed, and actually having confidence that you can be healed, your efforts will likely be met with resistance as you tell yourself, "I'll never get better; nobody recovers from this" or, "I saw the X-rays and the look on my doctor's face. This is serious; I don't think they can fix something like this." Let doubts of this nature go. Drop them like a hot potato.

---

[74] Bill Bauman's healing seminars. Also in: David Hawkins. *Healing and Recovery.* Veritas Publishing, Sedona, Arizona, 2009.

(2) **Don't identify with your illness; understand that your illness is not *you*.** Be vigilant about *not identifying* with the illness. Don't claim it as a part of you. Don't say, *"My* heart disease, or *my* arthritis, or *my* malignancy." It's only paying you a visit to help you heal in the deepest sense. Make friends with it and know that it will go. Remember, your body is on your side. The illness has come to help you become aware of the things you need to do differently. Remember, illness is a wake-up call. Aim to learn how to heed its messages.

(3) **Start developing emotional awareness by paying attention to your thoughts.** *Watch what feelings they evoke.* Emotions are our radar, our very own built-in internal guidance system. As early warning signals, any denial of painful emotions or discomfort is ultimately expressed in the body. If the denial persists long enough, corresponding areas of the body develop a dis-ease, an ache, a pain, a dysfunction, a resistance to the life force. If you don't acknowledge your emotions and what they are trying to tell you, maybe because you're not used to listening to them, *your body will let you know what you're feeling.* As Eckhart Tolle reminds us, when we look at an emotion or feel it in the body, "If there is an apparent conflict between what you're thinking and feeling, the thought will be the lie; the emotion will be the truth."[75]

The energy fields created by your thoughts and your emotions are very influential in your healing process. You could say they are the key to your healing. Positive energies—gratitude and appreciation, hopefulness, eagerness—will hasten your healing. Negative energies such as fear and anger will slow it down. Let yourself feel your emotions as they arise; become aware of them to the best of your ability, and of the thoughts that created them. If you can't trace the emotions to a particular thought pattern, don't worry. If the emotion or the feeling is

---

[75] Eckhart Tolle. *The Power of Now.* New World Library, August 19, 2004.

a vague discomfort, it's probably resting in your unconscious, waiting for the opportunity to come up and out. *Let it* come up and out. If it's not the right place or time to express it, find the right time and place to release it.

Clearing your emotions may be a challenge, but it is a critical process on your healing journey. (There are many techniques available to help you release repressed emotions; we will discuss a few of them later on.) Often, the lion's share of our negative emotions has been pushed down into our unconscious. We live in a society where it's not always acceptable to express emotion openly; and if it feels bad, we often run from it. We often bury our emotions only to have them rear their heads in unexpected ways and places.

> **(4) Focus your mind on the intention to heal.** *Treating your body is really all about treating your mind and your emotions.* Recognize that your thoughts elicit certain emotions and emotions certain thoughts; by shaping or repatterning your thoughts, you can change the way you feel. You can begin by putting yourself in a more healing state just by focusing your intention on becoming well. Our psychological processes, which have been described as having a quantum nature,[76] will then go to work to bring your intention to life.[77]

There is much scientific evidence supporting the use of intention to heal.[78] In fact, when you use holistic modalities such as acupuncture, Reiki, yoga, and meditation, you are putting the power of intention to work. Holistic approaches aim to get at the source of the illness. Many are validated by scientific research, and others are validated

---

[76] Karl Pribam, MD. *The Form Within: My Point of View.* Prospecta Press, Westport, Connecticut, 2013.

[77] In an energy field of probabilities, the power of intention itself collapses the wave function. To understand more of the wave structure of matter, see www.spaceand motion.com/physics-David-bohm-holographic-universe.htm

[78] Adam Dreamhealer. "Intention Heals: Truth Is Stranger Than Fiction," in Dan Brown's new novel, *The Lost Symbol.* Anchor Books, 2009.

experientially, by people's response. Many people respond to holistic measures that haven't been proven by science to be effective. Yet they are. Even though they may be considered "unscientific," they are extremely valid to the patient.

A physician tells us about his own experience: "When I mentioned acupuncture to an internist I know, he pooh-poohed it and said, 'You don't believe in that, do ya?' Well, I was one of the first patients in the United States to have acupuncture.[79] I had a hopeless chronic, recurrent duodenal ulcer that was going to lead to the necessity for a subtotal gastrostomy. It was in Washington, DC, and it was scientifically very well observed. You had to bring X-rays and everything with you to prove your medical condition."

"At the conclusion of treatment, they repeated all the same diagnostics, such as X-rays. From the third treatment, my hemorrhaging duodenal ulcer was cured and never recurred in all these years. This was fifty years ago; a permanent long-term cure for something that I had for twenty-five years. I had psychoanalysis and everything to try to cure it. So it may not be scientific, but it works. The holistic approach is far more inclusive than traditional medicine."[80]

We can direct our thoughts toward an intention to heal. We can train our thoughts and our minds, just as we have been taught to train our bodies at the fitness center. We all have a propensity for one illness or another. Some of us get sore throats a lot; some of us develop tumors more readily than others do. Others get ulcers; some of us have heart problems, high blood pressure, and so forth. But our *greatest* propensity of all is toward health and healing! However, we can hinder that tendency with doubts and fears. We often think the worst when we get a sore throat or the flu. We might say, "Uh-oh, what if this turns into strep throat and then I come down with rheumatic fever? Then I'll have to miss work, and if I'm out for too long, I might lose my job because

---

[79] Since that time, considerable evidence has scientifically validated the effectiveness of acupuncture. www.nccih.nih.gov/health/acupuncture

[80] David Hawkins. *Healing and Recovery.* Veritas Publishing, Sedona, Arizona, 2009.

they'll need someone to be in charge of the huge project I'm working on … and then my kids will have to drop out of college." On and on and on goes the worst-case scenario we often construct. What if we thought of only the best outcome instead?

We're all guilty of "awfulizing"—imagining the worst possible outcome. Why not instead take up "fantacizing"—imagining or fantasizing the *best* possible outcome? If you can do that, you will have taken a vital leap into the realm where healing occurs. Healing begins when you begin to understand the power of your thoughts and get your thoughts moving in the direction of intending, even expecting to heal. Even if you really feel sick, you can still reach for the best feeling thought; that is, find the hope instead of the fear underneath your illness.

THE UNCONSCIOUS IS KING

Suppose you're doing a great job of training your thoughts. Your mind is like a brain gym. You tell it to do sit-ups—meaning, to think in a certain way—and it comes right to attention and does twenty perfect sit-ups. Yet you don't see progress. Chances are your unconscious is pulling in a different direction.

How can you tell what your unconscious is doing? It is *un*-conscious after all. Whenever you're upset and something or someone is bothering you, look into your mind to find out what caused the upset. Discover the triggering thought and you'll find your mastership over the event. Or you can tell what's going on in your unconscious by observing what your natural pattern of thoughts looks like. When most of the time you see negative, fearful thoughts creeping around in your mind, or your mood is most often sullen or a downer unless you work at it, repressed negative feelings are lurking around in there.

If you want to heal, your journey will eventually lead you to the unconscious mind and the feelings and emotions that lie buried within you. Called the "habit mind" because it consists of a kind of enslavement to prior thoughts, habits, and tendencies, the unconscious is responsible for the large majority of our thoughts. Most people's behavior—unless you're one of the few who has trained yourself to be aware of the connection between what you're thinking and feeling and doing--- is driven by the unconscious. For most of us, only about 5 percent of what we do is conscious.[81] The rest of the time we're running on automatic pilot! We don't like to hear it, but most of our decisions aren't based on logic and reason.

The unconscious rules in every aspect of our lives. A French study sheds light on how it happens. France researchers hired a handsome young Frenchman to stand on street corners and proposition single women who strolled by. He gave half of them a light half-second touch to the arm or the elbow. He didn't touch the other half. The success rate in getting the women's phone numbers basically doubled from 10 percent to 20 percent with those who were touched. Unconsciously, being touched registered as feeling loved and cared for, and it was the key to the Frenchman's success.

The good news: unconscious bonds can be broken. You can break bondages to what's unconscious by breaking habits and tendencies. As you work to remove past tendencies, you will find yourself more and more in control. For instance, you may have a tendency to feel victimized, to take things the wrong way, to take offense at certain remarks. Or maybe you have a tendency to overeat or to feel anger when friends forget your birthday. You can eliminate those tendencies with a willingness to forgive and a willingness to let go of judging yourself or others.

> Every part of an illness comes from you. Listen to your body. What is it saying? Be that part of your body, once you have heard the guidance, and see what it's trying to tell you.

Beginning with your mind and moving through your day-to- day experiences, you can gradually learn to identify the habitual tendencies, the feelings of discomfort buried deep inside you as they surface in day-to-day

---

[81] Leonard Mlodinow. *Subliminal: How Your Unconscious Mind Rules Your Behavior.* Leonard Mlodinow, Pantheon, a Division of Random House, 2012.

situations. In addition, you can learn to release them. As you more fully recognize the patterns of your behavior, you can learn to feel and release the feelings associated with them. As you see that you repressed them at the time because they were uncomfortable, you will increasingly be able to draw on your power to heal. Because you will no longer be using your energy to resist repressed feelings, your natural healing power will flow more and more freely to the parts of the body where it's needed. From experience, physician and spiritual teacher David Hawkins says that this can actually be done rather rapidly.

(5) **Listen to your soul, the center of your being.** Listen to the still small voice within. It will be your infallible guide on your healing journey. Listen and heed its wisdom. In order to be still enough to hear your soul, to hear what the inner voice of your soul is trying to tell you, you need to be able to be quiet and still your emotions and pay attention to your emotional states so you can learn to clear yourself of negative emotions. Otherwise, when you listen within, you will hear negative messages, but that won't be the voice of your soul. It will be old tapes playing from repressed fears, habits, and hang-ups.

Every part of an illness comes from you. Listen to your body. What is it saying? Be that part of your body, once you have heard the guidance, and see what it's trying to tell you. Do a guided meditation to help you hear what your illness is saying. Abandon yourself to your body's wisdom. Listen as you would to an ailing five-year-old child. Be present to it with kindness and compassion. If you pay attention to it, your body will tell you what it needs. Putting your attention on something shifts the energy within it, bringing new energetic, healing impulses to your cells.

As you repeatedly go deeply enough within and learn to release unpleasant feelings, you gradually experience a sense of love that feels like compassion. It rises from within, and with it you will feel the soothing sense of peace and well-being that can heal anything. This is the pure energy of your soul. As you follow your soul's inner promptings, you will get more and more in touch with the wisdom of your heart—in the sense of having compassion for yourself and others. It is this alignment with love, with your soul, your source, that heals.

> It is this alignment with love, with your soul, your source, that heals.

Belief in external powers and medical experts too often leaves us feeling powerless. That's not to say Western medicine isn't important or even crucial at times to your recovery. But it doesn't heal. *You* do the healing. It's important to remember that no one knows your body better than you do. Listen to your body and what it needs to heal. When we activate our beliefs in our own ability to heal, the power within us is activated.

The crises of illness are like the trials of a hero's journey, experiences we all have, bringing us to the critical challenges we need to reach new heights.[82] Because the healing process is inherent in the life cycle—*we were born with it*---we are designed to overcome the challenges of illness. The series of stresses we encounter are custom made to force us to reexperience and reintegrate our inner conflicts, sometimes in a way that produces the symptoms of an illness, until we get the message. As heroes on our own journeys, we can, and in fact are meant to, overcome these challenges.

> Your illness represents a crossroads in your life where your soul is saying to you, "Honor who you are and pay more attention to what you need."

The illness represents a crossroads in your life where your soul is saying to you, "Honor who you are and pay more attention to what you need." Whenever people are suffering from a critical illness, it's a sure sign that *who they really are—from the depths of their souls*—is getting short shrift. Their energy is blocked, screaming to get through to the part of the body where the symptoms lie.

---

[82]   Joseph Campbell. *The Hero with a Thousand Faces*. Pantheon Books, 2008.

THE GIFT OF SYMPTOMS

Symptoms can be thought of as archetypal images from the unconscious; like Jung's concept of the shadow self, they represent parts of us we don't want to face. Perhaps it's anger that you've buried over feeling insignificant as a child. If you find yourself in the midst of a string of angry people and/or situations in your life, it's a sign that your shadow self, or that part of you that is unconscious, is attracting them.

> It's up to us to interpret the body's messages and take action to correct the situation instead of just running to take an Advil.

If you listen to your soul as you would a wise old woman, you can see what messages your unconscious may be sending. Since the soul is the embodiment of wholeness, connecting to the conscious *and* the unconscious, when seen as a wise sage, a wise old woman, it can be easier to tap into what it's trying to tell you through symptoms and to tap into its healing energy. Maybe the message is about something or someone you've driven away in opposition or conflict. If you leave a relationship with an unresolved conflict, for instance, it stows away in your unconscious and you're bound to meet it in your next one.

Your body is a great teacher that shows you, through its symptoms, what your deepest beliefs and unconscious thoughts are saying. In its wisdom, the unconscious finds a way to let you know, through symptoms, that something must be done differently. You must acknowledge what you have been afraid to acknowledge.

Symptoms are a clarion call. Like a reactor that produces and reflects the release of energy, your body vibrates to stress and produces outward symptoms that reflect your inner turmoil. As the body constricts under stress, its unfettered energy flow to a particular part of the body is constrained and the path is created for a physical manifestation of the problem.

Signs and symptoms of illness that appear in our bodies can be seen as helpers and serve as a wake-up call from the depths of us. They can actually lead us to grow, to start asking ourselves questions, to look more deeply within for a better understanding of the reasons for doing the things we do and the consequences.

> When symptoms begin to appear, it's a sign that you are ready to deal with whatever it is you've been resisting.

Symptoms are a part of the solution, not the problem. So respect them, knowing there is a purpose and a meaning to the body's defenses. When symptoms begin to appear, it's a sign that you are ready to deal with whatever it is you've been resisting. They are adaptive, creative achievements, the best solution a person has so far been able to come up with to what is seen as an otherwise unmanageable problem. However painful or disruptive a symptom might be, it can be assumed that the body would not have gone to the unconscious trouble of creating the symptom unless there was a need for it. To respect the symptom, then, means to recognize that it is serving an important purpose and to respect the person who has (unconsciously) created the symptom to serve just that purpose.

All illness is purposeful, a beckoning call to heed a disease process that is trying to get your attention, evidence that something is amiss in the workings of the mind, often unconsciously. It shows us—like a lit-up path—where the power to effect a change resides.

From this perspective, illness can actually be seen as a good thing in the overall pattern of your life. No matter what the illness, your body is trying to tell you something. Some part of your body is crying out for your attention. It is an important signal, a wake-up call from your inner most being, saying, "You must pay more attention to me! Listen to my feelings, my needs! Change the way you are treating me or allowing me to be treated."

When we get sick, we want answers. "Why me?" a close friend asked. "Why did *I* get breast cancer?" We want to know why this is happening to us. By listening within and accessing the wisdom of the unconscious, we can gain a new perspective on our symptoms and experience unique answers to our situation. In this way, we can rely on our own wisdom instead of following external pressures to do one thing or another to "fix" the problem.

A STORY ABOUT HEALING

When my friend JoEllen's daughter Kristen became critically ill, an American Indian assisted in bringing about this kind of soul communication and an awakening through an illness. As she tells the story in her extraordinary account, *Mother, Heal My Self*,[83] medical science had run out of answers at the sophisticated university hospital in South Dakota where JoEllen was vice president of nursing. Her daughter was being treated for cancer, and the diagnosis was grim.

One day a Sioux Indian chief named Wanigi Waci (Spirit Dancer), a dear friend and keeper of the Lakota Sioux healing traditions, came from his nearby reservation to the hospital to explain to the hospital staff the importance of cultural patterns in providing care to the Sioux people on the reservation. Many Sioux were admitted to the hospital from time to time. As vice president of nursing, JoEllen attended the meetings.

During their meetings, Wanigi Waci sensed Jo's distress about her daughter, Kristi, and offered to see her. When he saw Kristi, she was fatally ill and wanted to die. The wise chief could see that her soul was carrying the burden of many generations of repression of the women in their family. Kristi's epiphany of her illness as a wake-up call on her soul's journey came during one of the many long conversations with Wanigi Waci. He told her she had a choice to make: she could confront her deeply repressed fears and resentments or she could choose to die. Wanigi explained that by letting herself feel her deepest feelings of fear and guilt and anger and resentment, she could then release them. She could heal. In that way, she would put an end to generations of a pattern of repression by the women in her family.

---

[83] JoEllen Koerner. *Mother, Heal My Self: An Intergenerational Healing Journey Between Two Worlds.* April 15, 2003.

Kristi could choose to liberate herself and future generations of women or she could choose to leave this earth. Kristi chose to confront her demons. She mustered up the courage to face her deepest conflicts and fears, to confront generations of painful repression. She chose to listen to her soul, to listen to that inner voice and what it was saying to her. How did she listen? She waded through the emotional disturbances, the anger, the fears, and resentments. As she examined them one by one, she allowed herself to feel them. Then she let them go.

> Our fears surface because they are within us; not because of external circumstances. We attract situations and external events—usually not consciously—that will give them a chance to surface so we can deal with them, and release them. Illness is one such opportunity.

Eventually, she saw that her patterns of fear and resentment were repetitive. The same fears occurred repeatedly, in many different contexts, as they do with all of us. Our fears are the same, regardless of the external circumstances. In this way, Kristi's fears and resentments were the same, regardless of the people and events surrounding them. Our fears surface because they are within us, not because they are created by external circumstances. We attract situations and external events—usually not consciously—that will give them a chance to surface so we can deal with them and release them. Illness is one such opportunity.

As Kristi began to confront her fears, she learned to see the emptiness of their threats. Then she was able to release them one by one. It became easier and easier for her to do. The call is more or less the same for all of us. When we get sick, our souls are saying, "Wake up. There is a better way for you. This illness is only a stepping-stone to help you learn a better way. It is a stepping-stone on the path to your healing—a healing that will bring a healthy body as well as inner peace and more and more happiness. Confront this old emotional pattern, for it is causing you pain. This illness has come about to help you in your healing process."

The legendary Louise Hay, who healed herself of ovarian cancer many years ago and was among the first (maybe the *very* first) in the United States to discover that different illnesses characteristically affect different parts of the body, puts it this way: "I have learned that for every condition in our lives, there is a *need for it*. Otherwise, we would not have it. The symptom is only an outer effect. We must go within to dissolve the mental cause. It's like cutting down the weed and getting the root out."

Actually, your message from your soul is likely to be more specific. It might be more like, "Stand up to this person or situation; it is creating resentment in you. Release this resentment from your mind or get this person out of your life. Your response to the situation is creating your illness."

Louise Hay's, *You Can Heal Your Life*, now a classic in the field, set forth the thesis that different fears and attitudes create disease in different organs of the body. Enduring poverty as well as physical and sexual abuse as a child, she ran away from home at the age of fifteen because she couldn't take the sexual abuse any longer.

Years later, Hay was diagnosed with ovarian cancer. In her words, she went into a "total panic." Yet because of her work with clients, she knew that healing mental patterns—attitudes and beliefs—worked, and here she was being given a chance to prove it. As she tells of her experience, she "knew" that cancer was a dis-ease of deeply held resentment that eventually literally eats away at the body. Hay had been refusing to be willing to dissolve all the anger and resentment at "them" over her childhood.

She refused to have the surgery, under the pretense that she couldn't afford it, but really she was bargaining for time. Hay realized that if she didn't resolve the inner feelings of resentment and clear the mental patterns that created the illness, it would return, even if she had the surgery. Even if the surgeon manages to "get it all out," if the patient has made no mental change, he or she just re-creates the same illness, perhaps in a different part of the body.

She took total responsibility for her own healing. Hay recounts, "I read and investigated everything I could find on alternative ways to assist my healing process."[84]

> Treating an illness as a physical process only doesn't correct the origin of the dysfunction.

Louise Hay has gone on to help millions of others heal around the world. Her credo: by healing your attitudes and beliefs about yourself, you re-create your health and happiness. The call resonates deep within, where it remains either until it is silenced by other voices that will not allow you the freedom of following your own heart or until you acknowledge its importance and set out to change your circumstances.

Treating an illness as a physical process only doesn't correct the origin of the dysfunction. Yet we often experience a resistance to correcting the mental/emotional patterns, the thought processes that are creating the dis-ease. That's because it might mean that some part of the status quo in our lives is threatened—our jobs, our relationships or our marriages, the places where we live, the things that we identify with, the key elements of our comfort zones. Some or all of these things may have to change before our journey to healing can begin. As the changes occur along the way, the illness is saying to us, "You need to do things differently. Listen to what your soul—the still small voice within—is trying to tell you."

The main message? When your body doesn't feel good, it is actually doing its job. Remember, like your best friend, your body is on your side, designed to carry messages to you. It is then up to us to go within and listen, to interpret these messages and take action to correct the situation. Our problems can be helped or even completely prevented by the ways in which we act on these messages. To take a few simple examples, heightened tension can lead to a headache, an upset stomach,

---

[84]   Louise Hay. "My Story," in *The Light Connection*. December 2006.

or a stiff neck. Chronic anger has been shown to create heart problems.[85] Lower back pain is created by feeling insecure about your well-being; often financial problems show up as lower back pain.[86]

More complex is the experience of childhood trauma. But even then, your body is doing what it needs to do to help. Kalsched, a noted Jungian analyst, says that in situations like this, we see a remarkable wisdom in the psyche to assure survival of what he refers to as "the imperishable human spirit." In cases like this, our psyches' defenses operate to sabotage relationships to prevent further trauma in a way that is like the body's immune system, which possesses killer cells to prevent invasion of foreign bodies.

The idea that pain means injury or damage is deeply ingrained in the American psyche. Instead of thinking of pain as a warning signal that protects us—telling us to find a way to face our "demons," to relieve the tension or reinterpret the situation—we often ignore its messages and medicate it. We take a medication to get rid of it. It's easier. But if the root of the tension is not addressed, the problem will eventually take a greater toll.

The changes we need to make to begin to heal can be frightening and unsettling. Yet if we orient ourselves to the perspective that the cause of disease lies within and it is there to help us, we will make the changes we need to make with greater motivation and reassurance.

It is important to understand that in illness, the body is doing its best to help us heal by sending a message. Further, it is highly important to understand the relationship of mind, body, and spirit when considering the subject of how to heal. Healing doesn't only mean eliminating the symptom but getting to the heart of the problem, the origin of where the illness began. Due to the power of energy fields, healing comes out of our new attitudes, thought patterns, and beliefs. In the next several chapters, these relationships and how they operate on the path to healing will be explored and examined.

---

[85] Daniel Goleman. "Agreeableness vs Anger." *New York Times* Archives. April 16, 1989.

[86] John Sarno, MD. *Healing Back Pain.* Warner Books, New York, 1999.

VI

HEALING: THE POWER OF THE MIND

Power Step: Realize there is no limit to the power of the mind to heal.

Healing ensues from the willingness to accept the power of the mind and the willingness to never allow the mind to say something negative without challenging it and replacing it with something positive.[87]

—David Hawkins, MD, PhD

Think only what you want, and that is all you will get.[88]

—Lester Levenson

The mind is a powerhouse. A major key to healing lies in working with that power. First understand that the mind is a creator. It can create illness or health.[89] And it can heal. Having great power, your mind has the ability to bring into your life precisely what you ask for. The person who says, "My condition is hopeless," and believes it, is actually creating a condition that is hopeless. And it will probably resist treatment.

---

[87] David Hawkins. *Healing and Recovery.* Veritas Publishing, Sedona, Arizona, 2009, 134.

[88] Lester Levinson. *Stillness Speaks.* The Keys to Ultimate Freedom. Meditation with Quest. [PDF online].

[89] David Hawkins. Ibid, 124.

The moral? Don't ask what your mind brings to you; ask what you bring to your mind. Our thought patterns—not just one thought but our habitual thought patterns—actually create our experiences. Our thoughts are there for the choosing. Often we succumb to thoughts that pop into our mind, bothersome, pessimistic thoughts. We let them in and then they upset us! You are the master: don't let them in in the first place. To heal, choose thoughts that serve you, thoughts that feel soothing, reassuring, hopeful.

> "To own back one's own power requires realizing that it is the mind itself that is the cause of illness."

As Dr. David Hawkins, who recounts the many illnesses he healed in himself and others in his extraordinary work, *Healing and Recovery*, sums it up: "To own back one's own power requires realizing that it is the mind itself that is the cause of illness."[90] The main requirements for healing, says Hawkins, are a determination to move out of negative energy patterns and to move into positive ones, facing the truth about ourselves.[91]

An unwillingness to do that has consequences. A dear friend's recent experience illustrates the point. Suffering from continuous back pain after a fall, Allison had a surgical procedure designed to alleviate the pain. Unfortunately, it actually made things worse. As she became more and more discouraged and depressed, a downhill spiral of pain, pain medications, and a worsening condition of her heart and lungs sapped her energy to such an extent that it became difficult even to speak at times. The most challenging part of this picture was her refusal to try anything new: to change physicians, try new treatments, or adopt new mental attitudes. Fearful and convinced that her situation was hopeless, Allison grew weaker and weaker. Ultimately, more and more strain and stress on her heart led to her death. If Allison had been able

---

[90]   David Hawkins MD, PhD. *Healing and Recovery*. Veritas Publishing, Sedona Arizona, 2009, 122.

[91]   Ibid.

to be more hopeful, more sanguine about her prospects for healing, she might have rallied and recovered.

To understand how the mind works on the body, it is important to grasp that the mind isn't just located in the brain. It is in every cell of our bodies. In other words, our minds are in our lungs, our musculoskeletal systems, our hearts, and our reproductive organs. Neurotransmitters[92] and receptors throughout our bodies —triggered by our thoughts— transmit messages to our cells.

> Since the main driver of the body's health (good or bad) is the mind, we should aim to be much more aware of what we're thinking.

Disease, or dis-ease, originates in the mind, which vibrates in every cell of our bodies.[93] Disease actually has its roots in the French *desaise:* "des" meaning *without, away from,* and "aise" meaning *ease.* Dis-ease, the absence of ease or the absence of ease of the flow of the life force, called prana or ch'i in the East, originates from some disruption of the life force flowing through the body. Fear thoughts, pain thoughts, grief thoughts, and guilty thoughts that are held on to and not acknowledged and expressed or released cause dis-ease. If held on to for long enough, illness will develop.[94]

Since the main driver of the body's health (good or bad) is the mind, we should aim to be much more aware of what we're thinking.[95] It's important to watch what habits of thinking we adopt and what's competing for our attention. Most of us don't question how often we think about things that create fear, worry, and anxiety. Especially if you want to be healed, the thoughts that come up will be exactly the ones that need to be brought up, understood, reframed, and forgiven from the depths of you in order to be healed.

---

[92] A neurotransmitter is a chemical messenger that boosts messages between brain nerve cells and modulates signals between the cells.

[93] Candace Pert. "Neuropeptides and Their Receptors. A Psychosomatic Network." *Journal of Immunology.* August, 2001:135(2 Suppl):820–826.

[94] David Hawkins, MD. *Healing and Recovery.* Veritas Publishing, 2009, 66.

[95] Hawkins. Ibid, 66.

> It's important to watch what habits of thinking we adopt and what's competing for our attention, what we choose to focus on.

We have been taught to believe that our symptoms, our aches and pains, come from some external source, an external germ or "invader" over which we have no control. We are taught that diseases just happen; they occur in a random involuntary way. It doesn't enter our minds that a natural healing effect comes from reversing our thought processes. Most of us have no clue that we *can* reverse them.

It is well established that the greater the amount of negativity held in the mind, the greater the effect of the negative energies on the body.[96] If you are *not* repeatedly holding the thought "I am sick" in your mind, you won't be sick. We can only feel sick if we hold on to that thought. It's often unconscious, but often it is conscious. A little reflection will reveal that when the mind is distracted, illness can disappear.

SAM FORGOT HE WAS SICK

I witnessed firsthand a vivid example of this with my friend Sam. He had promised to take me sailing, and I called him that morning, excited to go. "What time shall I pick you up?" I asked. I had offered to drive us to the dock.

"Well," [cough, cough], "I'm not feeling very well." [cough, cough]

"Oh," I muttered, disappointed. But I quickly offered, "Not a problem! We'll just reschedule."

"No, no," he insisted. "I promised, and we're going."

We went back and forth for a while.

"Let's reschedule."

"No! We're going!"

---

96 Hawkins. Ibid, 108.

"No, it's crazy to go if you're sick!"

Sam again: "I'll manage it. We're going."

It went and on and on until I finally conceded. "Okay," I said, "I'll pick you up in an hour." And I did.

When we got to the dock, the weather was picture perfect. Gleaming with sunlight, Long Island Sound was awaiting our arrival when we stepped onto my friend's beautiful forty-two-foot sailboat. I was ecstatic. Sam, on the other hand, was looking a little pale, but he managed to act as if he was looking forward to the outing.

About an hour into the sail, things took an ominous turn. Unexpectedly, the wind kicked up and began heaving the sailboat from side to side, threatening to tip it over each time. As black clouds gathered overhead and the strong gales rushed the boat, I actually grew more and more excited. Having complete confidence in Sam, I was enjoying the sensation of flying over the waves. It was thrilling to me, feeling more like a speedboat than a sail! "This is sooooo exciting!" I bellowed enthusiastically over the roar of the wind and waves. My excitement was not well received.

"That's because you don't know any better!" Sam shot back with annoyance. It quickly became obvious that Sam perceived the situation to be more dangerous than I realized. I offered to help, which soothed his irritation, but we both knew that I knew very little about sailing. Since I couldn't be of much help, I sat quietly and hung on tightly, keeping my mouth shut and my enjoyment to myself.

Sam, an experienced sailor, skillfully navigated the sailboat through the labyrinth of whipping wind and razor-sharp waves, and we eventually made it safely back to shore. Surprisingly energetic and chipper, Sam suggested we have a drink and a bite to eat on the dock before we headed home. As we were sipping our drinks, I realized something that amazed me: there was no trace of the hacking or the gurgling sounds of congestion that had saturated his voice before the storm. His pallor was gone, replaced by a healthy pinkish skin tone. Sam was the picture of health!

As I expressed admiration for the experienced, skillful maneuvering it took to bring us safely to shore, I brought it to Sam's attention: "Do you see what I see?"

"What's that?" he asked. "Your cold or flu or whatever it was is completely gone." He looked startled. He obviously hadn't realized it.

"Hmm. Very interesting. I suppose it is," Sam acknowledged.

"Your laser-like mission to get us out of danger clearly took precedence in your mind," I suggested. "Well, maybe so. We'll see," Sam responded cautiously. He was struggling to integrate the whole experience. He actually seemed a little embarrassed that his spanking new state of health had returned so quickly.

At this point, you may be thinking, *Well, Sam had the flu. That's not so hard to heal. It probably wasn't that bad to begin with. What about cancer or something more serious? Can that be healed by distracting your mind or focusing your attention elsewhere?*

THE MIND'S STARRING ROLE

Actually, there are many cases where healings of more serious conditions have occurred precisely in this way. One of the most famous on record is the case of Norman Cousins, editor of the *Saturday Review*, who, stricken with a painful and life-threatening collagen disease, checked himself out of the hospital. He decided instead to check into a first-class hotel, figuring it would be cheaper and more relaxing than a hospital, with *much* better service. Convinced that his frame of mind and emotional well-being were key to his recovery, he proceeded to treat himself with massive doses of vitamin C and to order his favorite Marx Brothers films. Cousins laughed hysterically every day as he watched the Marx Brothers.[97]

---

[97] Norman Cousins. *Anatomy of an Illness*. W. W. Norton & Company, September 2001.

Within weeks, his condition improved. Eventually, Cousins healed himself. When he had a heart attack fifteen years following his earlier illness, he asked himself, "I wonder whether it would be possible to recover from *two* life-threatening conditions in one lifetime using the same approach?" His strong will to heal gave him the determination to try it.

As he was brought into the hospital on a stretcher following the heart attack, he sat up and said, "Gentlemen, I want you to know that you're looking at the darnedest healing machine that's ever been wheeled into this hospital." Cousins lived many more years than his physicians predicted. He died twenty years later of cardiac arrest.

Another well-known case is the more recent experience of David Servan-Schreiber, MD, PhD, who discovered his own malignant tumor of the brain as he was examining the brain scans of participants in a National Institutes of Health (NIH) study.[98] Servan-Schreiber held the prestigious position of directing the huge NIH study. One day he and his colleagues were in their imaging lab. It was a slow day because of bad weather. So Servan-Schreiber and his physician colleagues decided to take scans of their own brains as a test run through the research protocols. As Servan-Schreiber held a scan up to the light to examine it, he saw a tumor lodged in the brain's prefrontal cortex. Little did he know he was looking at *his own brain*! His fellow physicians squirmed and glanced nervously at each other, clearly dreading the thought of telling him that it was his.

Initially, because of his training in Western medicine, Servan-Schreiber did what he knew to do: he had the standard surgical removal of the tumor with follow-up chemo and radiation. With utmost faith in the world of the medical treatments he had spent his entire professional life learning and administering, he relaxed, assuming he was cured.

But Dr. Servan-Schreiber was in for a rude awakening. Three years later, the tumor reappeared in precisely the same spot. As his initial shock and disbelief subsided, he reasoned that because of his

---

[98] David Servan-Schreiber, MD, PhD. *Anti-Cancer: A New Way of Life*. Penguin Group, 2009.

privileged position as a top NIH researcher, he would take advantage of his access to the best scientists around the world and find out why this had happened to him. With fierce determination, Servan-Schreiber set out to find out what was causing the cancer and to heal it.

He called top experts around the world in psychology, nutrition, and the latest cancer treatments, also poring through the latest research covering every conceivable factor and how it might have contributed to his cancer. He talked to researchers on the cutting edge of how the mind's role may play a part.[99]

Servan-Schreiber's investigation led him to the discovery that in the mind-body arena, feeling helpless (which comes from *thinking* helplessly) in the face of life's challenges and crises is a strong contributing factor to developing cancer. Fortified with a rich array of research on the subject, Servan-Schreiber cites two important studies. One striking study focused on people who were healthy when the study began. They were asked a series of questions about any feelings of helplessness they were experiencing in their lives. Six years later—all other factors being equal—those that felt most helpless had a mortality rate from all types of diseases that was three times greater than those who had the lowest feelings of helplessness.[100] A second major study by psychobiologists at University College London in 2008 confirmed these results.[101]

Emphasizing the importance of nutrition as well as emotional well-being in cancer prevention, Servan-Schreiber points out in his book *AntiCancer: A New Way of Life* that *at most*, 15 percent of cancers can be attributed to genetic factors (for *all* human diseases, about 2 percent can be attributed to genetic factors).[102] In the midst of a divorce from the love of his life, working long hours, and living on junk food, once he

---

[99]   Ibid.

[100] Everson S.A et al, *Hopelessness and Risk of Mortality and Incidence of Myocardial Infarction and Cancer.Psychosomatic Medicine.* 58, no. 2, 1996, 113–121.

[101] David Servan-Schreiber. *Anticancer: A New Way of Life.* Penguin Group, 2009, pp. 156–159.

[102] Bruce Lipton. *The Biology of Belief.* Hay House, India. January 2013.

learned about the factors that contribute to cancer, his only question to himself was, "Why in the world didn't I get it a lot sooner!"[103]

> We're not always aware of it, but we create with our thoughts and self-talk.

Living through traumatic emotional experiences has been shown to be a huge factor in the lives of those with cancer. Especially the unresolved emotional pain of guilt and resentment has been pointed to as a major culprit in creating cancer.[104] Survivor's guilt is an example. "I can't believe I didn't see the car pulling out in front of us! I could've prevented the accident, and my friend would still be alive." Many clinicians, including nurses, physicians, acupuncturists, and psychologists, will tell you privately that in their work with patients, they see a marked connection between patients' core emotional issues and cancer.

We're not always aware of it, but we create with our thoughts and self-talk. We all have ongoing dialogues with the still small voice inside. It may be saying, "Damn, I could've done better. What I said sounded lame. Now they'll think less of me." Or perhaps it's saying, "I did a pretty good job on my presentation today. There were a couple of places I could work on to be even better for next time." Repetitive patterns of either of these avenues of self-talk will have a very different effect on your body.

Through our thoughts—what we think about the challenges we face—we are either healing an illness, bringing one about, or making one worse. How we choose to respond to whatever is going on in our lives is the key. Instead of having to wait for a storm to navigate, as in Sam's case, we can choose at any time to shift our focus of attention away from illness and toward a focus on health and healing.

---

[103]   David Servan Schreiber. *Anticancer: A New Way of Life*. Penguin Group, 2009.

[104]   David Hawkins. *Healing and Recovery*. Veritas Publishing, Sedona, Arizona, 2009.

THE POWER OF INTENTION

To shift our focus, we can use willpower to put mind over matter to work. Combined with a strong intention, if you really want to heal, if you want to recover, you can bring about changes in your body with your mind. You can heal. If you're in pain, it's more challenging, but you can still be hopeful in the midst of feeling pain, still feel optimistic underneath the pain, (my body is on my side and is doing what it knows to do to heal me), and *expect* to heal.

Intention that is rooted in the power of the mind, in what we call "willpower," may feel like an effortful, striving form of intention whose success is based on a strong, focused will. In the American "can do" way of thinking, if we want something, we strive for it; we push toward it. If we don't get it quickly, we push even harder. Many times this strategy serves us well, until we encounter situations where it doesn't.

WEI WU WEI, OR DOING WITHOUT DOING

> The wei wu wei approach involves filling oneself with a strong belief and feeling that the desired thing has already occurred and is on its way to you.

When you are ill, a different form of intention may be needed. An intention that is more subtle and suitable to healing approaches may feel more appropriate. This kind of intention feels more like a gentle wish than a strong, determined will. It is captured in the Taoist concept *wei wu wei*, or "doing without doing." In meditation, in creative pursuits, and in healing, this less effortful intention may well be more effective.

The wei wu wei approach involves filling yourself with a strong belief and feeling that the desired thing has already occurred and is on its way to you. In other words, removing your ego involvement, *feeling* the intention primarily from the heart, and letting the process take care of itself and unfold on its own brings success. This technique is rooted in an effective, natural energy flow that can be used freely in place of the more causal, goal-oriented approach.[105]

TRAIN YOUR MIND: HOW YOU INTERPRET A SITUATION IS YOUR CALL

You can use your mind to interpret a situation in any way you choose to make it work for you. Using the mind as a searchlight to find healing spaces around people and things you love, with good nutrition and lots of laughter, like Cousins, will shift your healing mechanisms into high gear. Just as the ability to heal lies within, the cause of your stress lies within as well.

A little reflection makes it obvious that our sources of stress are within us. If we want to get rid of stress, we can change the way we think about the situation. Many people, for instance, think that cities are stressful, noisy places. They are unnerved and put off by the crowds, the sounds of the city, the loud shrieks of the sirens, the shouting at night, the vrooom sound of the cars and trucks speeding down the avenues. I grew up in the country. Most of my family members aren't very fond of New York City for precisely these reasons.

But my Aunt Fanny, who grew up in the city of Philadelphia, loved these sounds. She loved visiting with neighbors draped on their doorsteps on hot summer nights. Constant processions of neighbors and friends in and out all day long, just to chat or to borrow a cup of something or other, was her element. A source of great comfort, they supplied her daily source of vitality. Walking along Market Street, with

---

[105] William Braud and Rosemarie Anderson. *Transpersonal Research Methods for the Social Sciences: Honoring Human Experience.* Sage Publications, Thousand Oaks, California, 1994.

its noises and bustle, thrilled Aunt Fanny. "I come alive when I'm on these streets!" she used to say. When she married my uncle, she moved to the country, to a beautiful estate with apple and cherry trees, grape vineyards, and rose arbors. Many commented that it was like a little Shangri-La. But in spite of the beauty that surrounded her, Aunt Fanny was lost. She missed the city terribly. The quiet and the isolation of the country were a source of great stress to her, and it took quite a bit of getting used to. I'm not sure she ever did. The beauty of the cherry and apple blossoms, the luscious rose arbors, and the sound of crickets chirping at night were the source of great peace and comfort to many who visited. To Aunt Fanny, it was all a source of stress.

But whether it's Aunt Fanny or the rest of us, the stress is always inside us. It attaches itself to external events because it's looking for a way to escape. How you react to stress is personal. How you react to situations, what kind of a mood you're in, depends on your internal state. If someone rams into the front of your car, you may not be happy about it, but if you're feeling good inside about other things in your life— maybe you just got a raise and you're having a great day—it might roll off your back. On the other hand, if someone hits your car and you just received bad news about your job or your health, it might be the straw that breaks the camel's back! No matter what the circumstances, "It's not the thing itself but what you think about the thing," as the famous philosopher Marcus Aurelius said.

We all have our own stress quotients, and we have to get to know what they are. One of my friends loves to listen to loud music in the car. To me, it's stressful and nerve-racking. But if I'm in a great mood, I can allow myself to enjoy the music, go with the flow, and not resist it; it can turn out to be an enjoyable experience. The reason is that it's not the event itself that sends you into a fit of anger, resentment, or self-pity—not to mention ill health—but your state of mind. You can change your reaction, thereby changing what's going on inside of you.

It's the same process with healing. All you really need to do is change your relationship to your reaction. Your overarching aim is to create a peaceful, warm, positive feeling inside. How you interpret a situation determines its effect on your health. But even if your reaction to your illness is stressful, if you accept your reaction, you shift what's going on inside you.

You can always reframe any stressful situation in your mind. A shift in attitude can eliminate the stress on your mind and body when you look for something positive, something you like in the situation, or simply allow yourself to feel good anyway. In this way, a shift in attitude can be the key to healing.

You can begin by telling yourself things that will ease your mind and make you feel better. You can remind yourself of something good about the situation: "This illness is offering me the rest I need; this illness is showing me there is something within me that I need to change, to let go of and to be forgiven so that I can be healed." Taken to the extreme, if your aim is to see things in the best light, you could see that even death has its positive aspects—for example, the person is resting in peace, is no longer suffering, was ready to die, and so forth.

SELF-TALK MATTERS: CHANGE IT FOR THE BETTER

In every situation, with every problem we face, we have a choice: we can expand our awareness or we can contract and hope to become small enough for it to go away. When we choose to contract, the energy pulls us down and we suffer more because the problem becomes our entire field of vision.

The idea is to change your self-talk to something that makes you feel better. If you can't seem to reframe the situation, embrace your reaction to it, even if it's anger or fear. Say to yourself, "I know it will all work out." Send comforting words and messages to yourself. The fearful reaction to stress is only there because of a need for more self-love and acceptance to begin with. By shifting your thoughts and attitude, you will change your relationship to your thoughts and your biochemistry. You will begin to secrete hormones that are soothing and healing.

For instance, you can say, "If this job or this new venture or this relationship doesn't work out, it's not the right thing for me. I know that something better, something that is just right for me, will come along." Or you can say the following: "Lately I've been meeting so many new people that I know there will be new opportunities waiting for me right around the corner." You can remind yourself that a challenging situation is a learning experience and that many famous people have "failed" many times before they finally succeeded. It's not your so-called failures that cause you problems. *It's how you interpret them that matters.* How you react to them is the key. They can just as easily be framed as "lessons and learning experiences." Your body will be the beneficiary.

You think you're unhappy because you lost your job. But that's not the reason you're unhappy. You're unhappy because there is unhappiness inside you that needs to be released, unhappy emotions that are looking for a way to escape. Your job loss can be that opportunity. It can be the best thing that ever happened to you—but only if you choose to see it that way.

In every situation, with every problem we face, we have a choice: we can expand our awareness or we can contract and hope to become small enough for it to go away. When we choose to contract, the energy pulls us down and we suffer more because the problem becomes our entire field of vision.

HELP YOUR MIND SEE THE GIFT IN YOUR ILLNESS

As you begin to understand the workings of the mind and the energy field it creates, you will begin to look for the source of stress or illness not in the world but in what you're holding in your mind.

The same goes for illness. You can always reframe your situation—that is, find a way to reinterpret the illness that sees the positive or as Bill, my teacher, would say in our mastery seminars, the "gift" in it. Find a way to see the positive in your experience of illness. If you truly understand that it's here to help you grow, and it is, you can learn from it. If you find the gift or the blessing in your illness and see that your body is actually trying to help you—no matter how bad the circumstances may seem—it will be a healing experience. You may have heard a person say, "The illness I had was the best thing that ever happened to me!" That's typically because the person saw it as a wake-up call that urged him to make the changes that needed to be made. The experience of illness helped the person turn his life into something happier and more satisfying.

> "You don't heal the body with the body; you heal the body with the mind."

Once you understand how the mind works, you will learn to reframe the circumstances of your illness so that you can feel better about what has happened. You can find a way to accept it. As you begin to understand the workings of the mind and the energy field it creates, you will begin to look for the source of stress or illness not in the world but in what you're holding in your mind. Where healing is concerned, the thing to remember about the mind is this: you don't heal the body with the body; you heal the body with the mind.[106]

If you learn to reinterpret failures or stressful situations as valuable lessons, and even learn to be grateful for them, obstacles in your path can be seen as helpful, even strategically well placed, to teach, to help, to inspire you. With a deeper understanding that accepts responsibility for all that happens to you, you can learn to put yourself in a positive feeling state much of the time. This is the best thing you can do for your healing journey.

You can learn to use your mind to gain more control over your body and reverse the symptoms that are causing you problems. Maybe your suppressed feelings of anger are creating high blood pressure. Perhaps you are ignoring anxiety and thereby creating asthma, irritable bowel syndrome, or chronic pain. By changing your thinking, you can create an entirely different feeling inside you, an internal environment that

---

[106]   David Hawkins. *Healing and Recovery.* Veritas Publishing, Sedona Arizona, 2009.

will strengthen rather than weaken your immune system. You can use your mind to create an internal environment that will enhance cellular regeneration, not hinder it.

GUIDING AND HEALING WITH THE MIND

Discoveries in neuroscience have demonstrated that the mind can heal as well as the body. Jeffrey Schwartz MD, a UCLA psychiatrist, and author of *Brain Lock,*[107] advocates treating obsessive-compulsive disorder by using a "mindfulness" approach—becoming aware of and responding to one's thoughts before acting on them. This approach has been helpful in obsessive-compulsive disorders, which are notoriously difficult to treat.

In the same way that a physical illness serves as your body's wake-up call, think of your anxiety as an alarm system. If your mind sounds an alarm, it's there to get your attention, just like someone trying to break into your home. The house alarm goes off and wakes you up. It's there to assist you to take some action to protect yourself. But what if the alarm system went off because the wind set it off? Your mind would respond in the same way that it would if there were an actual threat.[108]

The situation is similar with OCD. Instead of only warning you of real danger, OCD is an alarm system in your mind that responds to a variety of triggers as terrifying threats. By getting patients to repattern their thinking through a technique called "exposure and response prevention therapy," they begin with an understanding that a person driven by underlying fears, usually irrational, can be prevented from engaging in habitual, compulsive responses using controlled and prolonged exposure to the objects or situations that trigger anxiety.[109]

In the same way, it has been demonstrated with brain imaging techniques that using our minds, we can control our behavior. For

---

[107] Jeffreymschwartz.com

[108] Robert L. Leahy PhD. Anxiety Files in Psychologytoday.com

[109] Jonathan S. Abramowitz, PhD. "The Psychological Treatment of Obsessive-Compulsive Disorder." *Canadian Journal of Psychiatry*, 2006; 51: 407–416.

example, it has been shown that women and girls can control sad thoughts, men can control responses to erotic films, and people who suffer from phobias can reorganize their minds so that they lose the fear that accompanies them. Evidence of the mind's ability to control behavior is clear in all these studies.[110]

Our thoughts are creators of our reality. The thoughts we choose, whether we're aware of them or not, are constantly creating our realities. Actually, the body has no ability to create or experience itself. The body is experienced in the mind only.[111] Your body expresses that which you are holding in your mind.[112]

In this way, your mind and your thought processes can play a vital role in healing. As you become more aware of the thoughts that come into your mind, you can challenge the evidence of their truthfulness. I had an experience recently that called for challenging the truth of what I was thinking. I was in Paris this past spring. Although the weather was lovely, my room was air-conditioned and unseasonably chilly. I developed a terrible cold and a hoarse throat, but it didn't really faze me. I quickly chalked it up to a combination of a cool room and an immune system that was vulnerable because I needed a break. Because I rarely get colds, I assumed it would leave quickly, and I didn't pay much attention to it.

A month after I got home, although I was well rested and nourished, the hoarse throat was still with me. Over dinner at a restaurant, my voice was barely audible, no matter how much I tried to project it. I couldn't speak loudly enough for the person sitting across the dinner table to hear what I was saying. When I had to address a large group of people at work, my strained voice was embarrassingly hoarse and scratchy. I started to think more intently about what could be causing this. In a few days, I knew the answer.

---

[110] Mario Beauregard. *Brain Wars*. Harper Collins, 2012.

[111] David Hawkins. *Healing and Recovery*. Veritas Publishing, Sedona Arizona, 2009, 107.

[112] Ibid.

I had decided to "let go" of a project that I had put a great deal of time and energy into. The project meant a great deal to me, and it was taking longer than I thought it should to get started. I wanted to let go of it so that the feeling of deep frustration that was right below the surface would leave.

Knowing that the energy center of the throat represents the will, the power of choice, and the power to speak up, I realized what I had done. I had confused "letting go" of the frustration of trying to figure out how to make the project work, letting go of the anxiety and disappointment around the project, with thinking or *fearing* that I would have to give up on my dream completely! I decided my body was sending me a loud message to challenge the truth of that decision and rethink it. Soon after I realized what I had done, I changed my mind about it and my throat healed. My voice returned full blast in a very short time.

> Ignore the gloomy forecasts of others, no matter how well meaning.

During the time my voice was hoarse, it was important to point out what was happening around me. Well-meaning friends warned me in an ominous tone: "You better have it looked at. I know a great specialist; it might be something serious." The warnings and stories about so-and-so who didn't see a specialist in time and ended up at death's door went on and on. If you let yourself succumb to the fearful suggestions and concerns of others, don't be surprised if your condition worsens. If you don't have the conviction in your mind that you are basically healthy and can listen to the wisdom of your soul, the fearful predictions of others will make it worse! Ignore the gloomy forecasts of others, no matter how well meaning.

When it comes to other symptoms and conditions, the process is the same. A friend of mine was in tears because she couldn't walk more than a few feet without her knees being in pain. Her physician sent her to a specialist who said she needed a knee replacement. I knew she was going through a period of emotional strain, so I suggested she continually remind herself that the situation was temporary and would soon be healed. I suggested she massage her knees and see a physical therapist. If it didn't work, she could always have the surgery, I reasoned. The approach worked beautifully. Nearly ten years later, she is walking, dancing, and working out at the gym with ease!

You can use your mind to learn to love things that are good for you by focusing on the positive aspects of them, whether it's eating fish for the omega-3s, riding your bicycle, or meditating for the effects it brings. Dean Ornish is well known for having demonstrated that heart disease can not only be healed but can actually be *reversed* through diet—low fat, high fiber, and complex carbs—with moderate exercise three days a week and meditating several times a week.[113]

Doctors often report, however, that they don't recommend the Ornish regimen much because patients think it's too drastic. To which Ornish shoots back, "Drastic? What about the alternative? Do you think cutting someone's chest open for open heart surgery isn't drastic?"[114]

To heal, you must learn to use your mind to activate your will to heal. Your mind can help you find a way to stop resisting what's healthy and good for you, for starters. It helps not to think of your mind as a purely mental thing and of the body as a purely physical one; your mind and body are continuing, interweaving processes that are mental and physical all at once. Training your mind to accept and relish what's good for you and using it to *expect* to heal is very important fuel for healing the body.

MONKEY MIND

Buddha likened the human mind to drunken monkeys jumping around, screeching, chattering, babbling on and on. Buddha said that we all have monkey minds, like dozens of monkeys constantly clamoring for attention. What the Buddha was getting at is that for most of us,

---

[113] Dean Ornish. "Reversing Heart Disease: A Formula." *Annuals of Internal Medicine*. 2003.

[114] www.goodreads.com/author/quotes/35156.deanornish

thinking is virtually automatic, in that our minds are socialized, or programmed, to think in a certain way. Fear is a particularly persistent monkey, screeching all the time about what we're lacking, about all the reasons to be insecure and everything that could go wrong.

Buddha showed his students how to meditate to quiet the monkeys.[115] To fight with the monkeys or to try to banish them from your mind simply serves to energize them. What you resist persists. Instead, Buddha said that if you will spend some time each day in quiet meditation— simply calming your mind by focusing on your breathing or a simple mantra—you can, over time, tame the monkeys. They will grow more peaceful if you gently quiet the monkeys with daily meditation.

> But most of the time, we identify with our minds; in other words we believe we *are* our minds ... instead of realizing we *have* minds and can train them to do what we want them to do, the way the Buddha suggested, the way we train our bodies for a marathon.

Our minds are powerful, creative instruments. They can't help but create. But most of the time, we *identify* with our minds. In other words, we believe we *are* our monkey minds, instead of realizing we *have* minds and can train them to do what we want them to do, the way the Buddha suggested or the way we train our bodies for a marathon. Most of us don't realize we can guide them, control them, and quiet them. What our minds know to do is think, analyze, criticize, and believe the things they have been taught, regurgitate the things we learned in childhood. In this way, our thinking becomes habitual and ingrained, so we often go on "automatic pilot," letting the monkeys take over, when we should be challenging them, or ignoring them, or quieting them.

We can learn new ways to think, new beliefs, new assumptions that help us. My graduate school education taught me to do just that. I had a teacher named Martha Rogers, and she developed a new theory which

---

115   Thubten Chodron. *Taming The Monkey Mind.* Heian International, 1999.

she became famous for. According to her theory, diseases were the result of misguided energy patterns. Healing, she taught us, could be achieved by repatterning our energy through our thoughts and behaviors. So whenever I had a fever in graduate school or felt a little depressed, I reasoned that it was the result of misguided energy patterns. If I jogged, I could repattern the energy and heal. Therefore, well before jogging was popular, I started jogging whenever I didn't feel well. I even jogged when I had a fever. Unbelievably, it worked every time. My fever disappeared. My depression lifted.

All thought has form. If we identify with it or agree with it, the effect is to bring it into our own awareness, which then expresses itself in our bodies. Your body will do what your mind believes because the mind is in every cell in our bodies. It works like this: if you grew up with an authoritarian parent that stifled your individuality, you'll likely have a tendency to see all authority figures through the same lens. You may find yourself resenting anything that resembles your parental experiences of the past. Until you become aware of this tendency, you might impute motives to your husband or wife or boss or best friend that you perceive as trying to control you. Even though this might be your perception and not the case at all, continuously identifying with being a victim of authoritarian control could make you feel helpless and resentful, leading you to act with hostility and eventually creating dis-ease in your body.

MINDFULNESS AS A STARTING POINT

Mindfulness,[116] or paying attention to your parade of thoughts without judging them, will help you learn to train your thoughts in a way that is helpful to you and your healing. Instead of leaving the mind to its own

---

[116]   Mindfulness is a state of active, open attention to the present moment. When you're mindful, you observe your moment-to-moment thoughts, emotions, and sensations without judging them. Jon Cabot Zinn founded the Mindfulness-Based Stress Reduction, essentially a Buddhist practice, in 1979.

devices and indulging feelings of self-pity, anger, and resentment, you can simply become aware of the thought patterns leading you to feel like a victim of authoritarian control.

Let yourself (1) identify the roots of your past resentment, (2) acknowledge and feel it, (3) forgive your parent, and then (4) let the feeling of resentment go. Once you become aware of your patterns of thought, your thinking can then be shifted to override echoes of the past and see the people in your life with a fresh perspective, one that doesn't make you feel powerless. Through mindfulness, we can teach ourselves not to automatically assume that a person's actions are deliberately designed to upset or annoy us.

> The body will do what the mind believes because the mind is in every cell in our bodies.

In fact, if you shift your thinking to change the way you see a person, his behavior will change. Form a picture of him in a positive light and his behavior toward you will change for the better.

The energy of our thoughts—telepathy—operates constantly. We will delve more into the energy of our thoughts in subsequent chapters. For now, the important thing to remember is to look for repetitive patterns in your thinking. If you find yourself experiencing the same themes in your relationships—whether the theme is authoritarian control, accusing your partner of being selfish, feelings of jealousy that crop up in one relationship after another, or whatever your repetitive pattern of behavior may be—it's likely that it's *your* issue and you're seeing people and situations through the lens of your past.[117] This could affect your healing.

A wise friend of mine named Eric, a psychiatrist, always says, "One of life's most important lessons is this: no matter what happens—don't personalize it!" People are usually acting in a way that reflects their own

---

[117]   Your "issues" stem from your core beliefs, overarching beliefs you have about yourself in relation to the world (e.g., " I'm worthless or the world is an unsafe, unfair place.")

interests, in ways they think are best for them in a given situation. We don't have to react to what our monkey minds perceive as a problem. Because we are usually reacting to what we have experienced in the past, or what we have been socialized to think, it is essential to begin to be aware of your repetitive pattern of thoughts and unhealthy behaviors. Then you can begin to teach your mind to see things clearly (e.g., "I have a tendency to be jealous; maybe my partner really *does* have to work late"), not to overreact, and to entertain the best possible outcome.

> Ill health is more or less a set of distorted ideas and thoughts projected onto the body as symptoms, bringing your attention to what's bothering you so that you can clear it up.

We can use the very same strategy when we have an illness. We can think of the illness process this way: ill health is more or less a set of distorted ideas and thoughts projected outward onto the body as symptoms, bringing your attention to what's bothering you so that you can clear it up. Symptoms are barometers that show your patterns of thinking, your beliefs, are shaping your energy in a way that is creating your illness.

Symptoms are your clarion call. As soon as a symptom appears, that's your sign that it's time to look carefully at whatever you're holding in your mind. Since your mind is the dictator of your body, your body manifests your mind's inner stressors. "Take a look at what's happening!" illness says as it develops to call attention to the inconspicuous in our minds. Thoughts that need to be reexamined show themselves. In the process, the mind's major tributary, like rivers that flow toward a destination in the quest to triumph over disease, is the emotions. It is the emotions that lead us to the healing treasure within.

VII

EMOTIONS: YOUR BODY'S REACTION TO YOUR MIND

Power Step: Be aware of your emotions and especially aware of the thoughts associated with them. Then realize that when you continue to think thoughts that make you feel bad, you're investing precious energy in feeling bad. It's like continuing to sink money into a bad investment.

Awareness is the greatest agent for change.

—Eckhart Tolle

Illness pushes most of us to think deeply—and differently—about the biggest emotions: love, fear, cruelty, kindness, and compassion. Your greatest bellwether (remember, Norman Cousins laughed himself back to health!) on the mind-body continuum is your emotions. As the body reacts to your mind, you jump-start your healing journey by feeling good. Seeking to understand why you're feeling the way you do will unlock doors to healing. The thoughts that created your emotions will be revealed.

My friend Sam's father warned her, "Samantha, you'll always be a prisoner of your emotions!" Sam was prone to emotional outbursts that made her father uncomfortable. Actually, it was probably *her father* who felt imprisoned by his emotions, for he had a great deal of trouble expressing them. Either way, being at the mercy of your emotions is not a thing that promotes healing. Emotions must be felt in order to heal. Sometimes the emotions that break your heart are just what is needed to heal. Repressed tears can create anxiety, even chest pain. Anger must be felt too. But emotional upsets must be let go. Held on to long enough, they can be paralyzing and impede your healing.

> It can be said that the path to healing is an emotional one.

It can work the other way around: your dark feelings lurking in the unconscious can give rise to negative thoughts. Even if you can't understand why you're feeling bad at the time, just be aware of what you're feeling. Let yourself feel the emotion, surrendering your resistance to it. It's your resistance to it—refusing to feel it— that ironically keeps it alive. If you're in pain and suffering it may seem like a person or a situation is to blame. But it's not so. The resistance within you is what creates the suffering. When you stop resisting it, just allow yourself to feel it, it disappears like a patch of fog.

It can be said that the path to healing is an emotional one. If you become aware of your emotional reactions—actually moments of cellular healing—you will eventually see that what you're feeling is a theme of what's being released in your body.

UNHAPPINESS: FORMULA FOR ILLNESS

There has long been an association between unhappiness and negative emotional states in relation to disease. Galen, a prominent Greek physician who followed Hippocrates, observed two thousand years ago that depressed people were more susceptible to illness. This observation becomes self-evident to those who watch the reactions to their bodies when they are very worried, when they are having serious financial troubles, or when there are problems with close or important work relationships.

Yet the medical community has been slow to acknowledge the primacy of emotions in disease. Many *still* do not believe emotions are involved with cancer—or other diseases, for that matter. Among those involved in understanding the mind and its inner workings on a regular basis, like psychiatrists and psychologists, many are convinced that negative emotional states like deep fear, anger, guilt, and resentment lie at the root of most cancers.

My friend Jackie was a prime example of how severe emotional distress can create disease. Wracked with pain and bright red excoriated skin surrounding inflamed joints, she was stricken with a serious case of rheumatoid arthritis when her children left for college. Suffering from the loss of her mother's death at the time, along with one of her children leaving home, she feared facing the empty nest syndrome, facing herself, and the daunting prospect of feeling useless, abandoned, and alone.

As a member of a generation where women and men were taught to accept their lot and grin and bear it, she pushed painful feelings aside. Like many women of her time, raising her children had been her entire raison d'être. Now she felt as though she would no longer have a purpose or be needed. The world that had given her life meaning and purpose for years was falling apart.

Her physician made no such connection, however, and was basically unaware of her life situation, assuring her that rheumatoid arthritis was a viral disease; and though they weren't sure what caused it, they knew it was chronic and had no cure. The most they could hope for, the best medical experts assured her, was to keep it in remission with medication.

Meanwhile, deep down she had a vague intuition that her anger and the distress over the losses she was experiencing must somehow be connected to her disease. As she began to deal with the deep emotions that frightened her—to listen to them and face them, to cry and release them—she gradually began to see new possibilities open up for her. As she began to see her circumstances differently, her pain and swelling began to disappear.

With time, as she struggled to come to grips with new life circumstances, her emotional clearing allowed her to look at her situation with fresh new eyes. Through heeding her emotions, she learned to be more sensitive to her own needs, to nurture the desires of *own* soul, for the first time in her life. She found she had more time to do the things she had always wanted to do: gardening, cooking, and entertaining. Gradually, instead of fearing it, she began to enjoy her free time.

Jackie eventually embarked on a new career and became a successful insurance broker. I often marvel that while most people much younger than Jackie are worried about being laid off or forced to retire, at the age of seventy-nine, every time she threatened to retire, the management of her company urged her to stay. She works every day because she loves it, looks twenty years younger than she is, and takes no medication at all. She has not had a recurrence of her rheumatoid arthritis in twenty years. She is an inspiration to everyone around her.

As we begin to learn how to listen to our emotions, to express them and accept our present circumstances, knowing we can change things if we choose, new options open up to us, including the option to heal.

Embarking on a journey to release unconscious negative emotions is a vital aspect of healing. It seems difficult, but it can be done, and if your intention is to heal, you will succeed. As you learn to let go of or release memories of painful feelings, you will experience emotional clearing. As you become less bogged down with negative emotions—fear, anxiety, anger, apathy—your perspective changes and your awareness expands. This is the same as the shedding of an old lens we used to see reality and adopting a new lens instead.

HOW TO RID YOURSELF OF NEGATIVE EMOTION—LOVE YOURSELF MORE

When you dig deep enough it finally dawns: Negative emotions arise from self-disapproval, not feeling valued or good about yourself. When you compare yourself to others and come up short, when you feel rejected by a person you care about, when you fail at something, when your aim is to please the tribe (your long line of ancestors) instead of pursuing your own dreams and following your own path, negative emotions emerge.

Negative thoughts give rise to negative emotions. If you pay attention to how you feel about yourself and learn to be kind to yourself, as kind as you would a small child in pain, you'll see negative emotions dissolve.

So it follows: the best way to rid yourself of negative emotions is to repattern your self-talk. In the meantime, as negative emotions arise, embrace them. In other words, *allow yourself to feel what you're feeling* fully; allow yourself to feel, really feel, what's coming up to be released from your energy field. Then *let the feeling go.*

Be honest with yourself about what you're feeling. Admit how you feel, without judging or blaming yourself. It's important because on some level we often feel as if we've failed in some way, fallen short of the mark, when we feel bad, when we're in pain. We say to ourselves, "Uh-oh, I shouldn't have done that or said that; I hurt her feelings; I'm a bad person." However, we do things out of innocence, out of a misguided need for love. When deep down we are really searching for love, well-meaning though we may be, often we fear that we won't get it. We fear we won't be good enough to keep the affection of others that are important to us. So emotionally, fear dominates.

The solution? Love yourself anyway. You could be the most beautiful, most intelligent, most accomplished person in the world— and rich too. People can be dazzled by you. But if you don't feel it, if you don't know it, it doesn't matter. The voice inside will still moan, *They don't think I'm right or they don't like me because of the mistake I made, or the way I look, or the way I talk or walk, or*_____ (you can fill in the blank). When we feel this brand of emotional pain, it's a fear of rejection, a fear that we'll lose love and acceptance. In these situations, the answer lies in loving yourself, being good to yourself even more. If you made a mistake, remind yourself that you did what you did with good intentions and be the first to forgive yourself and love yourself even more.

> I made that negative remark because I was afraid. I can choose to forgive and accept myself and love myself more, not less. I will do better next time.

If you feel it, you're healing it. The pain we feel in these circumstances actually serves us. It occurs to expand and transform us. If you accept what you're feeling with heartfelt openness and compassion for yourself, the feelings that are bothering you will begin to dissolve. Furthermore, because we're all interconnected, your external circumstances will change as well (more on this in the next chapter). Let your mind follow suit and let your self-talk be accepting, compassionate, and kind. "I made that negative remark because I was afraid. I can choose to forgive and accept myself and love myself more, not less. I will do better next time."

> If we think of them [painful emotions] as helpful messengers and even welcome them, instead of fearing them and imagining they are harbingers of doom, it becomes clear that emotions are simply arising as energetic signals telling you that you have a need for more self-love and self-approval.

The space between what has happened in your life already and what's to come lies in how you shape your emotional terrain. As we learn to let ourselves feel painful emotions and think of them as helpful messengers, and *then* release them, we take major leaps forward onto healthier ground. It is not the negative emotion itself but our *reactions* to these painful emotions that matters. If we think of them as helpful messengers and even welcome them, instead of fearing them and imagining they are harbingers of doom, it becomes clear that emotions are simply arising as energetic signals telling you that you have a need for more self-love and self-approval.

Adopting this perspective will help it become more and more natural to let go of the negative feeling. Because of the way energy works, which we'll see in the next chapter, it's the process of feeling these negative feelings and then letting them go that is key to changing your circumstances; it is vital to healing. We are meant to be happy, to lead joyful, peaceful lives. Peace, happiness, and contentment always lie within. But the naturally good feelings that are your birthright can and often do get clouded over with doubts and repressed emotions.

How can we get in touch with the place where healing and happiness exists? How far within do we have to go to get in touch with it? Through openness to experiencing the lessons we're meant to learn, through repetitive patterns of self-forgiveness, self-love, and approval, we eventually tap the wellspring of happiness that lies within each of us. It lies beyond the mind, which will be discussed in a later chapter. But first back to the emotions; let's see what you can do to begin to heal right now.

THROUGH THE EMOTIONS, THE MIND BECOMES THE BODY

Feel good now. Feel good now. Feel good now. To begin to heal now, feel good now. Science shows that your mind and body are inseparable: the molecules of emotion in your body are seamlessly dancing with the brain receptors throughout your body. The radiant smile of joy, the blushing red cheeks of shame, the puckering features of pain, the wide-eyed glaze of astonishment, and the scowl of anger all tell the tale of inseparable emblems of feeling on the body. In this psychosomatic network of neuropeptides and their receptors,[118] emotions are the linchpin. Through the emotions, the mind doesn't just govern the body; it *becomes* the body immediately.[119] Happy thoughts secrete happy hormones. Unhappy thoughts secrete unhappy hormones.

As the nexus between body and mind, going back and forth, combines the two, emotions communicate what you are thinking to the cells in the form of biochemicals and vibrations. Referring to them as the "biochemicals of emotion," Dr. Candace Pert, who discovered this mind-body network, views emotions as messenger systems possessing a specific vibration, humming a signature tune, rising and falling, waxing and waning, binding and unbinding. In this way, emotions offer the key to an understanding of disease.[120]

---

[118] Candace Pert et al. "Neuropeptides and their Receptors: A Psychosomatic Network." *Journal of Immunology*. August: 135(2 Suppl):820–826.

[119] Candace Pert, PhD. *Molecules of Emotion*. Touchstone, New York, 1997, 187.

[120] Ibid.

According to Pert, communication back and forth through this network is the mechanism through which health and disease are created. As the messengers linking information to the major systems in our bodies—the neural, gastrointestinal, hormonal, and immune systems into one system—emotions unite the mind and body, serving as the bridge between the two.[121]

Just as TV airwaves carry information that beams onto your flat screen, this network of neuropeptides and receptors has been said to be *informational*, meaning that the mind-body creates a field *of* energy-carrying information as it flows among the cells, organs, and systems of the body. Pert explains that the information is transmitted as a chemical signal that is actually a fluctuation of energy by neuropeptides to their receptors in a kind of "lock and key" fashion. It's been demonstrated that the body simultaneously secretes the biochemicals that correspond to our thoughts and the emotions that accompany them. In other words, the biochemicals that flow through our minds and bodies are a sort of encoded communication triggered by certain emotions.

In this intricate network, the body actually mirrors the mind.[122] Happy thoughts, happy biochemicals. Negative thoughts, negative biochemicals. If you think positive thoughts, you feel good and your body secretes happy chemicals: endorphins, serotonin, interleukin. If your thinking is habitually negative, you feel bad and your body secretes unhappy chemicals like cortisol. Eventually, these unhappy chemicals wreak havoc on your immune system, creating an environment ripe for disease.

This flow of information can be conscious or unconscious. Eckhart Tolle refers to an accumulation of unconscious emotions that have been set aside because they're too painful to deal with as the "pain-body."[123] This pain-body develops a life of its own. Even though the emotions of the pain-body are unconscious, they are bound to interfere with our

---

[121] Ibid. 192

[122] Candace Pert. 181

[123] Eckhart Tolle. *The Power of Now.* New World Library, Novato, California, 1999.

healing. Unless we learn to release these repressed painful memories, we will continue being totally unaware of them and they will continue to get in our way—and in the way of our healing.

RELEASING UNCONSCIOUS EMOTIONS

Healing hits a roadblock as we send off to the unconscious emotions that are too painful to let ourselves feel. Never to be seen again, we still feel them. The extent to which we *clearly* feel an emotion is the extent to which it is conscious. If it feels vague and uncomfortable, and you have a hard time recognizing why you're feeling it, chances are it's a holdover from the past that has been banished to the dungeons of your unconscious. That's usually when you experience an intensity of emotion in a situation that doesn't call for it. You feel a barrage of negative emotions and say to yourself, "Where in the world did this come from?"

> All negative emotions come from your unconscious disapproval of yourself.

An overreaction like this is kind of like throwing up. It's a sign that your unconscious is looking for an opportunity to get rid of something it can no longer stomach, something it's been holding in for a while. Repressed emotion—"I can't believe he's treating me like this"—waits for a chance to escape, and it will often create a reaction to something that allows you to vent it, to release it. It wants to go. It may be an upset stomach. Or you may find yourself projecting your emotions onto others. When you accuse someone of something, saying, for instance, "You're such a selfish person" or, "Why can't you be more sensitive to others?" be on the lookout for an outpouring of emotions that may actually be yours. Emotions you may be unconsciously trying to release are fodder for your relationships with others. You are projecting them outwardly in order to let them go.

The pain-body, the cornerstone of buried negative emotion, prevents you from experiencing inner peace and connection at an emotional level. Down to your cells, it blocks your experience of vitality and health at a cellular level. As Tolle describes it, the pain-body takes on a life of its own, with its own energy field and cellular memory, whose primary aim is to hold on to the pain that you have accumulated throughout your life. When disease, dysfunction, imbalance, or lack of inner peace occurs at any level, you can be sure that the pain-body is active.

Tolle says the following:

> *There are two levels of pain: the pain that you create now, and the pain of the past that still lives on in your mind and body. This of course includes the pain that you suffered as a child, caused by the unconsciousness of the world into which you were born. The accumulated pain is a negative energy field that occupies your body and mind. If you look at it as an invisible entity in its own right, you are getting quite close to the truth—it's the emotional pain-body.*[124]

When a problem or a traumatic event happens, whether it is physical or emotional, and it is so devastating that we just can't face it, we can't handle it—we scream *nooooooo!* inside—we bury the event and the emotions that go with it down into the depths of us. We think, *I can't take anymore* or maybe even, *If this happens, I don't have any reason to live any longer.* In situations like this, we often say to ourselves, "This is too devastating to deal with. I'll ignore it; I'll face it if and when I can, when it is not life-threatening." We often underestimate our ability to tolerate discomfort, whether it is emotional or physical.

When we hold off dealing with anything traumatic—in other words, we don't allow ourselves to feel it—the negative emotion festers. In addition, we are allowing additional negative emotional energy to build and accumulate. Let's say your lover left. You thought that person

---

[124] Eckhart Tolle. *The Power of Now.* New World Library, Novado, California, 1999.

was the love of your life. You feel extremely upset. But instead of letting yourself cry and feel the loss, you act as if it doesn't bother you. Maybe you get angry at yourself and blame yourself. You say things to yourself like, "How stupid can you be? You took him [or her] for granted! Now you lost the best thing that ever happened to you! Now you'll be alone and miserable and you deserve to be."

> The first important step involves clearing your inner emotional pathway by giving your feelings the time and attention they need.

This kind of self-talk adds self-condemnation, anger, guilt, and fear to the original trauma. It becomes a vicious cycle that can go on and on if we think we can indefinitely put off something that we don't want to face right now. Negative energies of old hurts and hang-ups stay with us. We can try to put them out of our minds and deny whatever happened, but the more we keep the emotions buried deep inside, the more strongly they press to escape. The more unresolved issues we hold back, the more troubled our lives become.

Instead, you could allow yourself to feel the hurt, thinking, *There is a lesson to be learned here, and maybe it's good that this is happening. Can I think of other times when I learned a valuable lesson from situations that didn't feel very good at the time? I know one thing for sure. I will learn to change my actions so that when I do meet the right person, I won't make the same mistake again.*

What's often the case with many of us is that even if we're thinking positive things *consciously*, we're still feeling bad because of buried emotions of the past that produced the trauma. Even if you view your childhood as a relatively peaceful one, where your parents were nurturing and arguments over the usual control issues or struggles over money didn't come up all that frequently, we can all still recall painful stories. These stories, buried in our unconscious minds still affect us, manifest in our lives and our bodies, and play the same themes over and over again until we make peace with these hidden emotions and understand their insights.

> To explore this on your own, immerse yourself in an activity that will open your subconscious mind—painting, journaling, tapping, meditating, repetitive movement of any kind, keeping a dream diary, and so forth. Allow the answers to come to you—they've been waiting for a chance to reveal themselves.

Your healing mantra: become aware of painful emotions that may be repressed. By immersing yourself in an activity that will open your unconscious mind—such as painting, journaling, meditating, keeping a dream diary—the themes and patterns that are festering in your depths will be revealed. The Sedona Method of releasing negative emotion is also a powerful tool.[125] Just allow the emotions to come up and be released. They've been waiting for the chance. Actually, if you just keep your focus in the present moment and observe what you're feeling whenever you feel bad, if there doesn't seem to be any reason for it, it is almost certain to be emotions related to a past event. You repressed them at the time because they were too painful to feel, and now they are coming up to be released.

KEEP YOUR HEART OPEN

Clearing your inner emotional pathway by giving your feelings the time and attention they need brings healing. The best chance for a deep emotional clearing of the old energy patterns and issues lodged in our cells is likely to be your relationships. Through interactions with those closest to us, we can become more aware and begin to pay closer attention to our emotional reactions as they come up. By communicating gently and lovingly with our inner child, as some call it, we will be rewarded with more and more happiness and joy.

---

[125] Lester Levenson. *No Attachments, No Aversions.* Lawrence Crane Enterprises. Sherman Oaks, California 2003.

Keep your heart open. Through the ups and downs of the disappointments and fears in relationships, stay open. Don't shut down. By learning not to be afraid of your emotions, by feeling, accepting, and releasing a barrage of painful emotions, angry emotions, hurt, resentment, jealousy, and sadness, you allow them to pass away. These emotions make up an important part of your healing process, and they are not to be avoided but accepted, even embraced, as your opportunity for greater healing and expansion to higher, clearer, and healthier states. Acceptance doesn't mean you like it; it simply means not to deny what you're feeling. Then let them go.

> Remember, painful emotions are coming up to be released. *They want to leave.*

Remember, painful emotions are there because they are coming up to be released. *They want to leave.* At the root of all negative emotions, either the ones you may be feeling now or the ones that have been buried for a while, is your unconscious disapproval of yourself. Negative emotions represent energy that is going against your grain. The best antidote? Love yourself more. Be gentle with yourself; be understanding and show yourself the forgiveness and compassion that you would show to a dear friend or lover in pain. If you're not ready to forgive someone who hurt you, love yourself anyway. Love the part of you that isn't ready to forgive. Acceptance and self-love are the keys to emotional healing. Acceptance doesn't mean that you have to like it when something bad is happening to cause you emotional pain.

Not at all. *Accepting* your emotions simply means you let yourself feel them. You don't suppress them. Suppressing toxic emotions like anger, fear, and anxiety creates disease.

There is nothing wrong with feeling anger and fear and resentment. They can be natural responses to your circumstances. But if we think it's a bad thing to feel these emotions and we don't let ourselves *acknowledge* feeling them and repress them instead, eventually we're bound to run into trouble. We'll develop symptoms and conditions like high blood pressure, stress ulcers, headaches, or something worse. Toxic emotions create disease and tell us that something is wrong. The famous psychiatrist Wilhelm Reich recognized this connection long ago when he said, "The organs weep the tears the eyes refuse to shed."

> Toxic emotions create disease and tell us that something is wrong. The famous psychiatrist Wilhelm Reich recognized this connection long ago when he said, "The organs weep the tears the eyes refuse to shed."

Disappointments, losses, and pressures can mount. They can end up consuming us. That's when they create disease. The question remains, can we show ourselves kindness and compassion even when we're in the midst of life's most difficult challenges? If we can say yes, we are on the path to healing.

A vital approach to healing begins with the intention to take our focus off our problems and focus on all the things in our lives that feel good and to be thankful for them. Sometimes we might think, *I don't have much to be thankful for. I'm sick; I have expenses I'm having trouble meeting; I can't get a job. Thankful for what?* We all probably know people in tough situations who on the surface might not seem to have much to be thankful for. Maybe you're in that kind of a situation yourself. However, it's not about pointing to material things or even physical health. Being thankful begins with an intention, an intention to be grateful, even if it's for the sunlight streaming through the window, creating the feeling of warmth on your skin.

Thankful energies and repatterning the programs of the unconscious mind come from a sincere intention to change. It is not enough to try different healing modalities like visualizations and affirmations without addressing negative emotions *as they arise*. Repatterning these reactions or "programs" of the unconscious mind brings deep changes at the cellular level. By acknowledging and allowing ourselves to feel whatever we're feeling without reacting or judging ourselves for the way we feel, we jump-start the healing process. Being present to what you are feeling, just being aware of what you are feeling and then letting it go like soap bubbles, allowing it to pass right out of you, diffuses the negative emotion that has been buried deep in your cells and ignites the healing within you.

In summary:

1. Your thought patterns are conditioned—you can change them to serve you;
2. Your thoughts create emotions in the body and release corresponding "happy" biochemicals or "unhappy" biochemicals;
3. You can jump-start your healing process by learning to release unpleasant, painful emotions you're holding on to;
4. As you let go of negative emotions, your awareness expands; and as your awareness expands, your thoughts naturally become happier.
5. Your healing depends on self-love and acceptance.

Using a deliberate intention to love and approve of yourself, you consciously begin to reshape your thoughts in a more positive way, a way that makes you feel better and is helpful to you. Then, whenever negative emotions arise, you can train yourself to release them. Eventually you realize that you are *not* your mind, you are *not* your emotions, and that you *have* a mind and emotions, that you *are their master* and can shape your mind and emotions to work in favor of your healing. You can shape them as you wish, in ways that work for you.

Not only physical illnesses can be healed. The striking case of Dan Fisher, executive director of the National Empowerment Center, an MD, PhD, who suffered from schizophrenia for twenty to thirty years, is a powerful example of how mental diseases can be healed as well. Fisher completely recovered—as he puts it—*in spite of the system*. He then went to Harvard Medical School to become a psychiatrist. Fisher says, "The more of us who have recovered who can tell our stories, the more truth will displace falsehood. We welcome your letters by or about anyone who has made a complete recovery from mental illness." [126]

Dan points out that by "complete recovery," he means that the person has regained a meaningful role in society, can cope with life's stresses, and is not considered sick by others. The weight of personal testimony like this one will give credibility to the power of self-healing and the fact that most people are able to regain a productive role in society and recover from any illness. [127]

Our perceptions, beliefs, mind-sets, and values are a result of our level of awareness. Whenever we experience a shift in our awareness due to a new inner realization or understanding, we are actually breaking away from our old awareness and our old belief systems and attitudes.

As we release negative emotions, we let go of our painful conflicts and experiences at deeper and deeper levels. We become stronger, wiser, and more conscious of our own intentions and emotions. We become less driven by the automatic reflex patterns of our unconscious minds and freer to react toward other people with empathy, love, and compassion.

Illness is misguided beliefs and ideas projected outward onto the body as symptoms, and as you begin to clear up or release the repressed emotions associated with these ideas, the healing begins. More along these lines will be discussed in the chapter on energy. But first let's take a look at just how deep and far-reaching the mind and its effect on your emotions actually is. Let's look at the anatomy of our beliefs and how they work in our bodies and our lives.

---

[126] Dan Fisher. "My Story." Akmhcweb.org/recovery/My_Story.htm
[127] Ibid.

VIII

ACCORDING TO YOUR BELIEF IT SHALL BE DONE UNTO YOU

Power Step: Your beliefs are crucial to your ability to heal.

First you must believe that you can. Ignore well-meaning souls who would tell you otherwise.

Michael J. Balick, PhD, director of the Institute of Economic Botany at the New York Botanical Garden, tells a story about traveling on a bus in the backwoods of Brazil with a group of tourists. When they came upon a woman cracking open the nuts of a palm tree and extracting the juice, everyone jumped out of the bus, circled around her, and started taking pictures. The woman immediately became hysterical, had difficulty breathing, and went into a state of shock. She had to be hospitalized.

"She was convinced that the people had stolen her spirit," Dr. Balick explains. "And it was her belief, not the clicking cameras, that caused the physical reaction."

The woman in Brazil offers a dramatic example of how our beliefs become our biology.[128] It is well known that cultural beliefs influence health-related behavior all the time. It's been confirmed repeatedly that in cultures where belief in voodoo or magic exists, people will actually die after they discover a shaman has cursed them.[129]

---

[128] Michael J. Balick and Paul Allen Cox. *Plants, People and Culture*. Scientific American Library, 1996.

[129] Stephen Hawley Martin. *How to Master Life: The Science Behind the Secret*. Oaklea Press, March 2007.

Many Latino ideas of disease center around experiencing intensely negative emotional states like fright, anger, envy, bodily changes, and magical causes. Some Latinos refuse treatment, convinced that their spirit, or *espiritismo*, is in charge. Just the belief that an imbalance in either spiritual or physical terms is present can have a detrimental effect on the physical health of the body. Prayers or religious practices with a Curandero are often used to cure *susto*, or fright.

Beliefs work this way with all of us. As a pattern of deeply ingrained thoughts and emotions, beliefs are critical to healing. When you truly understand the latest science explaining the seamless inner workings of the thoughts and emotions coursing through our minds and bodies, it becomes clear why this is so. Fearful beliefs, like the ones held by the woman from Brazil, will trigger the release of stress hormones like adrenaline, noradrenaline, and cortisol; cause hyperventilating; and throw off the biochemical balance of our bodies. Illness follows.

What a person really believes will happen usually does. Tens of thousands of people have been healed after visiting the spring at Lourdes, France. Others become ill because of a belief in something that creates a sickness, a belief that some external thing is *the* primary cause of the illness, whether it's a shaman or a germ. Actually, the primary cause is a belief in the external factor—that a draft, for instance, will cause you to catch a cold. Oftentimes the belief is not conscious but something we've been taught to believe since childhood, and now it is tucked away in our unconscious minds.

The belief causes the result. The principle many healers subscribe to, in whatever various ways they may explain it, is that the basis of all healing is a change in belief.

> Belief is the X factor, the thing that has the most significant effect on the outcome, the major aspect of the power to heal.

Belief is the X factor. It has the most significant effect on the outcome, on the power to heal. We all have that power. However, we differ in our ability to activate it. Every cell in your body wants to help you to heal. If you think of an illness as your own personal wake-up call, your body's urgings to get your attention, you are on the right track.

The placebo effect, which has been renamed the "belief effect,"[130] has been shown to be very powerful in treating illnesses from depression to arthritis. In more than half of the clinical trials for the six leading antidepressants, the drugs did not outperform placebos. Studies supported by the Department of Health and Human Services found that 30 to 40 percent responded to placebos for treatment of major depressive disorder. [131] Dismissed as an irritating effect in well-controlled scientific studies, the placebo effect has been ignored by mainstream medicine. Actually, the placebo effect can be viewed as a stunning example of the body's natural healing ability, an ability that can be enhanced and expanded.

Healing is an art that we can all learn. There are many paths to healing, and different healing strategies exist in many different cultures. Healing modalities such as acupuncture, meditation, and therapeutic touch have been studied and shown to have healing effects.[132] Others have not been scientifically proven but people have experienced their effectiveness. What science *has* shown is that what works best is what a person believes in.

THE STRIKING CASE OF MR. WRIGHT

There is a striking and well-known case about the power of the placebo effect in the medical literature:[133]

---

[130] Bruce Lipton. *The Biology of Belief.* Hay House, June 2013.

[131] Bret R. Rutherford, MD, and Steven P. Roose, MD. A Model of Placebo Response. *American Journal of Psychiatry.* July 1, 2013; 170(7): 723–733.

[132] Herb Benson. *Timeless Healing.* Simon Schuster, New York, 2009

[133] Maj-Britt Niemi. "Placebo Effect: A Cure in the Mind." *Scientific American.* February/March 2009.

Dr. Bruno Klopfer was treating a man named Wright who had advanced cancer of the lymph nodes. All standard treatments had been exhausted, and Wright appeared to have little time left. His neck, armpits, chest, abdomen, and groin were filled with tumors the size of oranges, and his spleen and liver were so enlarged that two quarts of milky fluid had to be drained out of his chest every day.

But Wright did not want to die. He had heard about an exciting new drug called Krebiozen, and he begged his doctor to let him try it. At first his doctor refused because the drug was only being tried on people with a life expectancy of at least three months. But Wright was unrelenting in his entreaties, [and] his doctor finally gave in. He gave Wright an injection of Krebiozen on Friday, but in his heart of hearts, he did not expect Wright to last the weekend. Then the doctor went home.

To his surprise, on the following Monday, he found Wright out of bed and walking around. Klopfer reported that his tumors had "melted like snowballs on a hot stove" and were half their original size. This was a far more rapid decrease in size than even the strongest X-ray treatments could have accomplished.

Ten days after Wright's first Krebiozen treatment, he left the hospital and was, as far as his doctors could tell, cancer free. When he had entered the hospital, he had needed an oxygen mask to breathe, but when he left, he was well enough to fly his own plane at twelve thousand feet with no discomfort.

Wright remained well for about two months, but then articles began to appear asserting that Krebiozen actually had no effect on cancer of the lymph nodes. Wright, who was rigidly logical and scientific in his thinking, became very depressed, suffered a relapse, and was readmitted to the hospital. This time his physician decided to try an experiment.

He told Wright that Krebiozen was every bit as effective as it had seemed, but that some of the initial supplies of the drug had deteriorated during shipping. He explained, however, that he had a new highly concentrated version of the drug and could treat Wright with this. Of course, the physician did not have a new version of the drug and intended to inject Wright with plain water. To create the proper atmosphere, he even went through an elaborate procedure before injecting Wright with the placebo.

Again, the results were dramatic. Tumor masses melted, chest fluid vanished, and Wright was quickly back on his feet and feeling great. He remained symptom-free for another two months. But then the American Medical Association announced that a nationwide study of Krebiozen had found the drug worthless in the treatment of cancer. This time Wright's faith was completely shattered. His cancer quickly returned, and he died two days later.

Beliefs are the masters of our biology, as Mr. Wright's stunning example shows. The placebo response recounted here is the perfect case in point to demonstrate the power of belief, which reflects what we're thinking on an unconscious as well as conscious level. The placebo response in each of us is a response that naturally evokes the body's own repair mechanisms. It is a foundation of evidence that the mind-body can heal on its own.

Medicine has tried to ignore it by controlling for it. Nonetheless, anywhere from 30 to 80 percent of the time, depending on the study, a placebo performs just as well as the treatment. Instead of studying it, the scientific community has been controlling for it for decades, regarding it as a thorn in their side. Many in the scientific community are like the fellow that was looking for his glasses under the streetlight because that's where the light was, even though he lost them behind the bushes in the dark!

Remarkable healing stories are testament to the power of placebo, like the story about Mr. Wright. In spite of the medical community's resistance to seeing placebo as a great thing, its "healing is believing" effect has not gone unnoticed in other branches of science. In fact, much research has been done, mostly in the fields of psychology and psychoneuroimmunology, demonstrating the effect of our beliefs on our physiology and our biochemistry.

Not only medications are subject to the placebo effect. Another powerful example (briefly mentioned in chapter 1) is an account of knee surgeries performed at the Baylor School of Medicine. Dr. Bruce Mosely knew that knee surgery helped his patients. Like all good surgeons, Mosley was certain there is no placebo effect in surgery. Mosely was just trying to figure out which surgical procedure was giving his patients the most relief.

Therefore, he decided to do a study. He divided the patients in his study into three groups. In the first group, Moseley shaved the damaged cartilage in the knee. In the second group, he flushed out the knee joint, removing the material thought to be causing the inflammatory effect. Both of these constitute standard treatment for arthritic knees. The third group was a control group. This group got the fake surgery. In this group, the patient was sedated and Mosely made three standard incisions and then talked and acted as he would have during a real surgical procedure. He even splashed salt water to simulate the sound of the knee washing procedure. After forty minutes, Mosely sewed up the incisions as if he had done the surgery. All three groups were prescribed the same postoperative care.

Mosely was absolutely shocked at the results. The groups that received the surgery improved, as was expected. However, the group that received the placebo improved *just as much as the others*! In spite of the fact that 650,000 of these procedures were done annually at a cost of about five thousand dollars each, the results were glaringly clear to Mosely: his skill as a surgeon was of no use to these patients.[134]

TV news programs showed patients who had to walk with a cane prior to the surgery playing basketball with their children afterward. As one of the patients interviewed by the Discovery Channel put it, "In this world, anything is possible when you put your mind to it. I know that your mind can work miracles."[135]

Healing factors already present within each of us know how to counteract illness. Our beliefs are the trigger. Yet health care as we know it is focused on the physical, on the body, and the body is the least of it! The body is the effect, not the cause. Our bodies are simply mirrors of how we think and how we lead our lives.

MULTIPLE PERSONALITY DISORDER: PROOF POSITIVE THAT BELIEFS HEAL

More powerful, even astonishing, examples of the power of beliefs on healing and our entire physiology are detailed in Barry Cohen, Ester Giller, and Lynn W's brilliant work titled *Multiple Personality Disorder from the Inside Out.*

Vivid accounts of how different personalities brought forth in the same body spontaneously healed or became stricken with an illness or an allergic reaction in a matter of seconds leave little doubt of the power of beliefs on our entire physiology. Medical conditions possessed by one personality disappear when another personality takes over. Because of the completely different beliefs of each personality, the biochemical

134 Bruce Lipton. *The Biology of Belief.* Hay House, January 2013.
135 Ibid.

environments change radically when the other personality comes to the fore, creating striking examples of the power of beliefs!

Dr. Bennett Braun of the International Society for the Study of Multiple Personality in Chicago has documented a case in which all of a patient's personalities were allergic to orange juice, except one. If the man drank orange juice when he was being one of the allergic personalities, he would break out in a terrible rash. But when he switched to his non-allergic personality, the rash would instantly start to fade and he could drink orange juice with no medical consequences.

Dr. Francine Howland, a Yale psychiatrist who specializes in treating people with multiple personality disorder, relates an even more striking incident involving a patient and a wasp sting. At one appointment, the man showed up with his eye completely swollen and shut from a wasp sting. Dr. Howland called an ophthalmologist, wanting to get the patient treated for the sting.

Unfortunately, the ophthalmologist could not see the man for an hour, and because the man was in severe pain, Dr. Howland decided to try to bring forth the alternate personality. As it turned out, the other personality served as an anesthetic, and within seconds, the man was feeling absolutely no pain. The pain had ended, and by the time the man got to his eye appointment, the swelling was gone and his eye had returned to normal.[136] Seeing no need to treat him, the ophthalmologist sent him home.

After a while, however, the man's original personality took control back, and the pain and swelling returned with a vengeance. The next day, he went back to the ophthalmologist and was treated. The eye doctor phoned Dr. Howland because "he thought time was playing tricks on him." He wanted to make sure that it was the day before when Dr. Howland had phoned him about treatment for the man. Dr. Howland laughed and of course explained what had happened; that the man had multiple personality disorder and he had seen two different personalities!

Allergies are not the only things multiples can switch on and off. The control of the unconscious mind, which is in every cell in the body, as explained in chapter 5, can produce shocking biochemical shifts that

---

[136] Cohen et al. *Multiple Personality Disorder from the Inside Out.* Sidran Press, 2009.

control the reactions of drugs and alcohol in people with multiple personality disorder.

> By changing personalities, a drunk person can instantly become sober, and different personalities within someone with multiple personality disorder also respond differently to various drugs.

By changing personalities, a drunk person can instantly become sober, and different personalities within someone with multiple personality disorder also respond differently to various drugs. Braun records a case in which five milligrams of Valium sedated one personality, while one hundred milligrams had little or no effect on another. Often one or more personalities of a multiple are children. While an adult personality is in the fore and takes an adult dose of medicine, he or she is fine, but if one of the child personalities abruptly takes over, he or she may overdose.[137]

With a change of personalities in multiples, scars appear and disappear; burn marks and cysts do the same. The "multiple" can change from being right-handed to being left-handed with ease and agility. Visual acuity can differ so that some multiples have to carry two or three different pairs of glasses. One personality can be color-blind and the other not. Even eye color can change. Speech pathologist Christy Ludlow has found that "the voice pattern for each of a multiple's personalities is different, a feat that requires such a deep physiological change that even the most accomplished actor cannot alter his voice enough to disguise his voice pattern."

One multiple, admitted to the hospital for diabetes complications, baffled her doctors by showing no symptoms. Without warning, one of her non-diabetic personalities had taken control. The patient instantly showed no signs of being diabetic. There are also accounts of epilepsy coming and going with personality changes. Robert A. Phillips, Jr., a psychologist, reports that he has even seen tumors appear and disappear.

Multiples tend to heal faster. For example, there are several cases on record of third-degree burns healing with amazing rapidity. Most

---

[137] Ibid.

incredible of all, at least one researcher, Dr. Cornelia Wilbur, the therapist whose pioneering treatment of Sybil Dorsett (of the book and movie *Sybil*) is convinced that multiples do not age as fast as other people.[138]

How could such things be? We are deeply attached to the inevitability and the material "reality" of things. If we have bad vision, we think we have it for life. If we suffer from diabetes, we do not for a moment think our condition can heal with a change in beliefs or thoughts. But the phenomenon of multiple personalities challenges these long-held assumptions and offers further evidence of just how much our beliefs can profoundly affect the biology of the body. With a change of belief, our bodies can change in an instant.

Most amazing is the fact that after multiples have undergone therapy and reconciled their personalities into a single personality, they can *still* make these changes at will. This suggests that somewhere down deep in our psyches, we all have the ability to control these things by changing our beliefs.

BELIEFS: A FOUNTAIN OF YOUTH

Ellen Langer of Harvard believes that the biomedical model of the day—that the mind and the body are on separate tracks—is wrongheaded; and so is the belief that "the only way to get sick is through the introduction of a pathogen, and the only way to get well is to get rid of it," says Langer.

Just as beliefs can create disease, they can heal us and help us stay young. Ellen Langer of Harvard believes that the biomedical model of the day—a model that sees the mind and body on separate tracks—is wrongheaded; and so is the belief that "the only way to get sick is through the introduction of a pathogen, and the only way to get well is to get rid of it," says Langer.[139]

---

138 Cohen et al. Ibid.

139 Bruce Grierson. "What if Age Is Nothing but a Mind-Set?" *New York Times Magazine*, October 22, 2014.

She came to think that what people needed to heal themselves was a psychological "primer"—something that triggered the body to take curative measures all by itself. Gathering a group of men in their seventies together for a five-day retreat in New Hampshire, for a "counterclockwise study," as she called it, Langer set out to test this premise. The men weren't in good or bad health but what would be considered "age-appropriate" health. In other words, the men were a little slow, a little bent over, and easily fatigued.

Langer was determined to change all that. She re-created the world as it looked in 1959, with vintage programs on TV and mid-century music that was popular then. The men were treated as if they were younger. No one offered to help them carry their bags or get them things they needed, like blankets or snacks. Conversations were kept to the news and sports popular at the time: the Eisenhower White House, the Dodgers and the White Sox play-offs, and so forth. Lest the men be reminded of their aging, all mirrors were removed from the space.

At the end of their stay, Langer administered a series of physical and cognitive aptitude tests. The results were dramatic. The men's performance on the tests improved dramatically, at times exceeding the performance that would be expected of men a decade or more younger.[140]

Jeffrey Rediger, a psychiatrist and the medical and clinical director of Harvard's McLean Hospital, aware of Langer's original New Hampshire study, saw the made-for-TV version, which brought its tantalizing implications to life. "She's one of the people at Harvard who really gets it," Rediger commented. "That health and illness are much more rooted in our minds and in our hearts and how we experience ourselves in the world than our models even begin to understand."

Then in 2010, the BBC broadcast a re-creation, which Langer consulted on, called *The Young Ones*, with six aging former celebrities as guinea pigs. The stars were transported via period cars to a country house meticulously retrofitted to 1975, right down to the art on the

---

[140] Jeffrey Kluger. "Get Your Head in the Game." *Time*. February 23–March 2, 2015, 84.

wall. They emerged after a week as apparently rejuvenated as Langer's septuagenarians in New Hampshire, showing an amazing improvement on all the key health metrics. One who had rolled up in a wheelchair walked out with a cane. Another, who couldn't even put his socks on unassisted at the start, hosted the final evening's dinner party, gliding around with purpose and vigor. The others walked taller and looked younger. They had been pulled out of mothballs and made to feel important again. Perhaps, Langer later mused, that rekindling their egos was key to reclaiming their bodies.

If we believe that our bodies are subject to all sorts of influences beyond our control, and that this, that, or the other symptom causes such and such disease, then that's what will happen. In other words, this belief, impressed upon the unconscious mind, is accepted without question and proceeds to create bodily conditions in accordance with the belief. Again, if our fixed belief is that certain medical remedies are the only means of cure, then we find that this belief creates bodily responses accordingly. The theory of medicine corresponds with the measure of knowledge that those who rely on it can take in; and it acts according to their belief that in many cases medicine does a lot of good. However, it also fails in many instances.

For most of us who have been conditioned to have great faith in medical science, medicine is a most valuable aid in alleviating physical problems. The thinking we need to challenge is not the belief that, in its own way, medicine is capable of doing good, but the belief that there is no higher or better way.

Some scientists believe that other better avenues of healing are possible because our brains operate in a holographic way, which we will delve more deeply into in chapter 10. When we look at the electrical impulses traveling through our neurons and the patterns of billions of neurons interacting, we see they operate in the same quantum way as the wave/particle duality. When a photon of light is observed, it behaves either as a particle or as a wave. But both aspects are never observed simultaneously. Which behavior light exhibits—particle or wave—depends on the observer and what the observer expects to see.

So when we say our brains are holographic, a system of holographic surfaces within surfaces, we mean that each surface contains its own world of information, *depending on what you believe you will see*. Because our senses are the lenses or the surfaces through which we see things, if you change the lens/senses or surfaces from one personality to the next, or one belief to the next, you access a whole new world of information. The information that is stored in all the particles of matter and vibrations of energy in the brain is alive in the senses and in the patterns of neurons throughout our bodies. What information you access depends on you: your perceptions, what your senses perceive. What your senses perceive depends on your beliefs. Changing your beliefs is like changing your computer software, changing the disc.

The primary importance of belief in healing becomes apparent when you realize that believing you can recover from illness is the X factor or in itself a vital aspect of the healing experience. Many preeminent pioneers have pointed out this relationship. Dr. Herbert Benson, in his book, *Timeless Healing*,[141] and Deepak Chopra's book *Quantum Healing* have given us great insight. In *Quantum Healing*, Chopra discusses the key role of belief in Ayurvedic medicine:[142] "Ayurveda is ... a system for curing delusions, for stripping away the convincing quality of a disease and letting a healthy reality take its place. I spend much of my time just talking, trying to get people not to be so convinced by their disease. In Ayurveda, this is the first, most important step in healing. As long as the patient is convinced by his symptoms, he is caught in a reality where being sick is the dominant input."[143]

The reason meditation is so important in Ayurveda is that it leads the mind to a clear zone that is not touched by the disease. Until you know that such a place exists, your disease will seem to be taking over completely. This is the principal delusion that needs to be shattered.

Consistent meditation and many techniques that help to change the patterns of your everyday thinking are available to begin to help

---

[141] Herbert Benson. *Timeless Healing*, Simon and Schuster, New York, 2009, 189.

[142] Deepak Chopra. *Quantum Healing*. Bantam Books, June, 1990.

[143] http://www.chopra.com/ccl/healing-wisdom

you change beliefs that are not doing you any good. With conscientious daily mindfulness and repatterning of your thoughts and beliefs, your physical state is bound to improve … bound to heal.

IT'S GENETIC VERSUS IT'S BELIEF

Science has led us to believe that our genes are our destiny. When my father was seventy-six, he developed pain in his throat and saw many specialists for what he swore was throat cancer. His father had died of throat cancer when *he* was seventy-six, and my father was convinced, through years of having been told that there is a strong hereditary factor in cancer, that he had it too. Test after test and specialist after specialist showed my father that he was perfectly fine. But it took several specialists to convince him. He went on to live twenty-one more years in very good health because he fortunately believed in the results that specialist after specialist shared with him more than he believed in any hereditary aspect of throat cancer.

Genes don't tell the whole story. In fact, we now know that beliefs, emotions, and patterns of behavior in general can alter our genetic expression. We each have a genetic blueprint, but something causes the gene to *express itself.* In hundreds of scientific studies, beliefs and emotions have been shown to trigger the expression of specific DNA strands. Linking consciousness to genetic change, remarkable scientific discoveries in the new field of epigenetics are revealing the keys to healing.

As Dr. Bruce Lipton, an internationally recognized cellular biologist, explains, "Our health is not controlled by genetics. Conventional medicine is operating from an archaic view that we're controlled by genes. This misunderstands the nature of how biology works."

"Medicine does miracles," Lipton explains, "but it's limited to trauma. The AMA protocol is to regard our physical bodies like a machine, in the same way that an auto mechanic regards a car. When the parts break, you replace them—a transplant,

> "Our health is not controlled by genetics. Conventional medicine is operating from an archaic view that we're controlled by genes. This misunderstands the nature of how biology works."
>
> —Dr. Bruce Lipton

synthetic joints, and so on—and those are medical miracles."

Though medical professionals from all around may protest loudly, Dr. Lipton's research—and the research and empirical evidence of colleagues[144]—has shown definitively that the emperor has no clothes. Lipton's research is so compelling that it is a game changer and impossible to ignore. The entirely new field of epigenetics ("epi" meaning "above" genetics), or the study of gene expression caused by things other than changes in the underlying DNA sequence, came about because of these discoveries. Epigenetics means that lifestyle influences—how you eat, how you handle stress, your emotional IQ, and your environment—can modify your genes.[145]

> Science has taught us to mistrust our own instincts and intuitions about our health, instilling in us a sense of powerlessness.

Science has taught us to mistrust our own instincts and intuition about our health, instilling in us a sense of powerlessness. We defer to external powers. The power of medicine seems to reside in medications and technologies rather than in us as individuals. But the latest scientific studies are charting a new course. The question is not whether beliefs affect our health, but how. Now we're going to see how. It's all about energy.

---

[144] Erwin Laszlo, PhD. "Science and the Akashic Field." *Inner Traditions.* Rochester, Vermont, 2007, 46–47.

[145] Bruce Lipton. *The Biology of Belief.* Hay House Publishers, India. June 2013, 37.

IX

IT'S ALL ABOUT ENERGY

Power Steps: Be aware of your energy field. Ask yourself how you are shaping your energy with your day-to-day thoughts and feelings. Take responsibility for the ways in which you shape your energy.

The energetic consequences of your thought patterns will have very different effects on your healing journey.

Become aware of your thoughts and how they make you feel. Are you often irritated, impatient? Are your usual thought patterns negative? Or do you think thoughts like, Things always go well for me, or, I appreciate the people and experiences in my life that help me improve, help me learn, help me expand out of my comfort zone, bring me closer to my desires.

> *If you want to find the secrets of the universe, think in terms of energy, frequency, and vibration. The same holds true for the world in which we live, our interactions with each other, and indeed our interactions within.*

—Nicholo Tesla

We are walking, talking energy fields, living expressions of our inner energy. The last few chapters emphasized how the power of our thoughts and beliefs and the emotions that accompany them activate or impede the healing process. How is that accomplished? How *are* they activated? By the energy fluctuations of our thoughts and emotions. Predominant thoughts and emotions create certain energetic patterns that either resonate with who you are and your soul's mission or don't.

In most cases, illness is linked to an energetic loss; it's a leaking energy associated with the energy center (or chakra—meaning "wheel") that is connected with the choices and events driven by your ego or your social self, frustrating and blocking your soul's path. Actually, the condition has emerged to help you, to inspire change, to serve to wake you up. Having stored information such as stressors, negative thoughts, and emotions, your cells retain the energetic footprints or memories of past traumas. From this energetic perspective, it is easy to see why healing greatly depends on releasing and repatterning old habits of thought and developing a new pattern of positive thoughts and emotions that energize you and do not drain you.[146]

> It is in the energy field of consciousness that disease starts, in the energy field surrounding the physical body.

In chapter 3, we said that healing takes place on three levels: the level of the body, the level of the mind, and the energetic level. Now we're ready to talk about the ultimate level of healing: the energetic level. It is in the energy field of consciousness that disease starts, in the energy field surrounding the physical body. But what exactly *is* an energy field of consciousness? A little scenario will help explain it.

One night Cleve Backster, the foremost expert of lie detectors collaborating with the CIA, was sitting in his office with a little time on his hands. Being a creative kind of guy, he connected the plant in his office to a lie detector to see if it would register changes as he was talking to it. He talked to the plant for a while and saw that not much was happening. Being a veteran examiner on polygraphs, Backster knew that the most effective way to make the galvanometer jump was by making the person taking the test feel threatened. So as he was trying to figure out what to try next to get a response from the plant, he

---

146 Bruce Lipton. *The Biology of Belief.* Hay House, January 2013.

thought about lighting a match and *singeing* one of its leaves. To his great surprise, immediately the plant reacted. The lie detector signals flew off the charts! Backster was amazed.[147]

What does this tell us? It tells us that Backster created an energy field with his thoughts; and that the plant, which is sentient, a thing that *feels*, reacted energetically to those thoughts. It tells us that Backster's inner thoughts, feelings, and emotions created an energy field of consciousness that had an effect on the world around him—in this case, a plant. Further, it shows that the plant reacted with surges of emotion to Backster's thoughts. In fact, the plant's reaction made the galvanometer jump in much the same way a human being would. Now science is showing us that all living things react energetically to the world around them.

EMOTIONS: ENERGY IN MOTION

Just like the plant, every time you have a thought, feeling, or an emotional experience, it shows up in your energy field, even if you're not conscious of it. Our thoughts, feelings, and the emotions associated with them create an electromagnetic energy field that extends through our bodies and beyond. Our energy fields carry information and have an effect on the world around us. The information of our thoughts and emotions radiates to others and to the surrounding energy fields in which we all live and share energy. Our thoughts travel through the unified field of energy, the "mind that is the matrix of all matter."[148] In this field, telepathy and ESP operate constantly. In fact, we are all in constant

---

[147] *The Secret Life of Plants.* Peter Tompkins and Christopher Bird. Harper & Row, New York, 1973, 3.

[148] Max Planck referred to this as the matrix and said, "All matter originates and exists only by virtue of a force which brings the particle of an atom to vibration and holds this most minute solar system of the atom together. We must assume behind this force the existence of a conscious and intelligent mind. This mind is the matrix of all matter."

communication with each other. The clearer your energy field of fears, doubts, anger, and resentment, the higher the frequency of your field and the more efficiently and quickly your thoughts will travel. It's kind of like removing the static from your TV channel.

We're demonstrating an awareness of energy when we say people have bad vibes or good vibes, referring to the frequency of energy vibrations they're emitting. People who are said to have charisma often have a profound influence on others because of their high vibes of energy and enthusiasm.

Some of us are more aware of energy than others are. They can feel the energetic information being transmitted. For instance, my friend Jonathan says this about his grandmother: "My grandmother is ninety-two years old, but whenever I'm around her, I feel younger, livelier, and more energetic. When the family gets together 'Grams' is the life of the party. When she makes her grand entrance, the family lights up and the celebration begins."

On the other hand, Susan, a friend of mine, married to a fifty-year-old engineer, describes how she experiences her husband's energy: "He walks around on the verge of erupting with anger and thinks he has to control everybody and everything, and when he can't, he starts fuming and ranting and just brings all of us down. Even the cat runs away from him."[149]

> The stronger we feel about anything—take healing, for instance—the greater the energy behind the thoughts generated to manifest it, to bring it about.

The plant's reaction to Backster's thoughts flies in the face of conventional scientific thinking. Medical science doesn't take things like the energetic patterns and the frequencies of feelings and emotions into account where health and illness are concerned. As a scientist at NIH describes the scientific approach, she explains, "We're taught to strip our emotions

---

[149] Paul Pearsall. *The Heart's Code*. Random House, New York, 1998.

out of what we're doing."[150] Thoughts and feelings have historically been cast in two separate realms, where they have been presumed not to have too much to do with one another. Most people know intuitively that emotions have something to do with their health, but we've just begun to understand their electromagnetic effects on our bodies and far beyond the boundaries of our bodies. When you have an EKG taken at the cardiologist's office, the electrical impulses that create the rhythm on the printout that the cardiologist reads don't just stop at the paper!

Just like Backster's, our minds and the thoughts and emotions associated with them generate electromagnetic fields of varying types and intensities. They have an effect on our bodies and the world around us. People's electromagnetic fields have been measured from as far as six feet away from where they're standing, as was apparently the case in Backster's plant experiment.

Just as Backster found that the plant's "emotional" reactions became much more intense when his thoughts provoked fear in the plant, the more emotion our own thoughts evoke, the more power behind them. In other words, the greater the emotional charge behind your thoughts, the more powerful the feeling, the stronger the energetic reaction. In the plant's case, the intensity of emotion was a reaction to the prospect of having its leaves singed. In other words, the stronger we feel about anything, such as healing, the greater the energy behind the thoughts generated to manifest it, to bring it about.

YOUR THOUGHTS AND EMOTIONS CARRY INFORMATION

Energy patterns precede what we see happening in our own lives, just like we saw with Backster's plant. For instance, my sister tells the story of how she was driving along a country road when a picture of a deer

---

[150] Krista Tippett. "On Being. Ester Sternberg interview." *The Science of Healing Places*. www.onbeing.org/the-science-of-healing-places/4856

leaping out of the woods onto the road flashed into her mind. Sure enough, two seconds later, a deer leaped out in front of her car. These energetic patterns are at work in all kinds of situations.

One evening after one of our mastery sessions, we were invited to a beautiful lavish home in the desert. The majestic design inside flowed from a beautiful exterior facade with verandas and huge ceilings and glamorous living and dining areas. As we all waltzed in, a thought flashed through my mind: All that glitters is not gold! I was quick to banish the thought from my mind, chastising myself—just in case the thought was brought on by a hint of envy tucked away in my unconscious.

As cocktails were being served, everyone started buzzing about how our hosts for the evening, a lovely couple with all the money they could possibly ever need or want, were in the middle of a thorny, contentious divorce. Clearly, my mind had "read" the energy inside of this beautiful place as I walked through the entrance.

The same thing goes for illness. You don't feel well. You are achy, lethargic, and just feel generally down. When you go to the doctor, nothing shows up on your tests. They are all negative. The doctor tells you you're fine. "It's nothing. It's all in your head." This happens all the time because the pattern of illness exists energetically before it becomes a physical malady. Most of the trips we make to the primary care doctor's office are classified as "diagnosis of unknown origin" because the energy pattern creating the bad feelings hasn't shown up physically yet.

Your interactions with people bare the same energy footprints. Suppose you are nice and friendly toward someone on the surface, but deep down you really don't like the person. Maybe she has anger issues and just the thought of her feels heavy and burdensome. In the privacy of your own thoughts, you judge her: *Ugh. I don't like being around her. Why can't she get it together? Why is she so negative all the time?*

She'll get the message energetically, even though she may not interpret it as coming from you. If you think of energy as information, it helps to understand how thought/feeling waves are transmitted from one person to another. Your thoughts and feelings—your electromagnetic energy field—radiate a collection of energy waves of various frequencies and amplitudes. What you think of someone travels because your energy-carrying thought waves transmit that information—whether you're physically close to the person or not. This is especially the case if it's someone emotionally close to you. On some level, that person is receiving your energetic messages.

> The consciousness of one person is linked with the consciousness of another.

Energetic patterns are always operating regardless of separation in space and time. The consciousness of one person is linked with the consciousness of another.[151] Once you become aware of how others' thoughts and feelings "travel" energetically, you can become more mindful of how they could be influencing your own thinking and your own healing, and how your thoughts can be influencing the behavior of others.

THE HEART'S POWERFUL INTELLIGENCE

Because of the continuous information-carrying energy of the mind-body interaction, we can say that the heart thinks and its cells remember. One of the most extraordinary contributions revealing the energetic "thinking" power of the heart is the personal story of Dr. Paul Pearsall and how he used his heart's energy to heal himself from stage IV lymphoma. In his book *The Heart's Code* as he was close to dying, receiving round after round of chemotherapy, bone marrow transplants, and experiencing more and more difficulty breathing, Pearsall made an astounding recovery. He gives all the credit to the energy of his heart.

---

[151] Ervin Laszlo, PhD. *Science and the Akashic Field*. Inner Traditions, Rochester, Vermont, 2007, 150.

When his doctors kept telling him his illness was "all in his head"[152] (his doctors apparently didn't fully grasp the mind-body connection), Pearsall kept telling his family that he had a vague sense of dread that seemed to be his heart crying. As Pearsall tells the story, "Their inability and sometimes unwillingness to think with their own hearts and not just their brains almost killed me." Finally, a CAT scan revealed a "soccer ball–sized tumor" in his hip. By that time, the cancer had spread to his bones and he had little chance of surviving. He remembers thinking how ironic it was that the same doctors who doubted an energy they could not see, an energy that came from his knowing heart, were now using the invisible energy of the X-ray machines to try to save his life.

How did Pearsall recover? By listening to what his heart was trying to tell him. The voice of Pearsall's heart was profound. It told him, "You don't 'have' cancer; your cells have simply lost their memory of how to multiply in a connective, healthy way and, as a result, are engaging in thoughtless 'cancering.'" His cells were not getting the right information to teach them how to stay in harmony with his other body cells because they had somehow become disconnected with their coordinator of healthy energy, the heart.[153] What's the main message here? In matters of healing, let your heart rule your head. Listen to what your heart is trying to tell you.

Pearsall made a complete recovery. Everyone believed his recovery from stage IV cancer was nothing short of miraculous. Pearsall himself said the experience brought with it a profound realization that there is something immensely greater and wiser than our physical selves—and that it comes from the wisdom of the heart.

Heart-transplant patients lend rich testimony to the primacy of the heart's energy and unique intelligence. Transplant recipients have adopted strikingly similar behaviors to the heart's original owners, revealing that the donor's cellular memories reside in the heart. The donor heart sends along its information-carrying energy into the

---

[152]   His illness was in his head, but his doctors failed to realize the vital importance of the mind-body connection at the time.

[153]   Paul Pearsall. *The Heart's Code.* Random House, New York, 1998, 4.

recipient's body through the transplanted heart. Heart-transplant patients give firsthand accounts of dreaming about *actual* experiences of the donor or all of a sudden having a taste for things they couldn't stand before the transplant, like Chinese food or the opera. Friends and relatives expressed amazement that new behaviors after the transplant were so foreign that they knew for sure they *had to* have belonged to the original donor.

Pearsall relates an unbelievable account told by a psychiatrist at a medical conference, revealing this amazing information-carrying energy in the heart. Coming up to the microphone and struggling to hold back the sobs, the psychiatrist related her chilling story: "I have a patient who received the heart of a ten-year-old girl who was murdered. Her mother brought her to me because she was screaming at night, having nightmares about the man who had murdered her donor.

She said her daughter knew who it was." She continued, "After several sessions, I just couldn't deny the reality of what this child was telling me. Her mother and I finally decided to call the police, and using the descriptions from the little girl's nightmares, they found the murderer. He was easily convicted with the evidence my patient provided," the psychiatrist said. "The time, the weapon, the place, the clothes he wore, what the little girl he killed had said to him, everything the little heart transplant recipient reported, was completely accurate."[154]

The heart holds unlimited energetic potential for healing and healthy living. It has been shown to go well beyond its clinical role as a pump. "It thinks, remembers, communicates with other hearts, helps regulate immunity, and contains stored information that continually pulses through the body."[155] Our mind-oriented world trivializes its very own life support system by depriving the heart of its vital contribution toward a fuller, richer, healthier life experience. In reality, our minds are in every cell of our bodies, including our hearts. Our emphasis on the intellect to the exclusion of the heart short-circuits this intuitive heart connection with a pragmatic, rational, and often narrow, self-centered

---

[154] Paul Pearsall. *The Heart's Code*. Random House, New York. 1998, 7.
[155] Ibid.

interpretation of events. This kind of approach can undermine a fuller, more vital, energetic connection to life's experience, and to healing.

WHAT'S ON FIRST: THE HEART OR THE MIND?

The French philosopher Blaise Pascal famously said, "The heart has reasons which reason knows not of."[156] Pearsall seemed to be listening to Pascal's advice. Even though it didn't ring true in the minds of the physicians caring for him, Pearsall listened to what his heart seemed to be saying: "You are dying. Do something; say something!" Listening to our hearts can serve the same vital purpose for all of us. We don't have to be dying to heed the heart's sage advice.

Pearsall felt the energy of his heart connecting to people and objects. His heart's energetic voice was dominant over his mind's rational grasp of what his doctors were saying. Powerful feelings created a sense of urgency, tugging at him to listen to his heart. Most of the time, because we place such a high value on intellect, our minds come first. Motivated by the allure of logic and certain patterns of facts accumulated as evidence, we take our cues from science. Our powerful minds, directed to think certain thoughts, evoke corresponding feelings and actions.

However, it can work the other way around. As it did with Pearsall, our feelings and intuition about a situation can provoke thoughts that vie for your attention. If there is a question, if you are confused about whether to listen to your heart or your mind, listen to your heart. It will tell you more truthfully what is happening.

Pearsall did just that. His mind could have told him not to listen to his heart, that he was just being emotional and overreacting. Actually, many times we *do* ignore our feelings. Many of us, like the doctors in Pearsall's experience, don't listen to what our hearts are trying to tell us—in other words, what our emotions and feelings are trying to tell

---

[156] Le coeur a ses raisons que la raison ne connait pas

us. When it comes to medicine and healing, we're taught that they don't matter much in the scheme of things. The intellect rules.

But feelings matter a great deal when it comes to healing. The people and machines Pearsall's heart connected to energetically—or actually, the ones he was in communication with—made him feel better. Just as Cousins healed himself watching Marx Brothers films and laughing, learning what will make you feel better comes from the intelligent energy of your heart.

The powerful messages from the energy of the heart lie at the crux of the quantum notion that energy and information are the same. Because the heart thinks and the mind feels—because the mind is in every cell of the body—it's important to realize that they are actually working together. From a biochemical as well as an energetic point of view, they're inseparable. But one or the other can be dominant, depending on whether yours is a thinking nature or a feeling nature.

Scientists describe this "feeling, thinking" energy as non-local, meaning that it is not bound by space-time; it's outside of space-time. It exists not just in one place at one time but in many places at the same time. The feelings from the heart of Pearsall's family helped greatly in his healing, even though they weren't physically close by all the time. They didn't need to be.

> Once connected, people and objects forever retain the energetic connection.

Quantum studies tell us that people and objects on the opposite sides of the city, the country, or the universe, for that matter, like Pearsall and his family, have been shown to be energetically connected to one another. A change in one particle instantaneously attracts its information-energy sharing partner particle far away. There are no space-time barriers to experiencing this healing energy. In addition to his family, Pearsall felt that the machine's energy was assisting him in his healing. Once connected, people and objects forever retain the energetic connection.[157]

---

[157] Ibid.

IN HEALING, SYNCHRONIZE THE ENERGY OF YOUR HEART AND YOUR MIND

While the mind is an energetic powerhouse, it must have the heart's cooperation and fuel. If the mind is a Mercedes, the heart is the hi-test it needs to run well. Whenever we feel strongly about something, the energy of our hearts is behind it. Much more power is generated by our thoughts and beliefs when our hearts are "in it." The heart actually generates an electromagnetic energy field many times greater than that of the brain.[158] Scientists have found that when we create heart-based feelings of gratitude, appreciation, and compassion, we are generating a magnetic field inside our bodies that heals and extends far beyond us.

The key message? The heart is the real power behind the mind's activity. More importantly, it's the real power behind healing. While the mind is the initiator and interpreter of your life's activities and events, your heart has to be on board. In fact, as medical intuitive Carolyn Myss quipped in one of her seminars on understanding the energy centers in the body, "If your heart isn't in it, it's not happening!" As the Buddha taught, the heart is primal, the great foundation. Everything we do or say comes from the heart in varying degrees. In the Buddha's words: "All *dhammas* [truths] are preceded by the heart, dominated by the heart, made from the heart."[159]

> "All *dhammas* [truths] are preceded by the heart, dominated by the heart, made from the heart."
> —the Buddha

---

[158] Heart Math, LLC. In HeartMastery.com.

[159] Ajahn Mun Bhuridatta. "A Heart Released." http://buddhasociety.com

HEART-CENTERED AWARENESS HEALS

The key points of an energetic, heart-centered healing experience can be summed up as follows:

- Listen to the voice of your heart. The heart thinks and speaks and carries information. Each heartbeat carries information that affects the "matter"—people and places—within and outside of us. Energy that pervades matter is the information that is alive in our cells and becomes cellular memory.

- Do things that make yourself feel better. Continually practice forgiveness, surrender, and letting go as ways of empowering the flow of energy from your heart, releasing any resistance and allowing the energy to flow freely throughout your body, to others and the environment.

- Embrace your own heart as the object of your affection and develop a willingness to love and nurture yourself; cultivate the habit of offering yourself the love that others might withhold. Since the heart is the body's primary organizing energy force, it is through your heart that your cells' memories will be repatterned toward health and healing.

COHERENCE

"Coherence is created when your heart, mind, and emotions are in energetic alignment and cooperation," says Dr. Rollin McCraty, research director of the Institute of HeartMath. That state builds resiliency. Your energy is accumulated, not spent in conflicting intentions, leaving more energy to heal.[160]

When the heart is in sync with the mind, a high degree of coherence is created. However, most of the time, the degree of coherence between the mind and the heart can vary greatly. When the emotions generated by the heart are out of phase or dramatically different from what we're thinking, we expend much more energy, energy we could be using to heal.

Conflicting intentions of the mind, which is saying one thing, and the heart, which is telling us another, create "split energy." When this happens repeatedly, your overall awareness as well as the overall integrity of your health is compromised. A lack of coherence can have an adverse effect on our health at a number of levels, including vision, listening abilities, reaction times, mental clarity, feeling states, and sensitivities. These faculties are all influenced by the degree of mental and emotional coherence at any given time.[161]

Some suggest that a continued lack of coherence may lie at the root of diseases such as dementia and Alzheimer's. Conversely, as in my father's situation (described in chapter 5 on the Power of the Mind), if the mind is worrying about something that your heart (your feelings, your emotions) isn't engaged in, the disease could be "all in your head" and you will never get it. There is still a lack of coherence, but it isn't at the point where it's causing harm.

> The heart is the most powerful organ—the largest generator of electromagnetic energy in one's body.

In order to heal, when we can create a feeling of coherence inside our minds that is in sync

---

[160] Institute of Heart Math. "Articles of the Heart." Heartmath.org
[161] Ibid.

with positive emotions in our hearts, such as joy, compassion, and forgiveness, we create an optimal climate for healing ourselves. This will trigger major shifts in the electromagnetic frequencies we generate as well as the biochemicals they trigger. When we do create coherence, our immune systems become stronger, anti-aging processes are enhanced, and the level of DHEA—the life-giving hormone—surges. We think more clearly when coherence is high.

LEARNING TO SHAPE YOUR ENERGY

Just by believing you can heal, you begin to create more positive, higher frequency energy fields. As the energy flows through the meridians, or energy pathways of your body, it either flows freely, or it meets resistance from patterns of doubt and negative thoughts. By raising the frequency of your thoughts—that is, changing your thought patterns to more positive ones and releasing painful emotions—you can create the very energy fields needed to heal.

> You have to let go of the negative energy that is tugging at you to get your attention.

If you find your mind on automatic pilot and negative thoughts keep rearing their heads, try letting go of the bad feelings behind them. Tell yourself, "I don't have to pay attention to what my mind is saying. I don't have to let these negative feelings have their way with me either. I am in charge."

Self-talk is important here, and the key is to become aware of the energetic pull you feel toward your illness or pain. You have to let go of the negative energy that is tugging at you to get your attention. If not, you get pulled down into the disturbed energy. That's the last place you want your attention to be. But maybe you go there out of habit. Because you're used to looking through the disturbed energy, everything that once looked good, maybe even beautiful, now looks grim. Things you liked look dark and uninviting, maybe even depressing.

As soon as you start seeing yourself get upset, the minute you see it all getting negative, *let go*. The longer you wait to let it go, the harder it gets. If you don't let go, you get sucked in energetically. You start "awfulizing," thinking about how awful your life is.

> If you want to heal, your main goal is to raise the frequency of your energy field.

You can get out of this downward spiral by learning to be sensitive to your own energy as well as the energy of others. You can create the energetic changes you want by raising the frequency of your electromagnetic energy field. At high levels of energy, you will enable your body to heal itself. Let's look at some ways to do this.

HI CH'I: THE ENERGY OF BELIEVERS, VIVID IMAGINATIONS

Joel Osteen, the well-known spiritual teacher, gives a sermon on "magnetism" and how when you "put God first place in your life" and do good things for people, thinking kind, compassionate thoughts, you will "attract God's favor like a magnet." Osteen promises that God will send blessings that "chase you down." For true believers, Osteen is right! Why? Believers would say it's because of God's grace. Another explanation is because the high-frequency energies of belief in a higher power can activate the cell's healing mechanisms, sending signals that release healing biochemical frequencies.

We know this high-frequency energy by many names. The Chinese call it ch'i; in Sanskrit, it's called prana. Here in the West, we refer to it as spirit, or the Holy Spirit. You can strengthen it in your life when you learn to listen within. As you practice listening within for guidance, you will learn to recognize when it's the voice of your soul. If it's fear-laden, if it's an angry and punitive voice, it's not the energy of your soul speaking. As you learn to act from your soul's wisdom, you will accumulate higher and higher levels of ch'i and you will feel more health and vitality. You will begin to look younger and have more of the energy and vigor you need to heal.

> Feel the way you would feel if your desires had already come to pass! Whatever you would feel when you are healed and healthy, feel it now.

Abraham, a non-physical being channeled by Esther Hicks, who gives seminars all over the world, teaches participants to "tend to your vortex," or your electromagnetic energy field, by consciously creating high-frequency energies, putting yourself in a state of "feeling good" *before* your desired goal shows up in your life. In other words, behave as you would if it had already happened. Feel the way you would feel if your desires had already come to pass! Whatever you would feel when you are healed and healthy, *feel it now.*

WA SA´

Abraham is onto something! Acting as though your desire has already been fulfilled, getting into the feeling *now* of how it feels to be disease-free, can shape your energy in a way that brings about healing. This process of feeling as if you are well has been encouraged by many sages and mystics over the years. "Act as if, and you will become," say the spiritual leaders, and healing is a powerful case in point. Abraham's advice may be paraphrased to say, "Feel as if, and it [whatever you wish] will manifest," including your healing. Bringing the memory of feeling healthy into your present reality can bring about your healing. Your brain cannot tell the difference between what is real and what's imagined.[162]

---

[162] David R. Hamilton, PhD. DrDavidHamilton.com, 170

In a powerful presentation, scientist Greg Bradden shows this process in action. In a video production at the medicine-less hospital in Beijing, China, you can see on the ultrasound a woman's bladder tumor disappear as trained chanters surround the bed of the woman. Chanting "wa sa', wa sa', wa sa'," which can be translated to mean "It is finished, it is finished, it is finished," they are creating a new energy field. As they chant, you can watch the tumor disappearing on the ultrasound monitor.[163]

> As you do things that raise the frequency of your electromagnetic energy field and behave as if what you want is already in your life, you will attract circumstances that are higher in frequency and fulfill the feeling.

The mystic referred to as Neville has written extensively about the manner in which "capturing the feeling of the wish fulfilled" will bring what you want into existence. Popular in the States and the UK in the 1950s and 1960s, he cites numerous accounts of situations when this actually worked for everything from removing facial growths, to buying houses, to acquiring businesses and wealth, to healing.

> Feel as you would feel if you were healed. Live in that state. Feel the exhilaration, the relief, the peace that would be yours.

Neville advised, "Vividly imagine a scene that would not be possible unless your desire had been fulfilled. As you imagine it, feel as you would feel if it had already happened. See yourself and feel yourself there now." He made the distinction of thinking *from* the end, not *of* the end of its fulfillment. *Feel as you would feel if you were healed.* Live in that state. Feel the exhilaration, the relief, the peace that would be yours. Imagine yourself in a state of complete health and being totally healed.

---

163 YouTube.com. "The Medicine-Less Hospital."

Feel the excitement and the relief that you know you would feel if you were healed.

Then express gratitude for your healing—even if it hasn't come yet. Say thank you for your healing and then detach yourself. Don't keep looking to see if you're healed. Pay more attention to feeling the way you would as if you were already healed. Assume your healing is here. Be thankful that you are healed. Most important is to imagine that the state you want is already here. Feel it. Sleep on it. Drift off to sleep with the feeling that it's finished. You are healed.

Do your best to accumulate high-frequency energies through doing what you love. Play the music, watch the movies, read the things that inspire you, make you laugh, make you feel happy and good inside. When you begin to feel uplifted and "high," imagine a scene that vividly represents the fulfillment of your desire to have your health restored. Imagine yourself totally healthy and full of vitality and your physician saying with amazement, "It's incredible. Your condition is completely healed. We can find no trace of it."

These scientists and mystics are expressing one of the laws of the universe. The law of resonance is that like attracts like. As you do things that raise the frequency of your electromagnetic energy field and behave as if what you want is already in your life, you will attract circumstances that are higher in frequency and fulfill the feeling.

The feelings behind your state of mind make the difference in your energy frequencies. We say, "Become one with the state your desire." Vibrations of the same frequency attract other vibrations of the same frequency. We attract the people and things we resonate with, things of like frequency. Just as you get a certain radio station or television channel when you tune into a certain frequency, when you tune into certain thoughts, you get other thoughts and experiences of the same frequency.

The law of resonance is responsible for the differences in the manifestations of healings and other things in the physical world. Truly understanding the dynamics of energy forms lies at the heart of the coming new paradigm in science and medicine. The energetic vibrations of our mind and our beliefs, and the emotional and spiritual vibrations that accompany them, attract situations and people that correspond to the same levels of our own vibrating energy or frequencies. That includes healing.

AA knew these energy secrets a long time ago. It's the reason support groups like AA identify "sponsors" and encourage participants in recovery not to go back into the same environment and associate with the same people you were with when you were doing the drinking. Because you're going right back into the same energy field, it will pull you back in like a magnet.

> Just as copper conducts electricity when it's clean and a corroded pipe will not, our bodies become corroded with the nursing of grievances, feeling sorry for ourselves, constant criticism, and the blame and self-doubt we hold on to.

Much of the time, unless we become more aware, we act out of habit or compulsion. Our behaviors are governed by electromagnetic fields called "attractor" fields. They are energy fields generated by our attitudes, beliefs, and stream of thoughts. These fields create the lens of our consciousness or awareness and ultimately our worldviews. Therefore, while feelings of fear, resentment, grief, and despair attract other attractor fields of low frequency, feelings of love, joy, compassion, and gratitude vibrate at a much higher frequency and attract other higher frequency attractor fields. This is the reason things happen in our lives the way they do, not because of the causes we usually assign to the events in our lives.[164]

You say, "I'm depressed because I have problems in my relationship." But that's not why you're depressed. External events and situations do not cause you to be unhappy. The energy generated by your unhappy state attracts events and circumstances that resonate with the same energy frequency. This is the major reason that changing your thoughts and your state of mind to raise the frequency of your attractor field is vital to your healing efforts.

---

[164] David Hawkins. *Power vs Force*. Hay House, Carlsbad, California, 36–54.

Just as copper conducts electricity when it's clean and a corroded copper pipe will not, as electromagnetic energy fields, our bodies become energetically corroded with complaining and the nursing of grievances, feeling sorry for ourselves, constant worrying, fear, criticism, the blame and self-doubt we hold on to.

KEEP YOUR ENERGY FIELD CLEAR

An important key to healing, then, is to keep your energy field clear of negative emotional energies—clear of energies created by fear, anger, resentment, and doubt. Instead, keep it filled with positive thoughts, those of encouragement, hope, enthusiasm, and compassion. If you cannot, you create resistance and contraction in your energy field. Fear, pain, and anxiety trigger contractions in your energy field because your automatic response is to resist the painful emotional experience.

Bill Bauman, PhD, the spiritual teacher I had the good fortune of studying with, encouraged us to "embrace the pain" we were feeling. When I first heard that, I thought, *This is crazy. How can someone possibly do that?* But the idea is, in the midst of pain, find a way to feel the "space" or the positive feeling underneath the pain. *Love the one who feels the pain.* In other words, find a way to keep your heart open and receptive. You can experience pain in the context of hope or pain in a context of despair. Pain in the context of "What you're feeling you are healing" brings hope, and "This must be bad for me to feel this much pain" brings despair.

From an energetic point of view, keeping an open heart is key; it is very healing. In the absence of any judgment by your mind as to whether pain is good or bad, you can watch how the energy of your body behaves when it's in pain. It contracts. If you can think hopeful, healing thoughts that make you feel better, you will keep your body—as an electromagnetic energy field—from contracting and from resisting its natural health-giving flow.

Forgiveness, letting go, surrendering, and showing gratitude all serve to accomplish the same thing that "embracing the pain" accomplishes:

keeping your heart open and allowing the flow of energy through your body to be unrestricted. Allow your body to be in a relaxed, receptive state ... allow it to receive higher frequency healing energies. "Letting go, surrender," the advice given by many psychologists and spiritual teachers, means letting go of your preconceived thoughts, your resistance, and allowing yourself to be in a receptive state.

EVERYTHING IS MADE OF VORTICES OF ENERGY, INCLUDING US

Pure energy is behind everything once we break it down to its core. Scientific experiments in quantum physics and particularly those at CERN, the European Organization for Nuclear Research in Geneva, Switzerland,[165] continue to remind us of the energy composition of everything that exists. When we go down to the subatomic level, the minutest level of existence, we do not find matter, but pure energy.[166]

> We are all connected at the highest level by a dynamic field of energy called the unified field, or the matrix.

Every object in the universe moves and vibrates. Einstein taught us that everything in life is energy. Everything is vibrating at one speed or another. Nothing rests. Everything we see around ourselves is vibrating at one frequency or another and so are we.[167] We all have unique signature frequencies. Each individual thing is composed of vortices of energy radiating a unique energy frequency. Because our frequencies are different from other entities in the universe, it seems as if we are separated from what we see around ourselves—people, animals, plants,

---

165   Premiere research lab where physicists and engineers study the fundamental structure of the universe

166   CERN home.web.cern.ch/about/physics

167   www.physicsclassroom.com

trees, and so on. But we are not separated. In fact, we are all living in a continuous ocean of energy. We are all connected at the highest level by a dynamic field of energy called the unified field, or the matrix.

THE UNIFIED FIELD: LIFE'S MYSTERY AND MAGIC

Science is just beginning to investigate the properties of this all-encompassing energy field, although these properties have been part of Eastern spiritual practices for centuries. The properties of this field are so fantastic, even magical, that contemporary theoretical physicist Stephen Hawking, author of *A Brief History of Time,* refers to it as the "mind of God."[168] Some call it the divine matrix. Others are calling it the quantum hologram, or the unified field.

Science has found that something occupies what we previously thought of as empty space. Giving it different names and still exploring what it means, these are all names for a field of energy that scholarly peer-reviewed research papers[169] now agree exists. However, this information is so new that it will not become common knowledge for at least another decade. As a result, doctors and scientists are still basing their beliefs on our material world and still solving problems from the perspective that everything is separate from everything else and that what happens in one place has no effect on what happens somewhere else.

In his award-winning book, *The Divine Matrix,* Gregg Braden explains it this way: "There is a place where all things begin, a location of pure energy that simply 'is.'" The great scientist and Nobel Prize winner Max Plank called it "the matrix" and expressed it this way: "Underlying everything we see, there is a mind, and this mind is the matrix of all matter." The famous physicist David Bohm called it "the supraimplicate order"; Einstein called it "the zero point field"; Teihard De Chardin, a

---

168 Stephen Hawkins. *A Brief History of Time.* Random House Publishing Group. 1998, 193.

169 Edgar Mitchel. *The Quantum Hologram and ESP.* YouTube.com. October 3, 2013.

French philosopher and Jesuit priest trained as a paleontologist, called it "the theosphere," wherein lies the ultimate unity.

> A thought, in the pure energy of nature's mind, produces the thing that is imagined—in rapid manifestation.

Everything you see on Earth is made from this one original substance, this subtle energy. Edgar Mitchell, the astronaut who was the sixth man on the moon, calls it nature's mind, out of which all things come forth. Mitchell, among others, has pointed out that this energy from which all things are made is "thinking stuff." It transmits information, which, in its original state, permeates, penetrates, and fills the interspaces of the universe. A thought, in the pure energy of nature's mind, produces the thing that is imagined—in rapid manifestation. The closer we come to this energy, to this very high frequency energy, the more we can form things by our thoughts, and by impressing our thought upon the formless substance of nature's mind, we can cause the things we think about to be created.

How do we come closer to this energy? By aligning ourselves with our inner essence, our soul, or what some call our source. Through this alignment, our thoughts, feelings, and actions are saturated with higher frequencies of love, compassion, forgiveness, and gratitude. This alignment, which you can refer to as the coherence that comes from "centering yourself," or getting in touch with your inner self, your source, or your higher self, allows you to consciously feel the whole of your energy field inhabit your body. You will feel out of sorts and agitated when you are "splitting your energy," or feeling one thing and thinking another, or feeling one thing and *doing* another.

In this field of pure energy, everything is whole in the same way as a hologram, where every aspect of space contains the whole. As an aspect of this whole fabric of energy, this unified field, everything contains the whole, the positive and negative aspects of anything. In other words, there can't be an "up" without a "down." You can't ask a question unless there is already the potential of an answer. There cannot be a disease without a cure. In this field, you are aware that you are one with everything that exists.

This matrix of pure energy vibrates and creates a field around it. A vibrating field of energy attracts—like a magnet—and attaches to energy of the same vibrating frequency. Eventually, the energy field manifests into matter particle by particle. As the father of quantum physics, Max Planck once said, "All physical matters are composed of vibration."[170]

> "All physical matters are composed of vibration."
> —Max Planck

The scientific process of how this all works is called Bell's theorem; once energy particles are connected, they stay connected and can communicate with each other at great distances.[171] This discovery has been, perhaps, the most astounding discovery in physics to date. Great leaps forward were made when Bell, an Englishman, discovered that when an energy particle has once met with another similar particle, their energy states become entangled in such a way that however far apart they are, what happens to one happens to the other. This action at a distance seems to be almost magical in nature; it shows that this form of energy is in fact traveling faster than the speed of light!

Several experiments have demonstrated that Bell's theory is correct.

Experimental Proof

One astounding experiment, hailed by the *New York Times* as "the most spectacular yet of the mysterious long-range connections that exist between quantum events," was done by Dr. Nicholas Ginsin and his colleagues at the University of Geneva.[172]

---

[170] http://dkmatai.tumblr.com/pos January 13, 2013.

[171] www.Livescience.com/28808-spooky-quantum-entanglement-loophole-closed.html

[172] Malcolm Brown. "Far Apart, 2 Particles Respond Faster Than Light." *New York Times,* front page, Tuesday, July 22, 1997.

Dr. Ginsin sent pairs of photons (light particles) in opposite directions to villages north and south of Geneva. Then having placed fiber optic cable (the material used to transmit telephone calls) on both ends of the city of Geneva, a distance of several miles, he sent each half of the pair of photons simultaneously through the two cables on the outskirts of the city.

An amazing thing happened. At the end of their rapid journeys through the cables, each particle behaved in exactly the same fashion, making precisely corresponding movements, continuing to do exactly the same thing at the same time! Somehow, even though they couldn't see each other (they were on different sides of the city), they were still communicating with each other. Their decisions to go one way or the other always matched, even though there was no visible way they could possibly be communicating with each other. Classical laws of physics would have predicted that the particles would go randomly off into space, on their own separate paths ... infinitely. But that did not happen.

How can we explain why one particle immediately "knows" what the other is doing? The question is answered if we consider that each is a part of an inseparable reality, no matter how far apart they are. In that case, one doesn't need to send a signal to the other, for these two light particles stay constantly in touch through some mysterious interaction.

Science has finally uncovered the elemental oneness of the world that Buddhists and Eastern sages have known for thousands of years. This oneness cannot be diminished by spatial separation. An invisible wholeness unites the objects that are given birth in the universe, and we have stumbled onto this wholeness through modern experimental methods.

BELL'S THEOREM: WE'RE ALL CONNECTED

Bell's work tells us that there is a unity and interrelationship among all things—people and events are interrelated energetically. Once connected, energy particles, including people—human energy particles—are always connected. It also means that the particles carry information. Somehow they know instantaneously of the other's whereabouts and actions. Telepathy, premonitions, and clairvoyance operate constantly, beyond the space-time continuum.

The *New York Times* article reporting on the experiment above gives some hint of the vast implications of Bell's Theorem as it describes the fate of a prominent physicist: "Heinz Pagels was a very dedicated scientist. A distinguished physicist at Rockefeller University, he dedicated his life to research in understanding the strange mysteries of quantum physics. Like many other physicists, he believed that quantum physics is a kind of code that interconnects everything in the universe, including the physical basis of life itself.

In his book, *The Cosmic Code*, written in 1988, Dr. Pagels, an ardent mountain climber wrote the following: "I often dream about falling. Such dreams are commonplace to the ambitious or to those who climb mountains. Lately I dreamed I was clutching at the face of the rock, but it would not hold. Gravel gave away, I grasped for a shrub, but it pulled loose, and in cold terror, I fell into the abyss. Suddenly I realized that my fall was relative; there was no bottom and no end. A feeling of pleasure overcame me. I realized that what I embody, the principle of life, cannot be destroyed. It is written into the cosmic code, the order of the universe. As I continued to fall into the dark void, embraced by the vault of the heavens, I sang to the beauty of the stars and made my peace with the darkness."

The *New York Times* front-page article announced its startling conclusion: "Dr. Pagels was killed in a mountain climbing accident in 1988." His fate was communicated to him in a dream. This energy carries information and is not bound by the limits of space and time. It carries messages instantaneously across thousands of miles, and perhaps even across thousands of generations.

For many, Dr. Pagel's experience was eerily reminiscent of the Eastern image of the divine, not a ruler who commands from above but a principle that controls everything from within. For years, Eastern sages have professed an age-old truth that would explain Dr. Pagel's fate: that the stuff of the universe is essentially mind stuff.[173] It may well be the case that what was in Dr. Pagel's mind happened as a self-fulfilling prophesy. A highly respected physicist from Princeton, John Archibald Wheeler put it this way: "We are participators in bringing into being not only the near and here but the far away and long ago."[174]

Pagel's story lends credence to the existence of an all-encompassing energy field, the unified field, connecting man and matter. Scientifically, this is hardly up for debate any longer. Everything and everyone is connected with one another through this unified field and is continually in contact with this boundless sea of unlimited possibilities and no defined limits.

Many of the world's greatest thinkers and scientists, from the seventeenth-century philosopher Hegel to more contemporary figures like Carl Jung and prominent physicists like Ervin Laslo and David Bohm, have proposed variations on the theme of the universe as an undivided wholeness. Bohm proposed that all the separate objects, entities, structures, and events in the visible world around us are relatively autonomous, stable, and temporary "sub totalities" derived from a deeper implicate order of unbroken wholeness.[175]

Bohm's theory had well-known mystical connotations. His remark that this "implicate domain could equally well be called Idealism, Spirit, Consciousness" clearly had a mystical or soul-like flavor to it. But as it has been pointed out, the separation of the two—matter and spirit—is an abstraction. The ground is always one.[176]

---

[173] Paramahansa Yogananda. *Autobiography of a Yogi*. Self-Realization Fellowship, Los Angeles, California, 1998.

[174] "The Anthropic Universe." *Science Show*, a radio interview, 18 February 2006.

[175] David Bohm, *Wholeness and the Implicate Order*, Routledge & Kegan Paul, London, Boston, 1980, 48.

[176] Quoted in Michael Talbot, *The Holographic Universe*, HarperCollins, New York, 1991, 271.

THE SEPARATION BETWEEN US IS SKIN DEEP

We're all interconnected. By virtue of this energy field, it's not just our own minds and bodies; we are connected to others in a very real scientific sense. Our feeling of separation is not real. V. S. Ramachandran, director of the Center for Brain and Cognition and distinguished professor with the psychology department and neurosciences program at the University of California, San Diego, has done work with mirror neurons, demonstrating this in a profound way. Using PET scans, it has been shown that the same neurons in our brains fire whether we watch someone do something or we do it ourselves. It also works with touch. We have mirror neurons specific to touch.

But why, thought Ramachandran, *don't we actually feel it when we see someone touch someone else? … If the same neurons are firing, why don't we get confused and think, "This is me being touched"?* Is it because the neuroreceptors in the skin send signals to the brain that say, "Don't worry; it's not *you* that's being touched." Ramachandran decided to test his thesis and take the skin out of the equation. He anesthetized the brachial plexus, the network of nerves supplying the arm, including the skin, and then performed the experiment again.

> Telepathy and clairvoyance show that our thoughts are connected to all thoughts. Miracles, healing at a distance, are a function of the interconnectedness that occurs by virtue of this unified energy field.

This time the subjects *did* actually feel the touch when watching someone else being touched! His conclusion is that the skin is the only thing that separates us, in a very literal sense.[177] Telepathy and clairvoyance show that our thoughts are connected to all thoughts. Miracles, healing at a distance, are a function of the interconnectedness that occurs by virtue of this unified energy field.

---

[177] Ramachandran's TED Talk on YouTube.com

The new view of a universe that is interconnected has profound implications for healing and the way medicine is practiced. Offering possible answers to questions such as why spontaneous healing and healing at a distance work, many have tried to show that we can gain access to this interconnectedness for healing. Studies have shown the following:

- We can mentally influence biological processes in our own bodies as well as the bodies of others.
- We can mentally influence the thoughts of others.
- We can mentally influence the functioning of non-biological systems, other forms of matter.

Paul Pearsall's description (earlier in this chapter) of his own healing experience, fueled by the energy of communicating with his family members at a distance as well as the radiation machines that were treating him, drew life energy from these energy sources. As he described it, his heart knew what he needed to stay alive. He needed to draw on the energetic sources of love and positive support from his family to recover from an illness his doctors said would be fatal.

Pearsall also used his thoughts—his mind's energy—to turn the machines into "friends" whose energy came to his rescue. He showed that he was able, through conscious intention, to affect the behavior of physical objects, the machines. Other well-done experimental studies have shown similar results.[179]

Certain psychological conditions are more conducive than others when we're trying to make connections to the thoughts and feelings of others. William Braud, a scientist who did experiments demonstrating that someone's blood pressure can be altered by another using biofeedback

---

[178] William Braud. http://www.inclusivepsychology.com/uploads/HumanInter connectedness.pdf

[179] Paul Pearsall. *The Heart's Code*. Random House, 1998.

at a distance, cites five simple yet powerful mental steps that he has found to be effective:

MAKING CONNECTIONS

1. Relax and be quiet; breathe deeply.
2. Let go of all thoughts, especially troublesome, upsetting ones.
3. Focus your attention deeply within yourself (center yourself).
4. Think of your intention in a way that isn't forced or strained, in a way that feels good. Try it for five minutes several times a day.
5. Go about your business and expect results.

Many have successfully used these techniques and others like them. Research shows that our minds have the ability to function at a distance, regardless of the physical separation from the person or thing. Our awareness has some energetic quality that allows it to reach out across space and time to affect the physical course of a distant living organism—whether that's a human being or something else. For instance, we've all heard stories of how prayer can heal. Actually, there is compelling evidence about the healing power of prayer at a distance. Dr. William Braud has shown that people who hold positive images of a distant person in a way that is caring, compassionate, and prayer-like can actually bring about physical changes in that distant person.[180]

Prayer is not the only evidence that supports the ability of the mind to function at a distance. In his book *Healing Words,* Larry Dossey, MD, looks at several kinds of healing. Among these is "transpersonal

---

[180] WilliamBraud.http://www.inclusivepsychology.com/uploads/Human Interconnectedness.pdf

imagery," or using positive images to help your body or the body of another to heal.[181]

I have had such an experience. Encouraged by the writings of the mystic called Neville,[182] mentioned earlier in the chapter, I intentionally shifted the image I held of someone close to me. I went from thinking of him as ego driven and lacking in self-control and self-respect to a strong, kind, well-meaning, loving, and powerful soul. Gradually, an amazing transformation took place right before my eyes. He became kinder, less afraid, and more responsible in his relationships. He became more generous with his feelings and kindnesses toward others. Gradually, I watched as his behavior actually shifted to meet my expectations and new vision of him.

In cases like this one, obviously there is some communication of energy going constantly back and forth. But all particles are comprised of energy, which brings us to something suggested by Einstein's zero point field equations. These equations extend the individual energy fields of each particle into a single field that connects all particles, all matter, everywhere—including us and our thoughts. Thus it has been proven that there is ultimately one "super" energy field in and around us and everything is a part of it, everything is entangled within it, and everything arises from it.

Are we humans part of one energy? Yes! All matter is comprised of energy, and human beings are matter. Moreover, we have minds, hearts, and cells that generate their own energies, their own electromagnetic fields. From Bell's theorem, we know that every particle knows what every other particle it has ever interacted with is doing. If all electromagnetic fields are interconnected through this matrix, then so must be the energy of our minds, our thoughts.

This would explain such things as telepathy, how the thoughts of one person can be projected and picked up by another many miles

---

[181] Larry Dossey, MD. *Healing Words.* HarperSanFrancisco, 1993.

[182] Dr. Wayne Dyer referred to Neville in his presentations when he advised his viewers to "think from the end"—in other words, imagine that your desire has already been fulfilled.

away, and how a strong enough desire can manifest rapidly into reality. It is because our thoughts create a disturbance in this universal field of entanglement, shifting things around in the manner we intend, until a result arises that matches up with the desired thought pattern, the healing.

As if the divine matrix—you can call it the zero point field if you like more scientific language—with all its subatomic particles leaping in and out of existence inside us and between and among us were not enough to make "old paradigmers" in medicine a little crazy, evidence that the human psyche is not confined to the body or to particular points in space or in time is mounting. This evidence suggests that there is something about us that is infinite and eternal, something related to the idea of a soul, the individualized idea of the absolute. In the next chapter, we'll move beyond the mind and talk about it.

MASTERY

PART TWO

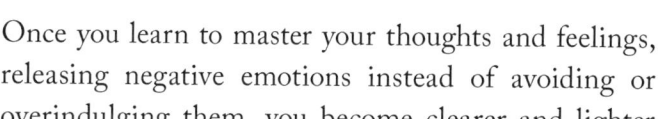

Once you learn to master your thoughts and feelings, releasing negative emotions instead of avoiding or overindulging them, you become clearer and lighter and move into the realm beyond the mind.

Meditation, singing, dancing, painting, can help you to go deeper into this realm of light and miracles, where anything can be healed.

X

BEYOND THE MIND

*Power Steps: Don't struggle with it (your mind); just disregard it. When it works against you, deprive it of attention. It will slow down and reveal that you **have** a mind but you **are not** your mind.*

Once you see its nature, you can go beyond it. You can transcend it, not allowing it to create imaginary problems. Memory and anticipation create problems of what you'll get or what you'll lose, colored by your likes and dislikes. The problem is not yours—it is your mind's only.

Begin by disassociating yourself from your mind. Resolutely remind yourself that you are not the mind and that its problems are not yours. How can an unsteady mind make itself steady? Of course it cannot. It is the nature of the mind to roam about. All you can do is to shift the focus of consciousness beyond the mind.[183]

Begin a daily meditation practice. To go beyond the mind, meditation is the best route.

Here [beyond the mind], there is no multiplicity whatsoever.

—The Uphanishads

During our mastery seminar, Bill offered, "When you let go of what you want, a much higher style of creation happens. Using intention,

---

[183] Nisargadat Maharaj. *I Am That*. The Acorn Press, 1988.

willpower can work, but it's a much smaller style of creation."[184] Real mastery in a high style of creation, is living from the inside out, beyond the mind. As you cultivate your inner reality, eventually you realize that you're standing at the point from which everything else emanates. You realize you can seriously influence the experience of your life from inside of you. You say to yourself, "If I can get mastery over my emotions, my thoughts, my own energy, and my attitudes, I will choose my own state of consciousness instead of always having it be imposed upon me by the circumstances of my life." Then happiness and healthiness become a way of life.

Going beyond the mind means going beyond the energetic mental barriers that the mind erects out of habit and past experience, high mental walls that arise from telling ourselves, "This is good, and this is bad." From the limited perspective of the mind, we really don't know what's good or bad for us.

"Forget all that you have learned!" Bill advised in the early days of our mastery sessions. Beyond the mind, a new world opens up to you. Everything is turned on its head. You move from person to presence; from your social self or your ego, to presence, to your higher self, your *God* self. You see life in a new way, from a larger perspective. You have a wonderful realization: everything happens *for* you, not *to* you.

As an example, you learn that pain is your friend. It provokes a kind of detoxing in you, forcing feelings to the surface and transporting you beyond former limitations in consciousness: "Pain is a signal that a powerful rite of passage is occurring, a foundational happening or primal ceremony in which a new and bigger version of me or you is being created. And pain is its imaginative producer, creative director, and primary actor. Always."[185]

If you go beyond the mind,[186] you aren't compelled to be *pulled* by the pain. As you focus your attention more and more deeply inside of

---

[184] Bill Bauman's Mastery seminar
[185] Bill Bauman., during his Mastery seminar, in St. George, Utah.
[186] In Bill's Mastery seminars, he would refer to the "little self" and the "big self," advising us to let the big self, the self beyond the mind, take charge. The

you, you find a sense of space. As you focus on it, you realize there is no pain in this space. The greater sense of presence within you lives there. As the pain dissolves, you begin to trust it more and more and you watch as this presence begins to guide you through life. You don't have to go with the painful feelings and be consumed by them as though they're part of who you are. Eventually, it transforms you, from identifying less with the person you are to identifying with the presence or expression of the absolute that you are.

Bill taught us how to listen to this presence. Learning when to go beyond our individual minds and listen to the universal mind represents true mastery: "Mastery is knowing when to go there [to your mind for answers] and when to not go there [to go beyond the mind for answers]. In addition, mastery includes knowing how the mind is fed for you. Bill explained, "My mind gets fed from you; my mind when we are here is our collective mind and is plugged into our collective soul."

He continued: "To be a master of not just your mind but the mind we all share is what happens beyond the mind. A lot of modern physicists are saying what Buddhists have been saying for years. Scientists are catching up and realizing there is this unified space that we are all connected to in a quantum way. So whatever information is there is here when you need it."[187]

Plato's allegory of the cave brilliantly depicted how the false images and thoughts in the mind can control us. Imprisoned in a cave since childhood, so the story goes, prisoners are shackled in chains and forced to gaze only at the wall in front of them. They can't look around or at each other or themselves. Behind the cave is a low walkway on which people carry objects and puppets as they walk. A brightly lit fire in the distance creates shadows of these objects and puppets on the cave wall. The sounds of the people walking outside the cave create sounds that the prisoners falsely believe come from the shadows on the wall.

The shadows and sounds constitute reality for the prisoners, who have never seen anything else. They don't realize that what they see on

---

"little self "implies the self that represents the limited human perspective.
[187] Bill Bauman's Mastery seminar

the cave wall are shadows of objects. In the same way as Plato's prisoners, our minds and bodies are like the shadows we falsely believe is reality.

Once you learn to quiet the mind, you're entering unknown, exciting virgin territory. In this brave new world, you see that your primary reality is within. Your focus, your pull, is no longer outward, on the "cave wall" of the physical world. Your focus is within; and gradually your inner essence takes on greater energetic power than your external reality. It's as if Plato's prisoners were freed and dragged out into the light of the sun. You begin building your life from that bright, peaceful, powerful space within, from inspiration, from your soul, from your own truth.

> **Beyond the mind, into the realm of pure energy, is where your real power lies. It's where the magic is.**

Beyond the mind, into the realm of pure energy, is where your real power lies. It's where the magic is. In fact, beyond the mind lies the most powerful energy in the universe, and it resides within each and every one of us. Unlimited insights of the soul can be experienced in this realm. Beyond the mind, we encounter the soul or the inner sanctum where healing takes place. Your innermost being, your soul, is the essence of who you are. You discover it beyond the mind. If you gain access to this inner essence, you can be healed quickly, even spontaneously.

When you enter this inner dimension of who you are—the very maker of your body—you gain access to your power to heal. Many doctors, philosophers, writers, and spiritual teachers have written and talked about this power for years.[188] Ironically, the deeper within we go, the further beyond the mind we venture, without regard to distance. Once you enter this realm, distance becomes a nonissue. In fact, the further within you go, the more far-reaching the power beyond the

---

[188] Among them: Tolstoy, William Blake, Ralph Waldo Emerson, and Dante. More recently, among the most well known, have been Joel Goldsmith; Lester Levinson; Bill Bauman, PhD; Carolyn Myss, PhD; Deepak Chopra, MD; Wayne Dyer, PhD; Larry Dossey, MD; Barbara Dossey, PhD, RN; Herb Benson, MD; and many others.

mind. Much like cell phone fields extend beyond the cell phone, our power beyond the mind is field-like, extending its influence beyond our brains and our minds.

Because in this materialistic age we have been so convinced of the importance of the mind and the supremacy of reason and the intellect, it has been very difficult, if not impossible, for most to embrace seriously the idea of a power that lies beyond the mind—until you experience it. Actually, to a greater degree than ever before, many seem to be experiencing an awakening of this power.

Prominent and highly educated scientists who dare to stand out in a world of scientific conformity are coming forward to talk about their own beyond-the-mind experiences. These scientists, whose personal experiences are game changers, recount extraordinary stories of the realms that lie beyond the mind. Life transported them there; and their experiences have opened up new territory for all of us that science has dared not tread in the past. Scientific discoveries leap from their expansions in consciousness, from these new spiritual realms beyond the mind.

> John Archibald Wheeler believed that reality arises from beyond the mind.

John Archibald Wheeler—a visionary physicist and teacher who helped invent the theory of nuclear fission, argued about the nature of reality with Albert Einstein and Niels Bohr, and worked with Enrico Fermi on the Manhattan Project–believed that reality arises from beyond the mind. According to Wheeler, information is fundamental to the physics of the universe. All things physical are informational in origin. [189]

Wheeler's work explains constantly operating telepathy, where thoughts come from, and why others can sense our thoughts and feelings. Wheeler's "it from bit" doctrine says that every "it"—every particle, every field of force, and even space-time itself—derives its

---

[189] John A. Wheeler. "Information, Physics, Quantum: The Search for Links," in W. Zurek, *Complexity, Entropy, and the Physics of Information*, 1990, Redwood City, California: Addison-Wesley.

function, its meaning, its very existence entirely from an immaterial source and explanation, "bit." In other words, what we call reality arises from an unseen source, and everything in it is informational in origin. In addition, Wheeler believed that this is a *participatory* universe, meaning the reality we experience depends on our participation in it. Reality depends on us. We are creators and shapers of a participatory reality.

TAPPING INTO THIS POWER

Turning inward is the first important step to tap into our unlimited creative potential to heal. Centering ourselves to reach that point of stillness within is the aim. The stillness or "singularity" within connects with the infinite energy, infinite wisdom, the peace, and the joy that lies beyond the mind.

> How do we heal? By going within, to that still, silent space within each of us that knows no illness. It's a space that is never sick, a space that is beyond fear. When you quiet your mind, you experience it.

How do we heal? By going within, to that still, silent space within each of us that knows no illness. It's a space that is never sick, a space that is beyond fear. When you quiet your mind, you experience it. That still space becomes more and more available to you as you clear negative emotions and give the power in the energy centers within you a clear path. Or you can develop tools that direct the mind and the power of imagination to take you beyond the limits of the temporal mind.

Actually, the process of creating health—or really, *whatever* you wish to create—is the reverse of the process of perception, how we normally perceive the world and everyday life. In the process of perception, our senses are primary players. Our senses translate physical experiences into energy fluctuations and information, and our brains interpret the energy fluctuations and information as our reality. In the process of creation, we begin with the energy fluctuations and information.

In other words, when we create, we consciously select energetic experiences, thoughts, and feelings, designed to create reality as we choose it to be, consciously focusing attention, immersing ourselves in what we choose to bring about. By bringing a new experience into our consciousness, it becomes alive energetically. Once it becomes alive energetically, it will manifest when the circumstances are right.

Through the ages, spiritual teachers have advocated meditation to transport you to this space beyond the mind. To move into mastery beyond the mind, Bill Bauman, my spiritual teacher, told us a different story of how he gained greater access to the energy beyond the mind. It occurred to him one day that he was thinking out of compulsion. On that day, he said to himself, "I'm addicted to thinking." Determined to stop the stream of thoughts running through his mind out of sheer habit, he learned to clear his mind and direct his thoughts.

As Bill told us, "I *trained* my mind to stop running on automatic pilot and to think only about things I *chose* to think about." As he recounted his experience, he revealed, "An amazing thing happened when I stopped thinking out of compulsion: I saw my heart open up! I became much more feeling oriented, much more in tune with people's emotions, much more empathetic and compassionate."[190]

When Bill stopped thinking out of habit, he freed vast amounts of energy from his mind, energy that gave new vitality to his feelings and his heart space. If you do what Bill did and learn to train your thoughts, become the master of your thoughts, become aware of what you allow yourself to think, you too will see an increased capacity to feel arise. Clearing your mind as Bill did will lead you deeper and deeper within, to your feeling realm, to that innermost self beyond the mind, your essential nature. Clearing your mind brings you to your inner essence. *This is the place where healing ultimately occurs.*[191]

---

[190] Shift Network teleconference presentation. October 2013.

[191] Many times the fixed positions of the mind erect a barrier to healing, assuming an intellectual position that believes the dismal statistics that may

In that place, your energy field emits higher frequencies and negativity no longer affects you. To arrive at that place, you have to rid yourself of the "ants,"[192] or *automatic negative thoughts* that we have all bought into because of our upbringings and other fear-based social influences. All the heavy emotional baggage you have accumulated needs to be released and cleared. Our minds constantly preach: "Don't do this, be careful of that, watch out here, look out for trouble there!"

ACT AS IF

Directing and training your thoughts, as well as emptying the mind, are powerful ways of tapping in to the space beyond the mind. Another powerful way to create health and healing (or anything you desire, really) is by using your imagination:

Feel as if you would feel if you were healed. Live in that state. Feel the exhilaration, the relief, the peace that would be yours. Imagine yourself in a state of complete health and totally healed. Feel the excitement and the relief that you know you would feel if you were healed.

Then, express gratitude for your healing—even if it hasn't come yet. Say thank you for your healing and then detach yourself. Don't keep looking to see if you're healed. Pay more attention to feeling the way you would as if you were already healed. Assume your healing is here. Be thankful that you **are** *healed*. Most important is to imagine the state you want *is already here*. Feel it. Sleep on it. Drift off to sleep with the feeling that it's finished. You are healed. The healing power here resides in your vital, vivid imagination. Many toss it aside, thinking imagination belongs in Disneyland, and not to be taken seriously. But that would be a mistake. Imagination serves as a vital link between your inner and outer worlds. Or we can say, imagination is the link between your conscious self and your Higher Self. Imagination creates

---

be associated with an illness or opinions that say a certain condition has no cure can throw roadblocks in the way of healing.

[192] Daniel Amen, MD, coined the term and presented it in his PBS special: *Magnificent Mind at Any Age.*

new electromagnetic energies fields that have the ability to shift your reality to embrace new states.

To go beyond the mind and access the realm of pure energy, your starting point is to be aware of your thoughts and release the low energies that accompany negative patterns of thinking and emotional baggage so that the mind can be stilled. As you learn to let go of negative feelings, you eventually learn not to be as concerned with your fears and painful emotions. You see that you can allow them to come up and then be released, even learn to welcome them, as they served a purpose. You can just watch them and let them go.

> As you learn to refrain from mental strife and struggle, to surrender anger, fear, and grief, your mind is overcome as a factor of power and it will resume its rightful place as an avenue of awareness, and the power beyond the mind will take over.

Gradually, you will feel the space underneath them and an inner peace will take root and release inner healing energies. As you learn to refrain from mental strife and struggle, to surrender anger, fear, and grief, your mind is overcome as a factor of power and it will resume its rightful place as an avenue of awareness. The power beyond the mind will take over.

As mentioned in the last chapter, in this clearing process, the unconscious mind has to be factored in. If not, healing processes can be encumbered by it. Anxieties, irritability, resentment, and anger can all be identified and released. If what you're feeling is negative but you can't put your finger on what it is, it's probably a leftover lodged in your unconscious. It's waiting for a chance to come up and be released. Uncomfortable feelings you've chosen not to look at are waiting to come up and be released, so you can just let them! Remember that *what you're feeling, you're healing!*

There are many techniques to accomplish the emotional cleansing of the unconscious, release techniques such as the Sedona Method, or the radical acceptance method, or the Byron Katie method.[193] When you are tired enough of experiencing emotional pain and your desire for relief is great enough, you will be led to people and situations and techniques that will help you find a way.

Many find a way to release negative emotions on their own. A friend of mine tells the story of how she had been depressed for quite a while. Her mother was ill and up in years, and she was depressed for fear of losing her. One day I called to see how she was coming along, and I was pleasantly surprised. She sounded fine, even cheerful. I commented on how happy I was to hear her sounding so "up" and asked what happened. She firmly replied, "I told my depression to take a walk!" It had obviously heeded her command.

My own path led me to Bill, who has assisted thousands of people, by virtue of his light, or you can call it his high-frequency energy field, to go beyond the mind. I am fond of calling this work with Bill "the lazy man's path to enlightenment," for Bill's amazing, magnificent light does (almost) all of the work.[194]

No matter what your mind is saying to you, it is only trying to protect you out of habit and past experiences. From this perspective, you can appreciate and love your mind, love yourself no matter what your mind is saying. It means well. Loving the one who is having the negative feelings has been called a new paradigm way of anchoring a new consciousness.[195] Instead of trying to purge the negative, focus on what is positive, everything about yourself you can love.

[193] See *No Attachments, No Aversions* for the Sedona Method; see thework.com, for Byron Katie.

[194] Bill Bauman, PhD, is a spiritual teacher who founded the Center for Soulful Living, along with his wife, Donna Bauman, PhD, who served as the founding executive director.

[195] Matt Kahn. "Anchoring a New Consciousness." YouTube.com.

I AM THAT

Eventually, as you go beyond the mind and rise higher in consciousness, whether by retraining yourself to focus on all that's good or releasing enough of the bad feelings you've accumulated[196] in your unconscious, your mind becomes a transparency. If what you identify with is red, you turn red. If it's blue, you turn blue. If you identify with wealth, you are wealthy. If you identify with health, you are healthy. (I am *that* … the essence of all that is).

Wherever you are in your heart and mind, you become a part of that. But nothing "sticks" to you. You become one with everything you encounter and there is nothing more to resist. When something emotionally challenging happens and you're confronted with pain or loss, your mind takes it in but has no inclination to reject it or to avoid it. It remains calm, open, and available. You may feel the pain or sadness for a short while, but it doesn't "stick."[197] You have experienced the "heart's release" that the Buddha promised. You stop seeing reality through your senses and mental states, where it is mediated, not directly experienced within. Your heart is opened, as Bill's was.

Because your mind has awakened, it becomes "transparent," one with the illuminating source of all life. You begin to experience more telepathy and clairvoyance and perhaps become more prescient. As you go beyond the mind, you develop a strong intuition and often "see" things or come to know things before they happen. In addition, beyond the mind, you go beyond time and space and gradually see that the answers, the knowledge you seek, arise spontaneously from within. Going beyond the mind, you go beyond time and space and have access to all the information that lies in the collective unconscious, the great database of humanity. Within this grand database reside the archetypes

---

[196]   Energy doesn't actually accumulate; it's information that is stored in the cells and becomes "cellular memory."

[197]   Phillip Moffitt. *Dancing With Life. Stage Three: Transparency.* Dharmatown.org

or energy patterns that are common to our experiences as human beings, as Carl Jung first described.[198]

By its very nature, the mind is turned outward. To experience the source of awareness from within, and no longer through the mind, is itself, in a profound way, the beginning of an entirely new worldview, a new reality. You begin to feel connected with all that is. At our foundation, in our very cellular depths, as Dr. Ramachandran discovered,[199] we are all interconnected.

Beyond the mind, you begin to experience that interconnectedness and become aware of the vast realm of intelligence that lies beyond the mind. As it becomes real to you, you begin to use your mind to draw from within the vast realms of your own being. The way you experience reality changes because your level of awareness changes. The idea of an objective reality is a goner. You see that there is no such thing!

EXPANSIONS IN CONSCIOUSNESS AND AWARENESS

Describing this vast realm of intelligence, German physicist Max Planck said it this way: "All matter originates and exists only by virtue of a force which brings the particle of an atom to vibration, and holds this most minute solar system of the atom together. We must assume behind this force the existence of a conscious and intelligent mind. This mind is the matrix of all matter."

As we go beyond the mind, we become more directly connected to this "matrix" and to one another by virtue of this matrix. In fact, it is the source of all matter, including us. We are made of this energy. It is the source of everything found within the universe, the stuff of which the universe is made, including you and me. *It is pure consciousness*, say an increasing number of prominent scientists. Consciousness is the basic

---

198   C. G. Jung, *The Archetypes and the Collective Unconscious*, 1996, London, 43.
199   Dr. Ramachandran, TED talk, YouTube.

element of reality, the source of everything. Nothing is outside consciousness.[200]

> When your consciousness has expanded into it—that is, has transcended the mind—knowledge is yours on demand.

One of the greatest physicists of all time, David Bohm, said that consciousness is basically in the implicate order,[201] as all matter is, and therefore it's not that consciousness is one thing and matter is another. Rather, consciousness is a material process, and consciousness is itself in the implicate order, as is all matter. Consciousness manifests in some explicate order, as does matter in general.

> Henry Stapp, another American physicist and author of *The Mindful Universe*, puts forth a "quantum theory of consciousness" that the state of the universe is a collection of "subjective knowings."

Many, many scientists have theories on consciousness as our physical reality. American physicist Nick Herbert, author of *Quantum Reality* and widely known as the foremost expert on Bell's theorem, explains what Einstein called "spooky action at a distance." Herbert reminds us that *matter is not solid at all*; it is mostly empty space and "ambiguous." Like Bohm, he thinks that consciousness is a process that pervades all of nature. Henry Stapp, another American physicist and author of *The Mindful Universe*, puts forth a "quantum theory of consciousness" that the state of the universe is a collection of "subjective knowings."[202]

---

[200] Amit Goswami, Richard E. Reed, and Maggie Goswami: *The Self-Aware Universe: How Consciousness Creates the Material World.* Jeremy Tarcher/ Putnam Books, New York, 1993.

[201] The "implicate order" is a term coined by Bohm to mean the deeper fundamental order of reality where we find that ordinary notions of space and time are not factors, as distinct from the "explicate order," which is the reality most humans perceive, and of course, space and time are factors.

[202] Henry Stapp. *Mind, Matter and Quantum Mechanics.* Springer, Berkeley, California, 1993.

All knowledge is contained in the universal mind. When your consciousness has expanded into it—that is, has transcended the mind— *knowledge is yours on demand.* You don't have to carry the information around with you. Whenever you need it, it's there. Sandra, one of the participants in our mastery class lost her daughter. She asked Bill for help. She was worried sick because her daughter had run away and no one could find her. In a short time, Bill knew where she was. He located her because he had access to the knowledge of her whereabouts through his mind as an infinite avenue of awareness.

Expanded consciousness is power. Whatever you feel needs to be done happens. Sometimes you hear experts refer to it as expanded awareness. Consciousness and awareness are often used interchangeably. Actually, awareness means transcending the mind, going beyond it. Awareness has also been referred to as super consciousness, pure consciousness, or supreme consciousness, meaning consciousness at very high frequency levels.[203]

Consciousness is fundamental to the workings of the mind, where there are divisions and duality like subject and object, good and bad.[204] When you transcend the mind, you move into a realm beyond good and bad and reach a state of holding nothing, or *no thing*, in mind. In this place, awareness is unlimited and takes the place of consciousness. Everything you can think of—all mental and physical things—exists in awareness.

Just as you can change your experience of reality by changing the frequency of your thoughts, or "lifting" your thoughts to ever-higher frequencies, your level of consciousness expands as you move to realms beyond thought. Quantum physics emphasizes that our minds' thoughts are not exactly physical in nature but represent energy fields and vibrations, as we discussed in the last chapter.

---

[203] Sri Nisargadat Maharaj. *I Am That.* Acorn Press, Durham, North Carolina, 2012, 310.

[204] The mind's job is to focus, to analyze, and to synthesize. Beyond the mind lies pure awareness.

The awareness space beyond the mind also possesses a frequency, a field of vibration. According to the law of resonance, the mind with a high-level frequency tunes in with other minds of high-level frequency. A low-level frequency mind tunes in with other minds of low-level frequency.

David Hawkins has devised a scale of consciousness starting with low-frequency states such as apathy and fear, on up the scale to states like desire, pride, and anger, to courage, acceptance, love, joy, and bliss.

> A mind with a high-level frequency tunes in with other minds of high-level frequency. A low-level frequency mind tunes in with other minds of low-level frequency.

As your consciousness expands in the space beyond the mind, into the higher frequencies and levels of consciousness, you begin to look at life differently. It's like tuning into a different radio station. You begin to see that whatever happens is in the service of your expansion, in the service of helping you expand and grow. You begin to realize that what seem to be adverse situations are actually designed to help you. They present opportunities for expansion.

For instance, someone with an expanded awareness will see the benefits of any situation. What may feel like adversity actually represents a situation to be mastered, a situation to help you on your path. A loss of an employee becomes an opportunity for someone better suited to the position. The loss of a lover becomes an opportunity for greater independence or someone you're better suited to. The loss of a tennis game becomes a great incentive for improvement. Instead of win-lose situations, people with expanded awareness tend to see life in win-win terms.

An illness can be seen as an opportunity to reverse unhealthy patterns. It is there to inspire you to change, to pull you back onto your soul's path. Even death looks different to people at expanded levels of awareness. They see that there is only a transition in consciousness, not death as we know it. As painful as it is to lose someone, you know that he is always with you. You can also choose to focus on the fact that he is no longer suffering, that he is reunited with loved ones he has lost, that caregivers are relieved of their daily stresses and burdens.

> At high enough levels of consciousness, Hawkins explains, anything heals.

As you go deeper within and experience a greater and greater expansion beyond the mind, you move up the ladder of consciousness that Hawkins and others have described. Eventually, you come to the level of unconditional love. When the mind is quiet enough and the emotional pain-body has been cleared enough, an intensity of pure energy arises. This is the energy of healing. At high enough levels of consciousness, Hawkins explains, anything heals.[205]

When we have access to this energy, we can direct our minds to act as "tuning forks," sending healing vibrations throughout our bodies. Practicing meditation with an intent to heal will bring forth these healing energies and vibrations. When you encounter these energies—which can come through another person as well as from within you yourself—if you are not resistant to it,[206] healing occurs, often spontaneously.[207]

In his book *The Black Butterfly*, Dr. Richard C. Moss sites many examples, including his own, of healings that occurred in this way with awakenings in consciousness. After having his own awakening years earlier, he decided to share the following experience: In one of Dr. Moss's conferences, a woman named Laura was singing a childhood hymn, repeating it over and over, for several hours—in the same way she would have if she had been meditating. Then all of a sudden, the quality of her singing changed. She was lifted to her feet, her arms raised to the sky, and she no longer felt as though she were singing. As she tells it, she *became* the song. She felt her hands extend into the air and her feet

---

[205] David Hawkins. *Power vs Force*. Hay House, Inc. Carlsbad, California, 2002.
[206] Resistance can arise unconsciously, forming a sort of energetic shield that won't allow healing to occur.
[207] David Hawkins. *Healing and Recovery*. Veritas Publishing, Sedona, Arizona, 2009, 29.

disappear. She felt no difference between her and them; she became one with the earth, the sky, the song. Her feet, her body, her arms, the sky, the song, and the singer all became one.

> The next day her terminal liver cancer was gone. The grapefruit-sized bowel metastasis was gone. Three days later she realized that for the first time in thirty-eight years she hadn't taken her daily insulin injections. In the ensuing weeks, all the secondary complications of her diabetes and cancer— kidney failure, fluid in her lungs, tumor-ridden lymph nodes, partial blindness, loss of sensation in her hands and feet, addiction to pain medication—healed.

Even a few recently broken toes completely mended within days. She was radiant; a palpable presence poured from her body like a gentle flame, and the whole understanding of her life was radically transformed. Dr. Moss offers workshops using dancing and singing as ways to expand personal awareness and consciousness to reach a state of balance between the body and the mind.[208]

HEALING MECHANISMS BEYOND THE MIND

The more we are able to still the mind, usually through meditation but also in other ways, as Laura did through dancing, or painting or playing an instrument, and go beyond it, the more we gain access to higher frequency energies, the greater the expansion of consciousness. When we connect with higher frequency energies, we can begin to let the lower frequencies pass through us as we would if we were walking through a patch of mist. As you expand your awareness, you learn to recognize negative thoughts as energy surges and not to judge them. You realize they are just feelings. They are not *you*, and you can just let

---

[208]   Richard Moss, MD. *The Black Butterfly: an Invitation to Radical Aliveness.* 1986, Celestial Arts, Berkeley, California, 1.

them go. The more you eliminate negative thoughts, the more peace you feel. Laura did it with dancing and singing.

In my own experience, I learned that in the company of a great soul like Bill Bauman, the mind becomes quiet spontaneously. You are effortlessly transported beyond the mind. Beyond the mind, you come increasingly closer to the space that is beyond duality, beyond good and bad. The poet Rumi called it a "field beyond right and wrong." It is not only the place where miracles happen; it is a place brimming over with health, energy, and life—actually, omnipotence, omniscience, and omnipresence.

BEYOND THE MIND: WHERE MIRACLES HAPPEN

When you are tired of pain and suffering, you can make the decision to refrain from mental strife, struggle, reason, or what you *think* is the thing to do. As you let go of your thoughts, the human mind is overcome as a factor of power. It resumes its rightful place as an avenue of awareness, no longer an avenue of ("I'm smarter than you are") power.

Many of us don't realize it, but our minds often serve as defense mechanisms. Just like overeating or overdrinking, overthinking can be a defense mechanism. You think to yourself, consciously or unconsciously, *If I know a lot, I feel more secure. It protects me.* Since our society places an extraordinary value on intelligence and the power of the mind, many of us have learned to love the mind and its intellectual approach to life's situations, myself included. The mind is a magnificent instrument. But the key is, as Eckhart Tolle puts it, is to learn how to use your mind, instead of letting it use you, as is the case with most of us.

As a result, many, like Bill, as described in his story earlier in this chapter, become addicted to thinking. As he began to release the need for compulsive thinking, his capacity to feel came to the front burner. He said, "Prior to that, I was minimizing it so I could think." As he stopped assuming he knew the answer to everything and let go of his propensity to think of the answer to something while the person was still talking, he said, "I found myself feeling scared." Because he lost his defense mechanism, he felt defenseless for a little while, as his mind was overcome as a factor of power.

> Ironically, when you empty the mind, you know more.

Ironically, when you empty the mind, you know more. You don't give up knowing. *Whatever you need to know is given to you when you need it.* In this state, you are merging with the highest potentialities of the unified field, the vast human database of awareness.[209] You become aware of *all that is* through the mind when the mind is used as an instrument to draw from within yourself. As your awareness of yourself is deepened and broadened, all blessings flow. You need not seek anything; all will come to you most naturally and effortlessly.

You'll know you've been lifted above the human mind when you are able to relax more and more. People who have attained this state meet everyday life with ease and happiness. If you ask them a question about a project or a relationship, you will often hear them say something like, "I'm not sure, but I know things will work out when the time is right." They realize that in the presence of this pure energy of awareness, there are no temporal or time-bound powers. This means that nothing in the material world has power over you any longer. Remember, Einstein taught us that time is an illusion.

When you are freed from the emotional baggage of the past, you are living in the "now." You have an abundance of energy. You are no longer trying to control what others do or say. You stop using your energy trying to anticipate what someone will say so that you can agree with it or refute it or come up with the right answer first. You are just with what is happening in the present, with your thoughts and actions.

---

[209] David Hawkins, MD. *Healing and Recovery.* Veritas Publishing, Sedona, Arizona, 2009.

LISTEN TO YOUR SOUL

> Then, in the light of calm and steady self-awareness, inner energies wake up and work miracles without any effort on your part.

Emptying the mind leads you to the depth and love of your soul … the path to healing. If healing comes from the center or truth of your being, from your soul, we can say that the key question to be asked is, what brings you closer to your soul? It's the light of your awareness, which expands and shines ever more brightly as you learn to quiet your mind. For you to get in touch with your soul, you must let go of any preoccupation with ego-driven behaviors and listen more deeply within. Then, in the light of calm and steady self-awareness, inner energies wake up and work miracles without any effort on your part.[210]

The soul binds us together, unites us, integrates us, and heals us. The soul is the glue of human relationship, the inspiration. Physicians and nurses have described scientific evidence supporting the soul's healing power.[211] After studying the research on healing at a distance, Larry Dossey, MD, author of *Healing Words* and the first director of the Center for Complementary Therapies at National Institutes of Health, saw as he observed healing at a distance through prayer that something of ourselves is infinite in space and time, omnipresent, eternal immortal. This infinite aspect is referred to as the soul.[212]

Whenever you are experiencing struggle, tension, or doubt (or illness!) you can be sure that the sense of love that comes from your soul is blocked. Like a copper wire that's corroded, the "charge" does not go through. Neither will the healing. This kind of love that comes from the soul has been described as a feeling of being limitless or unbounded, as

---

[210] Nisargdat Majaraj. *I Am That*. Acorn Press, Durham, North Carolina, 2012.
[211] Larry Dossey, MD. *Healing Words*. HarperSanFrancisco, 1993.
[212] Ibid, 6.

"oceanic" feelings. The feeling has also been described as "an indissoluble connection, a feeling of belonging to the world as a whole."[213]

When a person is fully aware, we say that she is "enlightened." Fully aware enlightened people are soulful soul-filled people in whom loving, compassionate thoughts, actions, and healing naturally arise. Enlightenment, or awakening to the presence of the one-in-all and all-in-one source of all things, and then expressing that realization in every aspect of your existence, is often a process of development, not a one-time event. Yet it can happen quickly, as it did with Laura. In Laura's case, her song absorbed her mind. Where there is focus on one thought or thing, a focus on the now, the power is all right there.

THE SECRET PATH TO HIGHER ENERGY FREQUENCIES: LET IT GO

To expand your awareness to higher energies—some would say to become enlightened—the Buddha and other enlightened souls stressed the importance of letting go of desires. Said the Buddha to the question "Why am I suffering?"—it's because you are clinging to something! But what does *that* mean? After all, desires are a natural thing. We all have them. The Buddhist approach doesn't appeal to some people because of this requirement to give up your desires! Yet that's not the whole picture, and perhaps many in the West don't understand the intent of it because our culture is so different from Eastern spiritual teachings.

The irony of letting go of something you want—including healing—is that *it's the quickest way to bring it to you.* Desiring something in the future keeps it there—in the future. If you let go of what you want, you're eliminating the energetic space that the desire puts between you and the thing you want. When you let go of the desire, something bigger and better is waiting to take its place. If I persist in clinging to what I

---

[213]   Robert Cloninger. *Feeling Good: The Science of Well Being.* Oxford University Press, 2004, Chapter 5.

want, the clinging energy blocks it from coming to me or locks me into some smaller version of who I am, only a version my mind can conceive. By its nature, that is most limiting. You get what you want most readily by *releasing* it into the pure energy beyond the mind. Letting it go means letting go of the clinging, needy feeling for it, whether it's your desire for an intimate relationship, or a job, or a healing. Releasing it instantly will bring it to you more quickly or open you up to bigger possibilities.

If your intention is to let go, life will start to tutor you and bring you situations that will give you the opportunity to learn to let go. I tried this "letting go" approach on small things first. Instead of clinging to the thought of it, I let it go, meaning I didn't worry. I didn't think about it any longer. I didn't give up on it; I just didn't dwell on it. I took my mind off it and moved on to the next thing on my to-do list, confident that the universe would bring it to me when the time was right. Sure enough, each thing I needed found its way to me at the right time.

However, you have to practice letting go. To have desires is a major aspect of human existence. It comes from deep within, from the soul's continual desire for expansion. Many believe that one of the reasons we're here is to learn to manifest our desires. It's almost impossible *not* to have desires if you are human. Desire is not wrong or bad. Desires are the fountain of life itself—desires to grow, to learn, to experience, to enjoy, to be happy.

The problem is that we tend to think fulfilling an external desire is what will make us feel better, what will make us happy. To imagine that fulfilling an external desire with fame, power, sex, or more money is going to make you happy or satisfy your craving and worries about lack is misguided. They are all well and good in their own place, but only something deep and lasting—alignment with your source, your soul, who you really are—will be fulfilling and ultimately make you happy. And it will bring you what you want.

So what does letting go of desire really mean? The thing to let go of is the neediness and clinging energy—the *need* for the desire to manifest, the *need* to make something happen. French philosopher Pascal said it this way: "We all have a 'God hole' that we try to fill with worldly things like money, sex, and worldly success."

We learn to possess and compete, to achieve, to accumulate knowledge and wealth. Then we strive to maintain it and keep it. We cling to things because we want to feel good. We want to be happy. But those things don't satisfy; no *thing* ever brings happiness permanently. We cling to our thoughts and emotions for the same reasons; we think we'll feel better. Even the negative ones are there for that reason—we place them there to protect ourselves and preserve our identities. But letting go, letting go of despair, of anguish, of the pain and doubt, and of everything we cling to and identify with, is the best thing to do to get what you want, especially a healing.

MEDITATION: PATH TO EXPANDED AWARENESS AND EVEN NEW GENETIC EXPRESSION

Anyone who has meditated for a while has experienced this magical realm beyond the mind. Some think of it as "nothingness," in terms of the fact that there is no *thing* or no thought form there. When you go *beyond* the mind, you are holding "no *thing*" in mind. I describe my own foray into this arena in the introduction of the book.

Actually, the space beyond the mind is as far from *nothingness*—in the conventional meaning of the word—as you can get! Within each of us lies the *all*, pure energy, teeming with potential and limitless possibilities, including our perfect health and healing. Because the pure energy of the divine matrix, or the zero point field, nature's mind, or the mind of God—whatever you choose to call it—is beyond thought, beyond reason, and reveals a new reality, it reveals an entirely new way of being. It's the place where miracles happen. It's also the place where healing happens.

As you go deeper within, often through meditation, you connect with the inner self that is drawn toward a "singularity,"[214] toward your

---

[214] Singularity is a physics term. When a physicist refers to a "singularity," he or she is generally referring to a quantity that is infinite.

center as a "singularity," toward the stillness within. This center has been found to be an axis of spin, as the Buddhist and Vedic traditions have represented it. By the vortex entering the crown chakra, or energy pathway, the kundalini spiral that meets at the heart chakra or the heart's energy pathway goes up and up and up.

A LITMUS TEST

As you move toward this "singularity," you merge with the soul. How do you know when the merger has happened? How do you know you have integrated this energy beyond the mind or the energy of your soul into your being? These characteristics disappear from your personality:[215]

- **Righteousness**—You don't feel compelled to judge and right the world's wrongs as a source of moral authority. Any sense of righteousness is replaced with a sense of love and compassion.
- **Neediness**—You no longer seek to draw your energy from others. Your happiness and well-being no longer depend on the care, the advice, the presence, or the opinion of others. You are no longer in a continual state of the need for attention, for emotional support, for help from others.
- **Victimhood**—You stop blaming others for things and circumstances that go wrong in your life. You realize that when you blame, you are relinquishing your power to an external person or source. You realize that you are the creator of whatever transpires.
- **Entitlement**—An attitude of gratitude replaces an attitude of feeling that you have a right to something, that whatever it is your due is coming to you.

Meditation is the ultimate letting go—letting go of discontent, letting go of fears and frustrations, letting go of all thoughts as they arise. It is a way of going beyond the mind to expanded levels of awareness

---

[215] Matt Kahn. "Anchoring a New Consciousness." YouTube.com.

and a way of gaining control of your mind. Spiritual teachers have said that everything that everyone is looking for in the world is far better gotten through meditation.[216] The deeper within you go, the greater the joy and the greater the ease of getting what you want and need in the material world.

For many, meditation is a mysterious thing. They hear about its magic and wonder how to do it. Meditation encompasses a variety of practices that help you focus your attention and control your thoughts. The origins of meditation can be traced to the East, where people have been practicing this art for thousands of years. Nevertheless, meditation doesn't have to be done according to ancient Eastern traditions. I learned to meditate reading Herb Benson's book *Timeless Healing*. There is a page in that book that systematically tells you what to do.[217] At the time, I had difficulty sitting still, so I told myself to sit still for five minutes a day to start. I did, and little by little it turned into a deeply rewarding daily practice.

Essentially, there are two types of meditation: mindfulness meditation, where you focus all your attention on the flow of your breath in and out of the body, and transcendental meditation, where you repeat a word or sound to prevent thoughts from entering the mind, both ultimately leading to a state of relaxed alertness. Benson has called it "the relaxation response." Best of all, you can spend as little as ten minutes daily meditating and still reap the benefits.[218]

THE MEDITATION EFFECT

Meditation states possess a high-energy vibration. With practice, your consciousness connects to higher and higher frequencies, to the energy that is the source of all creation. From that perspective, the benefits

---

[216] Lester Levinson. *Stillness Speaks. The Keys to Ultimate Freedom. Meditation with Quest.* [PDF online].

[217] Herbert Benson, with Marg Stark. *Timeless Healing.* Schribner, 1997.

[218] Herbert Benson, MD. *The Relaxation Response.* 162–163.

of meditation are extraordinary. Researchers at the Harvard Medical School have recently found that deep relaxation seems to switch off "disease-causing" genes while switching on genes that actively protect us from disorders such as high blood pressure, pain, infertility, and even autoimmune diseases such as rheumatoid arthritis. These health improvements have been shown to result from the "relaxation response."[219]

Recently researchers compared the genetic makeup of individuals who had been practicing meditation or yoga for a long time to a control group of individuals who were not meditation or yoga practitioners. In the words of Dr. Benson, who led the Harvard study, "We found a range of disease-fighting genes that were active in the relaxation practitioners but not active in the control group." But it didn't take long for the control group to catch up. In as little as two months after the control group began meditating, their genetic profiles changed to resemble those of the meditators.[220]

In a separate study conducted by Dr. Dean Ornish and colleagues, men diagnosed with low-risk prostate cancer were asked to adopt positive lifestyle changes—a plant-based diet, exercise, meditation, and participating in a therapy group—as a treatment for their disease because they had opted not to undergo conventional treatment. The researchers conducted two prostate biopsies on each individual, one before and one three months after following the plant-based diet, exercise, meditation, and participating in a support group. They reported that the biopsy samples collected after the lifestyle changes had a different gene expression pattern, with various disease-promoting genes switched off and various protective genes turned on. These studies certainly seem to have opened up a new frontier in healing, with huge benefits and without the side effects of medications and surgeries.[221]

---

[219]   Herbert Benson, MD. *Harvard Weekly.* 2013.

[220]   Ibid.

[221]   Dean Ornish. "Changing Lifestyle Changes Gene Expression." www.edge. org/conversation/changing lifestyle-changes-gene-expression.

Several studies designed specifically to understand the beneficial effects of meditation have shown that meditation helps to reverse heart disease,[222] reduce pain,[223] substantially slow aging,[224] lower blood pressure,[225] fight inflammation, and decrease anxiety.[226]

Researchers studying the effect of meditation on atherosclerosis, or plaque in the arteries, in African Americans showed an 11 percent decrease in the risk of heart attacks and up to a 15 percent decrease in the risk of stroke. Another study showed that cancer patients who practiced meditation for as little as seven weeks were significantly less depressed and anxious than their counterparts who did not meditate. Meditators also reported increased energy levels and fewer cardiac and gastrointestinal problems than non-meditators.[227]

It's difficult for many who have been taught that your genetic profile is a fixed thing to believe that such a diverse range of diseases can be helped by a simple meditation practice! But the physiological changes can be measured: Meditation has been shown to increase alpha waves (relaxed brain waves) and decrease production of the stress hormone cortisol. Many of the positive physical changes associated with meditation are related to the different biochemicals secreted when you meditate somewhat regularly. It has been shown to bring down levels of other stress hormones as well.[228]

Ever since the Buddha meditated under a banyan tree, the miracles of meditation have ranged from establishing mental resilience in a

---

[222] Ibid.

[223] Salynn Boyles. "Meditation May Reduce Pain." *WebMD News,* April 6, 2011.

[224] S. Black, PhD, MPH. "Can Meditation Slow the Aging Process?" www.asa. org/blog/can-meditation-slow-aging-process, 3/4/14.

[225] James W. Anderson MD. *Science Daily.* "Meditation Can Lower Blood Pressure." March 15, 2008. www.sciencedaily.com/releases/2008/03/080314130430.htm

[226] Julie Corliss. Executive Editor. *Harvard Health Letter.* January 8, 2014. "Mindfulness Meditation May Ease Anxiety, Mental Stress." www.health. harvard.edu/blog/mindfulness-meditation-may-ease-anxiety-mental-stress-2014. 10

[227] Ibid.

[228] Jeffrey A. Dusek, PhD. and Herbert Benson, MD. "Mind-Body Medicine." *Minnesota Medicine.* May 2009; 92(5): 47–50.

war zone to reducing the number of traffic accidents, and missed days of work.[229] Mindfulness meditation, pioneered by Jon Cabot Zinn, is your ability to recognize what your mind is engaging with and direct it. As Peter Malinowski, a psychologist and neuroscientist at Liverpool John Moores University in England, put it, "For some people who begin mindfulness training, it's the first time in their [lives] where they realize that a thought or emotion is not their only reality, that they have the ability to stay focused on something else—for instance, their breathing—and let that emotion or thought just pass by."[230]

Meditation can reduce chronic pain. One notable study conducted at the Texas Tech University found that meditation enhances the effectiveness of Western medical treatment. In another study published in the *Journal of Behavioral Medicine*, patients suffering from backaches, chronic migraines, and tension headaches were able to lessen or even stop their pain medication after meditating for several weeks.

Since the early sixties, scientists have shown that meditation improves mental functioning. Dr. Herbert Benson, founder of Harvard's Mind-Body Institute, has shown over and over again that meditation creates "the opposite of the physiological changes that occur during the stress response," including a decrease in oxygen consumption, heart rate, respiratory rate, and blood pressure and an increase in the intensity of alpha, theta, and delta brain waves.

Meditation is not just a way for us to get in touch with ourselves and calm busy minds. Meditation, by improving our spiritual and mental health, also has a vital effect on our physical and genetic health.[231] That includes aging. Carol Greider and Elizabeth Blackburn, with Jack W. Szostak, were awarded the 2009 Nobel Prize in Physiology or Medicine for demonstrating how telomerase works. Referring to telomerase as age counters or markers, telomerase activity is a predictor of long-term

[229] The Editors of *Ode*. "The Amazing Promises of the Zero Point Field." Ode Publishing Company, November, 2003, 45.
[230] Dan Hurley. "Breathing in vs. Spacing Out." *NYT.* January 14, 2014.
[231] David R. Hamilton. "Further New Evidence for the Benefits of Meditation." Hay House, United Kingdom. www.hayhouse.co.uk/david-hamilton-newsletter-march2011

cellular viability, which decreases with chronic psychological distress and aging. Meditation increases telomerase activity, somewhat like slowing or even reversing the "biological clock" that constantly seems to be ticking off a countdown toward the limit on the human lifespan. Scientists agree, however, that the current limit on the human lifespan is 125 years. Telomerase activity holds the promise of reaching that goal, bolstered by practices like meditation.[232]

According to research by the University of Wisconsin-Madison, meditation has been shown to produce lasting beneficial changes in immune system function as well as brain electrical activity. Studies have shown that 50 percent more electrical activity in the left frontal regions of the brains of meditators triggered more positive emotions and empathy while decreasing anxiety.

However, the premise of modern medicine, except for a handful of pioneers like Herb Benson, does not recognize the role meditation can play or the importance that going beyond the mind can play in healing. The common factor that all ancient traditions and Eastern teachings stress is that meditation, going beyond the mind, taps into the soul's wellspring and the vital force or the spirit of the patient. This is where the sail catches the wind, so to speak. Restoring this vital force and spirit, called different things in different cultures: ch'i in Chinese medicine, shakti in Indian medicine, ki in Japanese, vital force in homeopathy, is what healing is all about.

---

[232] T. L. Jacobs et al. "Intensive Meditation Training, Immune Cell Telomerase Activity, and Psychological Mediators." Psychoneuroendocrinology. 2011 Jun; 36(5):664–81. doi: 10.1016/j.psyneuen.2010.09.010. Epub 2010 Oct 29.

XI

THE HEALING PRESCRIPTION

Power Step: The first and most important step is to believe you can heal.

There is no such thing as an incurable or hopeless condition—
somewhere, at some time, someone has recovered from it.

—David Hawkins MD, PhD[233]

"The feeling is the prayer," says Greg Bradden. Chanting, saying the rosary, davening, and meditation all serve to evoke the feeling of peace and inner calm that arises from within. As you pray, the way you feel changes and the frequency of your energy field changes accordingly. To heal, you must find that prayer-like dimension of intelligence, of love, of energy within. It is the energy of your inner essence, your soul or your source. By gaining access to this inner energy, to the innermost dimension of who you are, and aligning yourself with it, you can heal anything. To heal anything from a sore throat or the flu to cancer or heart disease, your inner experience, or how you feel inside, must change.

By now, hopefully you're willing to consider that an ailment or a disease process arises as an indication of a deeper problem—a sign that something is amiss in the workings of the mind, most often the unconscious mind. An inner solution to the problem needs to be found where the power to effect change resides: within the depths of you.

---

[233] David Hawkins MD, PhD. *Power vs Force*. "Wellness and the Disease Process." Hay House, Inc., Carlsbad California, 2002, 222.

Accessing this innermost dimension of who you are—by transcending the mind—is the essential element in healing.

A problem or a disease takes shape first in your energy field as a pattern of energetic thought forms, and a change in those thought forms can heal you. Because the frequencies of our vibrations—remember, we're all electromagnetic energy fields—come from our habitual thoughts, our beliefs, it's possible to heal anything fairly rapidly with a change in your habitual thinking and the beliefs and attitudes that accompany it.[234]

> It's possible to heal anything fairly rapidly with a change in your habitual thinking and the beliefs and attitudes that accompany it.

Healers in cultures around the world have observed this relationship between the mind, the body, and our energetic essence for years. They have known intuitively what science is only now beginning to understand. We've all heard stories about someone with a "terminal" illness, say, stage-four cancer, who is told, after trying all that Western medicine has to offer, there is nothing more the doctors can do. The person is sent home to receive hospice care. Then, five years later, that person strolls into the doctor's office feeling great, with no further evidence of cancer.

I saw it happen many times. I remember a patient whose extremities were almost navy blue, signaling poor circulation after open-heart surgery. None of us—neither the doctors nor the nurses—expected her to live. Unconscious and on a respirator breathing for her, she was out cold for nearly two weeks. Then one day, miraculously, she began to respond to our touch, then to our voices. Slowly she began to open her eyes. Her blood pressure and pulse began to improve. In a few weeks, she came back, with rosy cheeks and the picture of health, to thank all of us, the doctors and nurses in the open-heart surgery unit.

It happens all the time with cancer patients. In the medical world, this is referred to as a spontaneous remission, which is defined as "the

---

[234]   Ibid.

disappearance, complete or incomplete, of cancer without medical treatment or with medical treatment that is considered inadequate to produce the resulting disappearance of disease symptoms or tumor."[235]

Remissions do occur, and more than one thousand cases (across all types of cancer) have been published in medical journals. Thousands more have most likely occurred but haven't been published, for most doctors don't take the time to write them up and submit them for publication, probably because they don't have time or consider it a one-time fluke or, at best, a miracle.[236]

Many cases have been occurring in recent years, enough so that the Institute for Noetic Sciences has undertaken the Spontaneous Remission Project, reporting thirty-five hundred cases of supposedly incurable diseases where the patients experienced complete recovery.

Physicians often don't know what to do with these occurrences. Many patients who are healed complain, "My doctor didn't even ask how I did it." The few researchers who have studied these cases have noticed that two groups of people were largely ignored in the research: the patients themselves as well as non-allopathic[237] healers.

Dr. Kelly Turner, a researcher from the University of California at Berkeley, investigated why these unexpected remissions occur. She traveled all over the world interviewing healers: in the United States, China, Japan, New Zealand, Thailand, India, England, Ireland, Zambia, Zimbabwe, and Brazil. She conducted phone interviews with the patients who recovered. Her work, partially funded by the American Cancer Society, revealed several themes, summarized below, that she found in these interviews with healers as well as those who were healed.[238]

---

[235] Kelly Turner, PhD, *Spontaneous Remission of Cancer: Theories from Healers, Physicians and Cancer Survivors.* PhD dissertation. 2010.

[236] Ibid.

[237] Allopathic means remedies using drugs and surgery to produce effects that are incompatible with the disease. Non-allopathic means remedies that do not use drugs and surgery.

[238] Dr. Kelly Turner. *Radical Remission: Surviving Cancer against All Odds.* HarperOne, March, 2014.

1. **In order to heal, you must change the conditions under which the cancer thrives**. The majority of those interviewed believe that cancer thrives under certain suboptimal conditions in the body-mind-spirit system. To remove cancer, those underlying conditions must change. A healer from Hawaii explained it this way:

The most successful recoveries seem to be strongly associated with major mental, emotional, or physical behavioral changes among the people with the illness. What is major for one person, of course, may not be the same for another. ... I know of one success where a woman left her family, took up a different religion, changed her clothing and diet, and moved to a different country. Maybe she needed all of those changes or maybe not, but overall it worked for her. I know of another person, a man, who simply stopped trying to outdo his father, and that worked for him.

2. **Illness results from an energy blockage that is slowing the flow of energy; health requires the movement of energy.** The majority of those interviewed by Dr. Turner also believed that any illness—including cancer—represents an energy blockage or slowing of energy somewhere in the body-mind-spirit system, whereas health occurs when there is a state of unhindered movement or flow.

One of the healers talked about his theory of "bypasses," psychological defense mechanisms that create a bypass around an energetic block. He said that this energetic block can be located on either the spiritual, mental, emotional, or physical level and that these bypasses become solidified over time. In his view, true healing only occurs when a person stops bypassing and releases the original blockage.

3. **A body-mind-spirit interaction exists, and energy permeates all three levels.** The third belief that the majority of Dr. Turner's interviewees expressed was the idea that a body-mind-spirit interaction exists and that energy permeates all three of these levels. According to an American-born Peruvian-trained shaman/healer:

> *To be healed it must be on all three levels, mind, body, and spirit. Most of us live in our physical bodies; we don't even know about spiritual or emotional bodies. So we have to connect with all three of them. But you see, in the mountains of the Andes, [the Andean people] are already connected.*[239]

We are living in an age where spontaneous remissions and the seemingly miraculous healings are becoming more and more commonplace. What's new is that now there is science behind it.

A NEW HEALING FRAMEWORK

The path to seemingly miraculous spontaneous remissions heralds a new scientific framework for healing. The new framework began to emerge with the advent of quantum physics and Heisenberg's uncertainty principle. The game changer that turned conventional science on its head, the principle says the act of human observation itself has a profound influence on reality. What we assume to be reality is affected and altered through observation. Further, it means that what we see is what we intend to see. What we see is what we believe we'll see. The implications of this principle shatter the very foundation on which our current model of medicine is built.

---

[239] Ibid.

Anyone who has worked in medicine for any length of time has seen spontaneous remissions and recoveries that cannot be explained by medical science. That is because we are looking for explanations within a narrow linear framework that has accomplished remarkable things; however, it is too limited to explain spontaneous remissions, or what we refer to as miracles. The current framework that physicians use for solutions is confined to the physical body and assumes the presence of an external invader, a pathogen, or a germ. But as cellular biologist Dr. Bruce Lipton expressed it, "Their healing abilities are hobbled by an archaic medical education founded on a Newtonian matter-only universe." He continues, "Unfortunately, that worldview is outdated and became inadequate with the arrival of the quantum revolution nearly eighty years ago."

Werner Heisenberg's uncertainty principle was a pivotal point in that revolution. His discovery showed us that the world that seems solid isn't solid at all. It is made of subatomic particles, little packets of energy that can't be measured or understood as separate parts. Also, these particles seem to take a particular shape if someone observes them. They "freeze into matter." Accordingly, many researchers began to reach the logical conclusion that consciousness creates reality.

Way out of the realm of Newtonian science, which was about a world of separate objects that we could see and touch and had an objective measureable existence without us,[240] the new world of the quantum ushered in a world that resembled the world of mystics. It's a world where particles at one time connected and remain connected instantly—communicate faster than the speed of light—across huge distances and over time.

As the new quantum framework continues to take shape, we have a better understanding of how healing can occur and why some cultures can heal instantly. Take, for example, the true story of Roy Martina,

---

[240] Newtonian science is an approach that looks at the world in separate parts; scientists likened the approach to a clock, or a "clockwork universe." Eventually, it was thought that by studying all the parts we would know all there is to know about medicine and curing people.

a doctor and a karate champion, who was at a party when a friend attacked him from behind as a joke. He reacted based on his training and instinctively put the man in a karate hold, accidentally breaking his friend's finger. Martina had heard that Aboriginals were able to heal broken bones almost instantly. Says Martina, "We thought [that] if they can do it, we can do it. So we 'tuned into' the aboriginal field … and sent energy to the broken hand. A couple of days later, my friend was back playing volleyball … X-rays showed no trace of a fracture."[241]

The Foundation for the New Healing Framework

New scientific discoveries that have been presented in earlier chapters begin to create a new healing framework and are summarized here:

- Our minds, bodies, and spirits are interconnected and integrated in such a profound way that to continue to think of healing only on the physical level with drugs and surgery is not only very superficial but it misses the mark. Healing needs to take place on all three levels: the physical, the mental, and the energetic.

- Fluctuations of thought create emotional energies that trigger biochemical molecules of emotion throughout the body. The energy fluctuations directly influence how neuropeptides, or protein molecules, shape our physiology. This energetic level, shaped by our thoughts and emotions, is the most important level of healing because everything takes shape energetically before it manifests physically.

---

[241] The editors of *Ode*. "The Amazing Promise of the Zero Point Field." *Ode*. The Old Publishing Company, November, 2003,

- Feelings and emotions are vitally important as energy forms; in fact, we now know that they have a profound effect on our own health *and* on the world around us. In the past science didn't give them any credence at all. In medicine, there still is no place (theoretical premise) for them, but you can select a physician or nurse practitioner who has the insight to know they matter.

- The space between us, in, and around us is not empty at all but is teeming with energetic fluctuations and information ... a matrix of energy that Nobel Prize winner Max Planck[242] called the matrix of all matter that connects all things and is the source of all things. Some scientists like Stephen Hawking call it the mind of God. Others call it the unified field, the quantum hologram, because it has been described as having holographic characteristics. (We will take a closer look at these characteristics in the next chapter).

- Key aspects of this quantum hologram are as follows:

  o   It carries information.
  o   It resonates with things like itself, things—people, music, places—that are on the same frequency, which means it responds to things we do, think and feel in like manner.

---

[242]   Max Planck is considered the father of quantum physics.

o It is non-local and can communicate (carry information in the form of thoughts and feelings) at a distance. In classical physics, the principle of locality has always prevailed, meaning it was thought that an object is influenced directly and only by its immediate surroundings. We now know that is not the case.

o It is holographic, meaning any one part contains the whole. In other words, nature has structured itself in the same way as a classic hologram!

Once we understand how this quantum hologram, the source of all that is, works, it allows us to create the events of our lives rather than feeling helpless about things like succumbing to disease. When we create the feeling of what we want—in other words, capture the feeling of how you would feel if you were healed—those feelings will literally rearrange the quantum hologram to create the thing we want, the thing we're feeling. Your mind and body are like an energetic mirror in that they create what you resonate with so that we must become the thing we are feeling, the thing we choose to experience.

• By virtue of this energy field, we're all interconnected; we are connected to others in a very real scientific sense. Our feeling of separation is not real. In other words, if others begin to think of you as healthy, begin to pray for you, send caring and compassionate feelings to you, they will greatly assist you in your healing. They may even heal you on the spot.

Remember that Ramachandran's work with mirror neurons has shown that when we anesthetize the skin in the arm, we feel touched when we see another being touched. His conclusion is that our skin is literally the only thing that separates us. Because of this unified energy field, telepathy, clairvoyance, and prescience[243] operate constantly because your thoughts are connected to all thoughts.

The way we think, the energetic frequencies created by our thoughts and feelings and their energetic signatures, is always being communicated to others. When we are consciously shaping them, we are creating on purpose, creating intentionally. When we're unaware of how we're feeling, we are still creating; it's just that we're not doing it consciously. We're creating by default. Consciously or unconsciously, we're still creating the electromagnetic effects of our feelings and emotions. Whatever you believe—in other words, whatever you are holding in mind—creates an energy pattern that is palpable to you and constantly being communicated to others.

- Meditation, or entering the realm beyond the mind, has profound healing power. Studies demonstrate the benefits of meditation in healing many chronic conditions and diseases—including hypertension, pain, and migraines—and is a key element in reversing heart disease, slowing aging. Meditation creates "the opposite of the physiological changes that occur during the stress response," including a decrease in oxygen consumption, heart rate, respiratory rate, and blood pressure and an increase in the intensity of alpha, theta, and delta brain waves.

---

243 Telepathy means transmitting information from one person to another without using any of the known sensory channels; clairvoyance means the supernatural power to see objects or actions removed from natural space-time; prescience means knowing something before it takes place.

REPATTERNING YOUR BEHAVIOR

As explained in prior chapters, your healing may take some releasing of old beliefs and patterns that are no longer working for you. This is why positive thinking often doesn't work. Friends and colleagues will say, "So-and-so was such a positive person; I can't believe she got cancer!" A person can be outwardly positive and seem happy yet unconsciously harbor internal conflict and turmoil, sadness, guilt, and fear. It is ultimately important that a person feels good and experiences peace inside to create healing and healthy molecules of emotion.

As you learn to become aware of your inner experience, of how you feel and monitor your thoughts on a regular basis, you will see how your thoughts generate the emotions you feel. This may require a daily, even hourly, practice of looking within and asking, "Am I feeling good, happy, hopeful, and healthy? Am I upset or feeling better? Am I still pondering the same problem I was wrestling with a month ago?" If you are, then there's a good chance that you're stuck on automatic pilot and old habits and compulsions in your unconscious are having their way with you! You can be sick and feel hopeful and optimistic or pessimistic and hopeless.

> The mind is so powerful that whatever we are holding in it, whatever beliefs, repetitive thought patterns we habitually hold on to, tend to manifest.

The mind is so powerful that whatever we are holding in it, whatever beliefs, repetitive thought patterns we habitually hold on to, tend to manifest. In other words, our bodies are affected by whatever we are holding in our minds. It is often, however, as pointed out in other chapters, not in our conscious minds. The source of illness is often unconscious guilt, aggravated by suppressed emotions, a consequence of pain and suffering.

Once you become aware of your thought patterns and feelings, you can begin the inner work of dropping habitual compulsions or tendencies—which will dislodge the negative thought patterns that are programmed in you from an earlier time, like software. *You must change the software.* This is true even if you don't yet see what the problems are. If you want to heal, you must be willing to let go of the attitude or habitual patterns of thought that created the dis-ease, because disease is an expression of your attitude and habitual way of looking at things.[244]

Through increased emotional awareness, watching your emotional reactions and gaining an awareness of them and why you have them—although knowing *why* isn't necessary—you will create a gap or a space in your emotional reactions to situations that will allow you to respond in new, more positive way. If someone accuses you of something, ignores you, or trivializes what you say, pause and watch your reaction. Feel what it's doing to your body. Do you feel heat? Do you feel queasy in your solar plexus? Are you sweaty?

> Releasing negative lower frequencies, energy fields in which disease can grow, will give you access to positive higher frequencies, energy fields in which disease can heal.

As you watch your buttons being pushed, you'll see why it is that you have reacted in this way and begin to change it. As you do, new emotions and feelings will begin to generate energy patterns of higher frequencies. Releasing negative lower frequencies, energy fields in which disease can grow, will give you access to positive higher frequencies, energy fields in which disease can heal.[245]

REMEMBER, IT'S ALL ABOUT ENERGY

As emphasized in earlier chapters, healing is an emotional journey, which is all about energy in motion. This energetic level is the most important healing level because everything takes form here first.

---

[244] David Hawkins MD, PhD *Healing and Recovery.* Veritas Publishing, Sedona, Arizona, 2009, 52.

[245] Ibid, 135.

To sum up the energy context of healing:

- The quantum physicists discovered that atoms are made up of invisible tornado-like vortexes of energy, constantly spinning and vibrating.[246]
- We all have a characteristic vibration, a frequency at which we vibrate, which our thoughts and emotions are creating. Our energy fields reflect our internal feelings, the degree of our self-love, inner peace, self-esteem, and integrity.
- Each atom we're made of is like a spinning top that radiates energy. Assemblies of atoms collectively radiate their own identifying energy patterns.
- Every material structure in the universe has a signature energy vortex radiating a unique signature energy, just as we do.
- As we go more and more deeply within, we move toward our center, a "singularity," wherein lies our infinite power to create, to heal.

> Whatever you believe, whatever you're holding in mind, creates an energy pattern that is palpable to you and is constantly being communicated to others.

The energetic level takes form and precedes all that is experienced on a physical level. This has been demonstrated by the research of Dr. Valerie Hunt, who recorded brain waves, blood pressure changes, galvanic skin responses,[247] heartbeat, and muscle contractions of subjects while others were observing changes in the patients' auras, or energy

---

[246] Bruce Lipton. *Biology of Belief.* Hay House Publishers, India. June 2013, 37, 70.

[247] Galvanic skin response means fluctuations in the skin's electrical resistance, often associated with emotional states.

fields. Hunt's research showed that the changes occurred in the subjects' energy fields well before they showed up in any of the physical indicators being measured.[248]

Hunt's research has a precedent. Earlier research on seeds and salamanders has shown that baby seeds and salamanders possess light fields around them in the shape of a full-grown entity. The seed has the light field of a full-grown plant, the salamander of a full-grown fish. In other words, they possess the energy blueprint of fully grown adults when they are babies. In the same way, researchers believe that we humans possess such an energy blueprint.[249]

So once again, how does disease develop? It begins to take form as our repetitive patterns of behavior form energy patterns that encumber the energetic life force flowing through us with clouds of negativity. These energy patterns always precede disease states. Some clinicians have spoken out about their frustrations of treating patients and watching them be treated for one symptom, only for another to appear soon afterward because the energy patterns that are creating the dis-ease are still operating.[250]

Once it becomes clear to you how this biomolecular communication network operates, you will begin to be careful about allowing yourself to think depressing thoughts or harboring anger for too long.

Once it becomes clear to you how this biomolecular communication network operates, you will begin to be very careful about allowing yourself to think depressing thoughts or harboring anger for too long.

---

248 Valerie V. Hunt, PhD. *Infinite Mind: The Science of Human Vibrations of Consciousness.* Malibu Publishing Company, 1996.

249 The Editors of *Ode.* "The Amazing Promises of the Zero Point Field." Ode Publishing Company, November 2003, 45.

250 Conversations with Bill Bauman, PhD, David Hawkins, MD, PhD.

MANAGING YOUR ENERGY IS A MUST

Besides the physical exam you get from a physician or a nurse practitioner, you can learn to do an energy reading on yourself that identifies your fears, deeply rooted insecurities, emotional stressors, and personal traumas. Just be on the lookout for situations that generate discomfort. The greater the discomfort, the more energy you have stored up in old habits of thoughts and fears. By observing what you are thinking and how you feel, you will learn to recognize where you are "leaking" energy/power—in other words, when you feel drained and when you are investing your energy in the wrong place. And you can learn to restore it and manage your energy toward healthier states and healing.

Our bodies also have an energy anatomy.[251] Energy resides at the core of all matter, including us humans. As electromagnetic energy fields, the ways in which we use our life energy matters a great deal. Whether we choose to experience resentment and fear or happiness, joy, and love makes a big difference energetically.

We have energy centers up and down our bodies. Energy travels throughout the body in pathways called meridians. When we entertain negative thoughts, emotionally resisting people and situations that come into our lives, we are hindering the energetic flow of our electromagnetic fields. Repeated patterns of resistance create dis-ease.

Energy fields dominated by fear, anger, and guilt—what we can call negative emotions—will deplete your energy. Habitual disruptions of the energy flow brings dis-ease or some form of impairment on the physical level. An acute emotional disruption can bring it on rather quickly.

Repeated patterns of resistance—resisting the emotions or the natural flow of energy through your body—create disease. Blaming, complaining, reacting, impatience, excessive storytelling about your problems or ailments or what's wrong are all forms of mental resistance

---

[251] Carolyn M. Myss, PhD. *Anatomy of the Spirit.* Three Rivers Press, 1996.

to whatever is happening. The resistance is physical too because the mind and body are connected. Your muscles tighten and you feel stressed and tense. Excessive eating, drinking, and shopping to cover up your feelings are more obvious forms of resistance that won't facilitate your healing.

> Repeated patterns of resistance create disease. Resistance creates power leaks. Power leaks create disease.

Resistance creates power leaks. Power leaks create disease. You can learn to recognize when energy is leaving your body, recognize when you have a "power leak." Marta is a good example. From a very well-to-do family, with a cheerleader smile, she attended the best schools. Her older sister is a Harvard-educated physician and in a successful marriage. Marta didn't do well in her relationships with men; and although she was well educated, her career wasn't as illustrious as her sister's, or even as illustrious as her family would've liked.

Marta successfully lived through a diagnosis of breast cancer. Now the cancer has returned. She has stage III colon cancer. Colon cancer affects the third energy center, or chakra, the center having to do with self-responsibility and self-esteem issues. A lack of self-esteem, feeling bad about her life situation, created major power leaks in that energy center.

The lesson of the third chakra or energy center is about self-love and self-respect. It can become about survival intuition, which we tend to disregard when our self-esteem is low. This chakra houses the solar plexus, which warns of danger and negative action or energy coming to you.

Medical intuitive Dr. Carolyn Myss has brought to light extraordinary knowledge of our energy anatomy and how it works. In talking about the characteristics of this energy center, Myss reports that she has often seen depression develop in people who break promises to themselves because of the lack of self-respect that results. Issues concerning self-responsibility, caring for oneself and others, self-esteem, fear of rejection, and oversensitivity to criticism eventually manifest as ailments in the abdomen, stomach, upper intestines, liver, gallbladder, kidney, pancreas, adrenal glands, spleen, and middle spine. Myss has found that arthritis, anorexia, and bulimia often relate to third chakra issues as well.[252]

The third chakra demands that we respect ourselves and the guidance we receive from our intuition. Referred to as the emotional body, it's the area through which emotions located in a person's energy field, such as fear and anger, enter the body. Marta's anger at herself for not keeping up with her sister—personally or professionally—created deep resentment in this energy center.

Many of us, like Marta, progressively give away or "leak" the power of our energy fields into what we perceive as external sources of power—people, things, or situations that we believe will validate who we are, that will make us feel worthy and important. Looking for power in all the wrong places—in a world that is actually powerless and only has the power we endow it with—will create problems in this energy center.

By reclaiming the power of our thoughts and emotions, the thoughts that we repeatedly hold, our beliefs, we can create the healing we want. Regardless of what her sister's life is about, Marta could choose to learn to feel a deep satisfaction in herself and her own circumstances or to make plans to shape them in a way that would be more satisfying, give her hope, and stop the energy drain. If she could capture these feelings and hold on to them every day, several times a day, her energetic integrity would be restored and she would be healed before long. In fact, if she could become happy and enthused about her life, her heart-based feelings and emotions would change the electrical energy fields in her heart and produce quantum healing effects throughout her body.

---

[252] Carolyn M. Myss, PhD. *Anatomy of the Spirit.* Three Rivers Press, 1996.

EVEN YOUR DNA CAN BE HEALED

The world is full of people who believe that bad genes are a curse that cannot be overcome and that one day their genes will turn on them. Perhaps the biggest game changer of all is the discovery that if you change your electromagnetic energy field, you change the atoms; if you change the atoms, you change the molecules and even the DNA. DNA is not immutable, as we have always thought.[253] We have been taught that we're all subservient to our genes. Angelina Jolie's recent example garnered national headlines. Because her mother died of breast cancer at the age of fifty-six and Angelina found out she was carrying a "faulty" BRCA1 gene, which is thought to sharply increase the risk of developing breast and ovarian cancer, she decided to have a double mastectomy as a preventative measure.

Yet it has recently been discovered that the holy grail of DNA is not etched in stone. The age-old science that our genes are destiny has been resoundingly refuted by cellular biologist Bruce Lipton and Harvard Mind-Body Institute founder Herb Benson, MD. Lipton's discoveries have shown that science got it wrong, paving the way for a significant paradigm shift in science and biology. This discovery has changed Lipton's life forever, and it can change ours. According to Lipton, belief is the ultimate arbiter. If Angelina or anyone else believes the faulty gene will cause cancer, then it probably will, says Lipton.

Lipton's groundbreaking discovery set into motion amazing implications for medical science. He discovered that you can remove the nucleus and its DNA from a cell and the cell continues to work normally. We have always thought the nucleus is the main part—the central aspect or the "brain" of a cell's functioning. But Lipton discovered it's not the cell's brain at all. In fact, the cell is intelligent without its genes. Actually, Lipton found that DNA functions as the "reproductive gonads" of the cell. Without DNA, the cell cannot reproduce.

---

[253] Sue McGreevey. "Mind-Body Genomics." *Harvard Medical School News.* May 1, 2013 (study published in the open access journal *PLOS ONE*, May 1, 2013).

The DNA of a cell works like a constructing blueprint for the cell. The DNA is inside the chromosome, covered by regulating proteins. Stored in an inactive state, it is not working as a functioning part of the cell most of the time.

CELL MEMBRANE, CELL'S BRAIN

The kingpin in the picture seems to be the cell membrane. In Lipton's words, "The genes do not program the cell! The cell membrane is a structural and functional equivalent of a silicon chip." An Australian research group confirmed this in 1997.[254] Silicon chips are at the heart of any electronic device. They are able to carry electrical current and play a part in the electrical operation of the device.

If you destroy the cell membrane, the cell dies. That's why the cell membrane is Lipton's candidate for the brain of the cell. Most importantly, the cell membrane has the job of interacting with the environment. It is aware of its environment and sets in motion appropriate responses to environmental signals. Says Lipton, "The nucleus of the cell is simply a memory disk, a hard drive that contains the DNA programs that encode the production of proteins. We can edit the data that goes into our biocomputers just as we choose the words we type!"

> The energetic fluctuations in your cell membrane, or the cell's environment, meaning your beliefs, your emotions, your behavior, create the energetic vibrational blueprint that becomes your physical body.

The energetic fluctuations in your cell membrane, or the cell's environment, meaning your beliefs, your emotions, your behavior, create the energetic vibrational blueprint that becomes your physical body. This is an example of how science has progressed far beyond Newtonian science, into

---

[254] Bruce Lipton, PhD. *The Biology of Belief,* Hay House, 2007, 61.

the realm of energy and a new paradigm that tells us that the world we see is a world of effects. This new approach ushers us into a vital aspect of healing: to heal, you must raise the vibration of your electromagnetic energy field, and when you do, you ignite the healing process at the deepest level, the level of the cell membrane.

A new paradigm that will empower each of us is needed, one that encourages us to take a more active role in realizing our own power to heal, in managing and taking charge of our health. The science is here to back us up, and in many ways, the new paradigm is already emerging. In addition, it's the most natural thing in the world. Mainstream medicine's approach is inside out: an external invader, or a germ, causes the problem. When the real issue, as Lipton says, actually is this: what's being created in the cell's internal environment?

IN A NUTSHELL

I. **We have to begin with the X factor.** This means that the first vital step in self-healing is that *you must believe* it can be done. Belief is a critical factor. Think about how you feel when you hear these miracles of healing. Do they sound way out? Or do you see yourself trying them and think, *I could do that?* If you want to heal (and you must *want* to heal), you will have to have an open mind and let go of what you think are "the facts" of your illness. Avoid well-meaning people who want to tell you about all the latest statistics about your illness, about what might happen. Tune them right out!

Read about the successful healings of others and do not be overly concerned with all the scientific literature that says the statistics are against you. What is considered science today will change tomorrow, and your own body's intelligence is a much better barometer of how you're doing. Medical evidence is constantly changing, and there are always cases that defy statistics and beat the odds.

As a nurse, I can tell you that many situations occur on a regular basis where all the patient's "numbers" or indicators looked great and the person died anyway. The opposite is also very true: many times, we see patients whose vital signs and lab tests look grim and the patient recovers easily, despite "expert" predictions. So you must believe you can heal and make sure you have a physician or other clinician that deeply believes in your recovery.

If you cannot convince yourself completely, then at least be open to the possibility that healing comes from within and disease can be quelled from within.

Also know that there is no order of difficulty, no matter how serious the problem may sound. Understand that your body's functioning is orchestrated by your mind. Illness is a result of what you are holding in mind. The unconscious mind is usually the culprit because your unconscious mind is the result of habitual thinking and programming. You can learn to recognize the behaviors and the consequences of your unconscious mind, how they come about, and how not to give in to them. Ask yourself, "Do I want to be healed? Do I believe I can be healed? Do my thoughts and actions reflect that intention? If not, can I at least have an open mind about it?"

II. **Take the view that your illness is on your side.** Know that your body is doing what it's supposed to do to help you see that a change is needed. Have a willingness to accept whatever is being expressed on the physical level with an understanding that something in you is coming up to be healed.

Your illness is an indicator. Your body's way of helping you is to bring your attention to whatever it is that is coming up to be healed and be grateful that your body has this capacity. We actually *want* to be able to bring up whatever it is that needs to come up, so the illness is a sign of progress, not a falling back.

All illness is merely our consciousness calling attention to something that needs to be looked at, something we are feeling fearful or guilty or upset about. It may not be conscious. If the feelings are vaguely negative, you know it's something lodged in your unconscious, something trying to come up to be healed.

Illness means there is a belief system that we are holding that has to be let go of and cancelled—something that has to be forgiven, something within us that has to be loved. So be thankful it's been brought to our attention. Now we can ask the following:

a) What is it trying to tell me?
b) What is it that I'm supposed to learn?
c) What is the gift in it?

The illness is not you so don't identify with it. You do not have to accept illness as a permanent condition. Your mantra: you have the power to heal.

III. **Begin to be aware of your emotions.** Remember that organs weep the tears the eyes refuse to shed. Healing is an emotional journey—learn to monitor your emotions and release those that are toxic—deep anger, resentment, depression—understanding that repeated resistance to them creates disease. *Feel them and then let them go.* Listen to your body and put yourself first (forgiving yourself and self-nurturing); ask your body what it needs, what it would like. Several prominent scientists, like David Hawkins, MD, PhD, have commented that deep resentment and unresolved guilt are at the heart of most cancers.

IV. **Intend to heal. Focus on things you like, things that make you feel good, give you energy, and help you heal, not on your illness.** As Hawkins says repeatedly, you can't be sick unless you're holding it in your mind.

If you're truly sick, you probably think this sounds crazy. You're weak and nothing tastes good. Maybe you're nauseated and depressed. And there's somebody telling you that you have the power in you to heal, that you can heal quickly, that you have energy to spare, and that every cell in your body wants to heal.

So you can begin by thinking of something to make you happy, to make you feel good. Maybe hearing your favorite song or getting something to eat will help you feel better, even if it's only lemon sherbet! But the important thing is to ignore, meaning *take your attention away from,* the present reality of your illness.

Refuse attention to your sickness. You have to want to look away from your sickness. Distract yourself from your sickness and tune into the wholeness you're becoming, the wholeness *underneath* your illness.

If your intention is to heal, you will seek out situations and people that feel good to you—calming, peaceful, soothing. Intentions and expectations create an energetic searchlight that will look for people and situations. Your expectations will raise the frequency of vibrations of your electromagnetic energy field. Your "sickness" reality doesn't mean as much as your vibrational reality.

Learn to monitor your thoughts and watch how they make you feel. Especially watch what your self-talk is like. Are you thinking self-defeating thoughts like, *I'll never get better* or are you thinking vital thoughts like, *I'm doing better each day; I'm on my way to a full recovery*? Positive expectations of healing in your thought patterns are vital to your recovery.

Words of caution: All the people around you, maybe even those caring for you, may give you all the statistics, all the depressing "scientific details." Listen with half an ear; tell yourself that you will beat those odds easily. Remember Sam's story in chapter 5, when he was forced to take his mind off his illness to navigate the boat in the storm? When it was all over, his flu had disappeared.

V. **Don't identify with your illness.** The example of Stacey's healing in chapter V, "Anything Can Be Healed" makes this point clearly. She said to herself, "This illness is not me, and it will go the same way it came!" And it did. Don't identify means don't claim it as a part of you. Don't feel it as though it is you or a major part of you. Don't invest your energy in it. Let go of any tendency to be preoccupied with it. When you identify with something, you make it more powerful by imbuing it with your energy. It becomes an energetic part of you. Tell yourself, as Stacey did, "This illness is not me, and it will go the same way it came."

VI. **Understand that healing takes place on three levels: (1) the energetic, (2) the mental, and (3) the physical.** The lack of vital energy flow creates diseases. If these levels are not aligned, disease is created. The energetic forms first, as a blueprint. As an example, if the "eyes" of the energy body— are resisting something, there is something you don't wish to see or accept—your "energetic eyes," will not be in sync with the eyes of your physical body, and you will have problems with your eyes.

As your awareness increases, you will see that your disease has arisen from splitting the energy between your innermost instincts—self-preservation and fear-based limitations and becoming the limitless being that you are. As your attitudes, awareness, and understanding shift, you will radiate higher frequencies and your energy body will change and begin to create new healing energies.

VII. **Create a positive energy spiral, with feeling good as your goal. You must become the vibrational equivalent of what you're asking for, your healing.** Begin your day with feelings of gratitude. Notice how your body feels when you express gratitude. Even if you're in the throes of an illness, find something to be thankful for. Maybe all you can come up with is the weather—giving thanks for a sunny day—or someone's support. But that's a good start. "The key that explains how energy heals, how mind becomes matter, and how we can create our own reality is the emotions," says Dr. Candace Pert, former head of molecular biology at NIH.

Dr. Pert, who studied brain biochemistry at NIH, explained that emotions are energetic signals that are hardwired to communicate with the chemical and electrical makeup of every single cell in your body. "When you change the electrical state, you change your inner world, and in turn this affects your outer reality," states Pert. "We're not just little hunks of meat. We're vibrating like a tuning fork—we send out a vibration to other people. We broadcast and receive."

Our emotions orchestrate the energetic interactions among all our organs and systems to bring about healing. To create a healing energy spiral, think of things that evoke positive emotions. There is a vibrational currency for money, and there is a vibrational currency for healing. Every thought you think is causing a vibration to be created. If you're disappointed in your state of health, as you begin to feel that disappointment, you can learn to reframe it to feel hope.

- First thing in the morning, begin by playing your favorite song.
- Spend time in quiet with an intention to communicate with your inner essence, your source.
- Make something for lunch that is healthy and that you love.

Engage the energy of your heart. Your heart's electromagnetic energy field is a lot stronger than your brain's. Find something many times a day to engage the energy of your heart: Express gratitude. Let go. Forgive. Surrender. Greg Bradden traveled to many foreign lands and talked to indigenous people chanting and meditating. To all of them he asked repeatedly, "What do you feel inside?"

- The response he got: the feeling is the prayer. In other words, you chant, you meditate, you go beyond the mind to reach for the energy of the source; changing your inner emotional experience to engage your heart, changing how you feel inside to an inner feeling of deep peace, is essential to healing.
- Capture the feeling of calm, of peace and happiness in your heart. Align yourself with the energies of your inner essence, your source.

VIII. Capture the feeling of already being healed or remembered wellness. Use your imagination to feel as though you would if you were completely healed, just like the trained practitioners did in the medicine-less hospital in Beijing, when they chanted WaSa' around the bed of the woman healed of the bladder tumor. Rehearse in your mind scenes and situations where you are celebrating your remarkable healing. Picture your physician telling you that she's never seen anything like it—you healed so quickly!

Keep in mind that there is a vibrational precursor to everything that's physical. Everything is a vibrational reality before it manifests; your energetic reality precedes all that is experienced at a physical level.

IX. Meditate, or "move beyond the mind," daily for at least ten minutes. Meditation is extremely helpful to healing. Probably more than any other technique, meditation, expanding your awareness by quieting the mind and connecting with your inner guidance, can help you heal and can accomplish anything else you wish for, with much greater ease than all our perceptions and rituals.

When you meditate, you bypass thoughts of limitation such as "I have troubles; I am sick." When you are able to quiet the mind, you will see your infinite nature. You will experience the energy of your source. The deeper you go, the more you will experience the pure healing energy that is soothing. The deeper you go, the better the feeling is.

You don't have to meditate according to any formal instruction. Sitting in a relaxed, quiet place in a comfortable position and focusing on your breathing or thinking of one word or phrase and continuously repeating it so that other thoughts drop away is all it takes. When I began to meditate, I did it for only five minutes a day because it was difficult for me to sit still! It gradually became easier. Eventually, you get to a point where you enjoy it; it draws you in. (For step-by-step instructions see Herb Benson's *Timeless Healing*, page 52.)

The threshold at hand in medicine seems to be the crossing of the threshold of the outer self to the inner, learning to look within to activate our own self-healing mechanisms. As David Servan Schreiber, MD, PhD, put it in *AntiCancer: a New Way of Life*, "In the conventional model, we turn over our health care to doctors. I hope it will change. As it stands now, they do very little to help your body do its part to fight the disease. They do not support the terrain; they only target the tumor. We need to know we can go further." Going further leads to entirely new possibilities of finding the healer within, and that journey ultimately leads us to see that that's where much of our power lies because we are living in a holographic universe.

XII

HEALING IN THE QUANTUM HOLOGRAM

Power Step: Become that which you desire to be. Live in that state; make it come alive in you.

There is one original, formless substance from which all things are made. In its original state, it permeates, penetrates, and fills the interspaces of the universe. A thought in this substance produces the thing that is imagined by the thought. A person can form things and can cause the thing he thinks about to be created.

—Wallace Wattles

Reality is merely an illusion, albeit a persistent one.

—Albert Einstein

What we see out there in the world is a projection of what is within us. Like a mirror, the holographic universe reflects back to us, through our senses, what we see. Before delving more deeply into what a hologram or a holographic universe actually *is*, a little warm-up is in order. One morning in a quaint little church in East Hampton, suddenly—in a flash—everything around me shifted into one continuous, vast two-dimensional space. People and objects with no clear boundaries all blended together into an immense flat surface, a surface with height and width only. It looked like a continuous mural. There was no depth. Depth came only when I focused on one aspect of it. My focus made

219

it "pop" forward into three dimensions. I was being shown how our perceptions, through our senses, bring something to life.

Our senses act as 3-D glasses. We create whatever we're focusing on with our senses. Settled into the peace and serenity I found in that little church, as I listened for guidance about my next career move, *whoosh!* Things zoomed into being as if my senses were powerful binoculars. First the priest and the altar popped into three dimensions as I gazed at them. When I stopped looking at them, they receded back into the flat, two dimensional background. When I focused on the organist, she and the organ burst forth in 3-D, just as the priest and the altar had. Something supernatural was happening. The force of the moment was unmistakable. I was so deeply moved down to my core that tears poured out of me for a long time. Fate had chosen to reveal something profound, a truth of some sort. At the time, I took it all to mean that I was receiving an answer to my career question.

My epiphany didn't *really* make sense until years later, when I read David Bohm's concept of a holographic universe. It was an aha moment, when things fell into place and a clear picture of what Bohm was saying shone brightly in my mind.

While our physical experience is dominated by hard objects that seem to be separate and have clear boundaries, this is far from the case. What physicists like Bohm and Wheeler and others have discovered is that at the quantum level, an ocean of waves of probability flow constantly. It is only when we observe and focus on something, like the priest and the altar, that the wave function collapses and we see solid, specific physical people and objects. In this way, we create through our senses; we bring things to life.

THE HOLOGRAM: OUR PRIMARY REALITY

What we focus on comes to life as a hologram does when light illuminates it. Bohm imagines the source[255] as "coherent light that illuminates the vast unlimited space of all that is unseen." He named this unlimited, unseen space the *implicate realm*. As it is illuminated, it gives rise to the physical world we see through our senses. Bohm called the world we see the *explicate realm*. According to Bohm, the universe is super-holistic and unified, very different from a universe of separate parts modeled after Newton's clockwork universe.[256] Bohm thought of our consciousness as an essential feature of the holomovement and our senses as the lenses through which we bring things into reality. When we see through the lenses of our senses, it's like wearing 3-D glasses in a movie theater.

In Bohm's view, *space defines matter*, not the other way around. He considers this holomovement to be our primary reality, "the implicate order", or the invisible substance from which the physical world arises. The seen comes from the unseen. Bohm is in good company. Several of the most prominent scientists of our time have also advanced the idea that a special energy exists, an "immense background of energy" that is one whole and unbroken movement. In fact, way before our time, Leibnitz, the discoverer of integral and differential calculus, also held the view that a metaphysical reality underlies and generates the material universe, the universe we see through our senses.[257]

---

[255] David Bohm. *Wholeness and the Implicate Order*. Routledge Classics. London, England, 2002.

[256] Newton's analogy for the universe, which he described mathematically, was a clock. Separate components make it tick.

[257] Leibnitz's philosophy. http://philosophos.org/philosophical_connections/profile_062.html

> "By the entity's [person's] thoughts, attitudes, and actions, transformational changes occur in the dense and subtle matter, which can produce a refined structure in the matter."
> —W. A Tiller

Dr. Tiller, prominent physicist from Stanford, agrees. Describing how humans can shape matter, Tiller says, "By the entity's [person's] thoughts, attitudes, and actions, transformational changes occur in the dense and subtle matter, which can produce a refined structure in the matter."[258] Tiller believes we've entered a stage in our evolution where we're heading in the direction of developing the capabilities that will enable us to manipulate space, time, and matter consciously.[259]

Ken Wilbur, who has been called the Einstein of consciousness, agrees. He says that this "immense background of energy" is the realm of the spirit and it is our primary reality: "The material realm, far from being the most fundamental, is the least fundamental; it has less being than life, which has less being than mind, which has less being than spirit."[260]

> What we believe, what we feel inside, makes an energetic imprint on this holomovement.

What we believe, what we feel inside, makes an energetic imprint on this holomovement. Because everything is vibration, changing this imprint by changing our beliefs and feelings can change our physical world. It's all about how we resonate with the holomovement and the energy frequencies of what we think, what we believe, what we feel. That's why all the mystics say of the reality we live, "As within, without." In other words, the beliefs and feelings inside us

258   W. A. Tiller. *Science and Human Transformation: Subtle Energies, Intentionality and Consciousness.* Pavior Publishing, 1997.
259   Ibid.
260   Ken Wilbur, editor. *Quantum Questions: Mystical Writings of the World's Great Physicists*, 2001.

determine what we focus on and what we perceive in the physical world. When two people look at the exact same objects or circumstances, they see very different things. From this perspective it is said, "When you change the way you look at things, the things you look at change." As we change our thoughts, feelings, emotions, we change matter. How? By impressing different energetic frequencies on the holomovement.

Bohm used the metaphor of the hologram, borrowing from holographic photography or three-dimensional photographs, to convey his idea of how we create or bring things to reality. Holographic photography relies on wave interference: energy wavelengths of differing frequencies "interfere" or combine with each other and create a pattern. Further, every point on the film is completely determined by the overall configuration of the interference patterns.[261] In other words, every part contains the whole.

> You define your external reality, not the other way around.

When it comes to our senses, what we perceive to be reality we bring to life in the hologram in the same way and every part of our lives contains the whole. We project our perspective, the energetic patterns of our thoughts, feelings, and beliefs in every aspect of the hologram. That's what led John Cabot Zinn to say, "Wherever you go, there you are." You define your external circumstances, not the other way around.

---

[261] To understand Bohm's idea, you must first understand a little about holograms. A hologram is a three-dimensional photograph made with the aid of a laser. To make a hologram, the object to be photographed must first be bathed in the light of a laser beam. Then a second laser beam is bounced off the reflective light of the first and the resulting interference pattern (the area where the two laser beams comingle) is captured on the film. When the film is developed, it looks like a meaningless swirl of light and dark lines, until another laser is shined on the film. Then a three-dimensional image of the original object appears.

> Our brains are holographic transmitters and receivers.

Many scientists now believe that our primary reality is in the unseen ocean of waves of varying frequencies.[262] Because mathematical proof exists, there is a consensus among theoretical physicists that the universe is holographic.[263] Bohm's view that the reality we see doesn't actually physically exist, and that reality is in fact a very sophisticated hologram, has received much scientific and experimental support. Leonard Susskind, theoretical physicist from Stanford; Andrew Newberg at the University of Pennsylvania; and Amit Gotswami, professor emeritus at the University of Oregon, are among the many other distinguished scientists that share this view.

Focusing on something collapses the wave function. In this way, our senses, through perception, make what is actually the two-dimensional reality of the universe come to life.[264] In the same way, imagination, if vivid enough, can bring the thing imagined to life. We have all learned to trust the evidence of the senses—what we see and feel and touch. But that's not the whole story.

WHAT HAPPENS IN ONE PART HAPPENS IN THE WHOLE

Like a hologram, anything contained in one part is contained in the whole. Shine a light on any part of it and the whole image will come to life. As it turns out, Bell's theorem gives us a great example of how

---

[262] David Bohm called this the implicate order. He described it as a deeper, more fundamental order of reality where space and time are no longer dominant factors determining the relationship between elements. Rather, an entirely sort of basic connection of deeper elements from which our ordinary notions of space and time are abstracted as forms derived from the deeper order.

[263] http://www.crystalinks.com/holographic.html

[264] Leonard Susskind, theoretical physicist at Stanford. "The Fabric of the Cosmos," with Brian Greene. NOVA.

the parts are contained in the whole. If you remember, Bell's theorem, discussed in the chapter on energy, tells us that when a particle was split and each half was sent sailing along to different corners of the city, and then the spin on one particle was shifted in the opposite direction, the other particle did exactly the same thing. It simultaneously followed suit. The second particle changed its spin to mirror what the other was doing, and it changed it *at the same time*! When a particle is split and sent off in different directions, then one particle is directed to spin left; the other particle spins right. It does exactly the same thing at the same time, even though it's many miles away.

Initially, scientists reasoned that somehow the particles were communicating. But after more study, scientists concluded that there was much more to it. In the holographic model, the particles communicate simultaneously *because they are connected at some deep fundamental level.* Further, they are connected in a holographic sense, meaning that what happens in one part happens in the whole. With a hologram, you shine a laser through one part and you see the whole image. The parts each contain the whole. If you alter one part, you affect the whole.

What does that mean in our day-to-day lives? If you change one aspect of your behavior, even a small aspect, everything in your life will change. The reason is that every part, every act, every thought pattern contains the whole. As an example, if you decide that you will be more forgiving of everyone, including yourself, you will see more and more forgiveness coming your way, in every aspect of your life. Generosity and giving work the same way. When you're generous to others, the universe is generous to you. When you give, you get. Because every part contains the whole, when you give, the universe gives back to you.

The hologram mirrors who you are. You impress yourself—your thoughts, beliefs, and feelings—on the hologram. What you create comes from within you. If you want to see what you have created, look around you. If you think life is unfair, the holographic universe will deliver unfair situations to you. If you believe you are fortunate, healed, favored, life will bring you more fortune, more healing, more favorable circumstances.

OUR BRAINS: HOLOGRAPHIC TRANSMITTERS AND RECEIVERS

Even though matter is mostly space,[265] we experience everything as though it were solid, including us. "Why is that?" many physicists asked. We all know that matter is much different from space. Yet the apparent difference comes from the rapid motion of the electrons in their orbits around the nucleus. The force fields created by the motion of the electrons give the appearance of the solidity of matter. The space is only empty in that it is devoid of massive particles, but it is filled with force fields of varying strengths.[266]

Again, the holographic explanation works. Our brains are holographic transmitters and receivers. The brain uses holographic principles to convert the frequencies it receives mathematically through the senses into the solid physical world.[267] As our beliefs change, so do the frequencies of our energy fields and the realities we construct through our senses.

> Our brains construct what seems to our senses to be concrete reality by interpreting frequencies from an unseen dimension, a hidden realm of primary reality energy patterns, carrying information that transcends time and space. The brain seems to be operating like a hologram, interpreting a holographic universe.

In the holographic domain of consciousness, frequencies are sorted out. Our minds and bodies seem to be constructed to cooperate with the holographic world we live in. Our neurons convert waves and frequencies into the images that make up our world. This means that our

---

[265] https://www.physicsforums.com/threads/is-matter-mostly-empty-space.509327/
[266] Ibid.
[267] Michael Talbot. The Holographic Universe. Harper Perennial; Reprint edition (May 6, 1992).

brains construct what seems to our senses to be concrete reality by interpreting frequencies from an unseen dimension, a hidden realm of primary reality energy patterns, carrying information that transcends time and space. The brain seems to be operating like a hologram, interpreting a holographic universe.[268]

HEALING IN THE HOLOMOVEMENT

When it comes to healing, the idea that treating a disease is really only addressing the symptom was a huge motivator for the work of Bohm and another of the world's most prominent scientists, Karl Pribram. Pribram, born in Austria and a neurophysiologist at Stanford University, predicted the holographic nature of perception and memory. These two scientific giants were the main architects of the great theory that the brain is a hologram enfolded in a holographic universe, a view that is drastically different from conventionally accepted ideas.[269]

Frustrated because existing theories couldn't explain any of the ideas encountered in quantum physics or questions related to the workings of the brain, Bohm and Pribram came up with the theory of a *neural hologram*, made by the interaction of waves in the cortex, the outermost layer of the brain, formed by the wave interactions of the world we see. All matter is composed of these interactions of the tiny particles that make up an atom (protons, neutrons, and electrons). Pribram and Bohm advanced this view, that the brain operates in a manner similar to a hologram, in accordance with quantum mathematical principles and the characteristics of wave patterns,[270] and it operates in a holographic universe.

The implications for healing are profound. If you think of everything existing as an ocean of waves of potential, vibrations of

[268] M. Ferguson. "Karl Pribram's Changing Reality in the Holographic Paradigm," New Science Library, Shambhala, Boston and London, 1985.

[269] Ibid.

[270] Ibid.

varying frequencies containing information—like radio or TV waves—enfolded in a two-dimensional surface, when you focus on something, you impress or, "I'm-press" your conception of yourself onto the ocean of potentiality, and collapse the wave function. In this way, you are actually creating physical reality.

Experiments originally performed by Dr. Masaro Emoto, author of the *New York Times* best seller *The Hidden Messages in Water*, offer a glimpse into how this works. As you read it, keep in mind that since the composition of the human body is 65 percent water, the same processes could take place in your body at the molecular level. Every cell in our bodies contains water.

Emoto's experiments showed that projecting positive emotional energy on to distilled water causes the molecules to rearrange their patterns. The opposite is true concerning negative energy, where the molecules became erratic and disorganized.

Dr. Emoto also performed an experiment with rice. He put an equal amount of white rice into two containers and labeled one "Thank you" and the other one "You fool." There was also a control container of the same, which had nothing written upon it and was kept to the side. He asked schoolchildren to say the words written on the containers, talking to the containers out loud. After thirty days, the "You fool" and the control had become black and rotten. The "Thank you" specimen remained white and largely unchanged. This experiment has been repeated many times, yielding the same results, with varying amounts of rotting. Positive thoughts and intentions consistently produced clear water and preserved rice, and the negative produced dark, discolored water and moldy black rice.

It's interesting that the control specimen, which is always ignored, also turns black. Perhaps this is a hint that ignoring people in our lives, or ignoring our own well-being in the absence of love for the self as well as others, is likely lowering our own energies and creating something in our bodies akin to the moldy rice!

Self-healing, then, can be accomplished by self-talk that is aimed at seeing yourself, feeing yourself, immersing yourself in *believing* yourself to be healthy and whole. Ten or twelve times a day, focus on this healed, healthy conception of yourself.

> Ten or twelve times a day, focus on this healed, healthy conception of yourself. Tell yourself you're thankful to be healed, even if the healing is not yet apparent. You're operating in the primary reality of the holomovement, impressing upon it the state you wish to create in the physical world.

Tell yourself you're thankful to be healed, even if the healing is not yet apparent. You're operating in the primary reality of the holomovement, impressing upon it the state you wish to create in the physical world.

CELEBRATE FIRST, BEFORE THE PARTY BEGINS

That's why all the mystics say to *act as if*, give thanks *first*, even if the thing you want hasn't shown up in your life yet. Celebrate first, even if things don't seem to be going your way. It's the impression on the holomovement you're changing. It can't tell the difference between what is "real" and what is from your vivid imagination.

When you occupy the desired state and express gratitude for it—"I am healed"—the holographic nature of the universe resonates with the high-frequency energies of gratitude and celebration and reflects these energies back to you. If we can so vividly *imagine* ourselves—in other words, feel *as* though we are healthy and well, so much so that we are *thankful* for it, we will resonate in the hologram, with energetic blueprints of healing.

If we are inspired with vitality when we see someone being healed of the same disease we have—since every part of this holographic world contains the whole, the energetic blueprint for anything and everything—we can heal too. Like the hundredth monkey principle, the energetic blueprint exists for us to inhabit.

GOING BEYOND THE SENSES—
BETTER FOR HEALING

When we go beyond the senses, through meditation or imagination or another way of getting into the "zone" beyond the mind, we begin to see *why* the "relaxation response" described by Herb Benson, MD, founder of the Harvard Mind-Body Institute, greatly helps us in healing. You don't have to worry about maintaining a particular focus or intention. You bypass thought altogether.

> Many scientists now believe that our primary reality is in the unseen ocean of waves of varying frequencies.

As you go more and more deeply within, beyond the external world you create with your senses, you connect directly with the implicate order, or the energy of your source. As you tap into the energy of your source, you are directing the light of your source toward healing and resonating with the healing frequencies that bring the energetic blueprints associated with healing to life in the hologram. As you rise higher and higher in consciousness,[271] healing becomes an easier, less effortful experience because you are more in alignment with the informational blueprints or higher energy frequencies that resonate with healing energies.

As you align with these higher energy frequencies and rise higher in consciousness, you see the world differently. Your beliefs, judgments, and thought patterns naturally change. Then your physical surroundings change to resonate with the new frequencies and your physical body changes too. It doesn't take effort. Different experiences are simply mirrored back to you as a reflection of your higher energy frequencies in the holographic field. If you want to live in a loving world, love yourself; then all the people in your world will change their "dance" to match that loving energy. If you want to live in a healthy world, heal yourself,

---

[271] Rising higher refers to higher energy frequencies.

minister healing words and actions to yourself, and healing energies will gather like a magnet around you to match the energy frequencies of your soothing, healing energy, energy created by your new thoughts and feelings.

ALIGNMENT WITH SOURCE

When you align yourself with the energy of your source, by adopting new thoughts and feelings of higher energy frequencies, either consciously shifting your thoughts and feelings or through meditation, and often both, you resonate with the high-energy frequencies encoded in our holographic universe. There you have access to an infinity of information contained in the energetic blueprints stored in the hologram. You connect to the high-frequency blueprints that give healing messages and guidance. When you align yourself repeatedly with source energy, the vital energy of the life force flows freely throughout your body and your senses resonate with high-frequency healing energies. Then constrictions or constraints in that energy flow are gradually or sometimes rapidly released, for you no longer resonate with them.

As our brains and the world we perceive combine to form an interference pattern that acts like a hologram, our senses bring the energetic blueprint to life. To reiterate, our act of focusing collapses the wave function in an ocean of probability waves, as our perception brings the object of our attention to life. Like donning 3-D glasses in a movie theater, the lenses of our senses bring the energetic patterns of our thoughts and feelings in the hologram into form. When you put 3-D glasses on, everything becomes three-dimensional. In the same way, our senses bring our energetic reality into a three-dimensional physical reality. When it comes to healing, focusing on ourselves as healthy and vital, imagining it, feeling as if it's already here, we can bring it into physical reality. We can manifest it.

If we believe in the image of ourselves as healthy and whole, whether we feel it, "see it", or imagine it with the help of a role model—someone who has been healed of the same illness—our consciousness will automatically express health and wholeness, for that's how the holographic universe works.

> What we "impress" upon our consciousness or our awareness will be created as if it were mirrored back to us. That's how the holographic universe works.

What we "impress" upon our consciousness or our awareness will be created as if it were mirrored back to us. When you shine the light of your consciousness on believing, seeing yourself as healed (as you would shine a light on a picture of a hologram to bring it to life), your healed image of yourself comes to life. Your consciousness will automatically express whatever you register upon it, whatever you think and feel. In other words, whatever you see and feel—what you *believe* to be the case.

Science is veering more and more in the direction of a nonmechanical reality. The universe is beginning to look more like a great thought than a great machine. To put the conclusion crudely, the stuff of the world is mind stuff. [272]

Of major importance here is the ability to *ignore the appearance of your illness;* ignore its present reality as best you can. A good story is told along these lines in *An Autobiography of a Yogi*. As Yogananda became known for his spiritual powers, his sister developed a severe strep throat. She asked him to come over and heal her throat. He put his hands on her throat and transmitted healing energies. He told her she would be fine in a little while. After Yogananda left, his sister went to the mirror to see how her throat looked. She panicked when she saw redness and inflammation, and in a little while, the infection reappeared full blast.

The mind stuff of our consciousness, which encompasses the energy field created by your thoughts and feelings, is projected onto the hologram. It can be likened to sensitive film. Whatever you impress upon it will be expressed—in the form of a motion picture if we're talking

---

[272] Sir James Jeans and Sir Arthur Stanley Eddington, in *An Autobiography of a Yogi,* Copyright 1993, Self-Realization Fellowship, 313–314.

about film, in the form of health or illness, if it's your consciousness. In its "virgin" state, it has an unlimited potential to record anything impressed on it. In the same way, we receive impressions; everything we see is "I-am-pressed" in our minds. What is impressed on the film or in our minds depends on what "picture" we focus on and how our senses perceive the day-to-day world we see. It is then expressed in our worlds.

In this context, if we "impress" messages of health, healing, happiness, and well-being—messages of wholeness—we can be healed. If we wake up each morning and during the day take the time to impress health on our awareness; *feel* ourselves to be healthy, happy, healed; feeling the way we would feel if the condition were removed, we can be healed.

Energy fields are decoded by our brains into a 3-D picture, giving the illusion of a three-dimensional physical world. In spite of its apparent material reality, the universe is a kind of 3-D projection and ultimately real in the same way as a hologram. In actuality, we are one with all that is; what we see is our own view; what we choose to see, our subjective focus, a projection in bas-relief, onto what is actually a continuous undifferentiated two-dimensional surface.

> The real power is in how we see things, what we choose to focus on.

If you want to heal, you can reach into the implicate order with your feelings and imagination—impressing upon the unseen energy of the universe—and imagine yourself healed without resistance. In other words, don't let yourself get hung up on how this is all happening. Our real power to heal is in how we see things, what we choose to focus (shine the light of our consciousness) on. No matter your condition, if you want to heal, choose to focus on health and *feeling* healed. That's what the hologram will mirror back to you; that's what the hologram will create.

This is a key reason that role models, coaches, videos of the thing you want to become are so important. This is the principle the AA approach to healing is based on. A sponsor is continuous living proof that the person with the addiction can be healed. He is joined at the hip, by design, with a living example of success that it can be done; that it *has* been done.

The world we see is one of our own making. Our brains do the processing like a big searchlight that brings to light whatever we focus on; our minds select the thoughts and images we use to interpret what we see. Edgar Mitchell, astronaut and founder of the Institute for Noetic Sciences, expresses his belief that once we realize who we are and how it is that we create our own reality, our power to heal—in fact, our power to do anything at all—is unlimited! According to Mitchell, we are omniscient, omnipotent, omnipresent.[273] Our brains act as a "phase gate,"[274] mathematically constructing aspects, *phases* of reality. It interprets what we see through the lens of our senses as *frequencies*—the way a radio or TV would—from an unseen dimension that is beyond both space and time. Matter is expressed by the quantum hologram itself.

Understanding that there is a more fundamental energetic reality that is invisible, that is not comprised of parts but an inseparable interconnectedness, is an understanding that can be vitally helpful in healing. In this dynamic way of seeing the world, there are no "material things," only energetic events. It is a scientific fact that all matter emits and reabsorbs "quanta," or packets of energy. That these emissions are coherent and carry information has been validated by MRIs.[275] Mitchel uses the example of a lighthouse to describe how this information is carried. From the lighthouse, when the fog lifts, we can see the light shimmering on the waves. If we could still the waves, we could see the information stored inside them.

In this light, the quantum hologram is actually a storage place for information that anyone can tune into at various frequencies, at any time. This is how telepathy, clairvoyance, and intuition can be readily

---

[273] Edgar Mitchel Lecture. "The Quantum Hologram and ESP." YouTube.

[274] A phase gate transmits information in holograms as a selective resonance. It occurs when two interpenetrating wave fields contain synchronized oscillations at the same frequency; it's what makes two alternating jump ropes appear to be one.

[275] Edgar Mitchel. Lecture. "The Quantum Hologram and ESP." YouTube.

understood. The world as a quantum hologram can be seen as a place where information is stored, and we can tune into it the way you would put a new disc into your computer.

Therefore, when your desire is to heal, your aim is to "tune into" this energy field of information, meaning put a new disc into the computer of your mind, insert *new beliefs that will help you to heal.* See only yourself as healed. Relax and allow yourself to become one with the energy of the image of yourself as healthy and healed. Resonate and become one with it. More than merely concentrating, let go of thoughts and allow yourself to feel as if you are healed. If you think, you think of pleasant things. A feeling of ease, of happiness, of well-being is your aim.

As information carriers, we all have a mass of shimmering energy in the background of our existence. According to physicist Erwin Lazlo, even the information in our memories isn't stored in our brains. It is "stockpiled" in the quantum hologram. Our brains are the rivers and processors that gain access to this information when we resonate with certain frequencies.[276]

Even if you feel sick, you can begin to let those thoughts go and begin to intentionally think of things that are pleasing, things that feel good, things that you felt when you were well. In fact, you can aim to capture the feeling you had when you were well. As you do, you are creating a new reality by resonating with new holographic information. Remember, your brain does not know the difference between what is actually happening now and the reality you're feeling because you remember it. It goes by what you're feeling energetically; it is resonating with and retrieving the information or memories stored in the quantum hologram. The brain retrieves old and new information in the same way. This quantum hologram is an ocean of information, a storage place that anyone can tune into.[277]

The "hologram wave flux" includes the flowing nature of what is, and also of that which ultimately takes form. In the well-known wave/

---

[276] The editors of Ode. *The Amazing Promises of the Zero Point Field.* Ode Publishing Company, November 2003, 45.

[277] Ibid.

particle duality of the quantum world, the holographic universe is a sea of waves. As we tune our consciousness into a focus on healing perceptions, feelings and thoughts which have wave function equivalents, their energetic frequencies or oscillations resonate with similar situations, sensations and people who reflect healing energies.[278]

ASPECT REPLICATED BELL'S EXPERIMENTS

Alain Aspect validated Bell's original work. Aspect's experiment demonstrated that the web of particles that composes our physical universe—what we might refer to as the "fabric of reality itself"—possesses what appears to be an undeniable holographic property---every part is contained in every aspect of the whole. Aspect's experiment revealed that a photon, a particle of light, could travel as a wave through two places at the same time, even if it could only be observed in one location. Aspect concluded, "A pair of entangled photons should be considered as a global, inseparable quantum system."

Aspect's finding offers compelling evidence that the universe is a hologram. His experiment is one of the most important of the twentieth century and will probably change the face of science forever. The implications of Aspect's findings are remarkable: by virtue of the holographic principle whereby every piece contains the whole, we are, or can be, literally "in touch" with almost any part of the world.

Holographically embedded information stored in one place in the seemingly empty space around us can have an effect on every cell in the body of someone miles and miles away. Distance doesn't make any difference. Because what happens in just a small fragment of the holographic energy interference pattern affects the entire structure simultaneously, there is a tremendous connectivity between all parts of the holographic universe.

---

[278] Erwin Laszlo, PhD. "Science and the Akashic Field." Inner Traditions. Rochester, Vermont, 2007, 115.

EXPERIMENTS WITH CLAIRVOYANTS REVEAL HOW THE HOLOGRAM WORKS

A scientist named Puthoff, who worked with the CIA at one time, conducted experiments with clairvoyants. Puthoff asked clairvoyants to describe locations that subjects visited, after showing them a map of where they were located. The clairvoyants were told nothing else at all about the locations. They were only shown where they were on the map. Their results were astoundingly accurate. The clairvoyants described the locations to a T.

Then Puthoff got bolder. He asked clairvoyants to describe *beforehand* the locations of places that the subjects intended to visit but had not yet arrived at. Once again, the clairvoyants knew nothing of the locations but were nonetheless astonishingly accurate, making it apparent that the information must have been available [in the hologram] before the events actually occurred.[279]

What does this have to do with healing? This is where the key healing revelation comes in: the information stored in the energy waves is accessible and recoverable through resonance. In other words, if you want to heal, your prevalent vibration must resonate with healing vibrations that are higher frequency, positive, healthy energies. The frequencies of the energy determine what information is retrieved.

Using the principle of resonance, we can actually increase the speed at which the energy fields of our bodies and minds vibrate, through entertaining higher frequency thoughts of gratitude and compassion, through celebrating all that we love, listening to music that we love, or being around uplifting people. We can access higher and even higher consciousness states through meditation and other activities like painting, dancing, praying, chanting—activities that allow us to go beyond the chatter of our minds.

---

[279] The editors of Ode. *The Amazing Promises of the Zero Point Field.* Ode International Publishing Company, November, 2003, 45.

The quantum hologram inspires wellness and healing in that infinite amounts of information are stored in a vast energetic sea and are always accessible—unaffected by the limits of time and space. The information to heal is always available to us, provided we resonate with it.

Here's a review the characteristics of the holographic universe and the new potential for healing it offers:

- A holographic—whole in every part—universe can explain such things as distant healing, healing through prayer at a distance, and spontaneous remissions because information blueprints are always available to heal in the sea of holographic energies.
- A holographic universe can explain archetypal experiences,[280] encounters with the collective unconscious, and other unusual phenomena experienced during altered states of consciousness. Current neurophysiological understanding of the brain is inadequate to explain these occurrences.
- A holographic universe explains paranormal and mystical experiences.
- Near-death experiences can be explained by a holographic universe, in that death is a shifting of a person's consciousness from one level of the hologram of reality, one energy level of information, to another.
- Synchronicity, the simultaneous occurrence of events that seem related but have no apparent causal connection, can be explained by the idea of a holographic universe and directly by Aspect's research. In fact, synchronicity tends to peak just prior to a new realization or insight.
- Telepathy, precognition, mystical feelings of oneness with the universe, and even psychokinesis, or moving things with your mind, can be explained through the holographic universe,

---

[280] Jung first described and used the term "archetypes." Archetypal experiences are those in which energy forms that are contained in the universal consciousness of humanity are recurring and experienced by most of us. Some archetypal experiences are of the helper, the victim, the saint, the sinner, and so forth.

essentially when you tune into or become one with the object, the person, or situation. For example, I have seen my own teacher, Bill Bauman, succeed, through telepathy, in locating a friend's daughter who had run away and was lost somewhere in the United States.

- A holographic universe can explain how so many memories and so much information can be stored in so little space (our brains can store billions of bits of information).[281]

- A holographic universe can also explain how we are able to recall and forget, how we are able to have a deep knowing of something, how we have déjà vu, how we have the ability to transfer new skills, how we have the ability to construct a world out there.

- It explains how we are able to have phantom limb sensations and how we are able to have photographic memories. In actuality, we are tuning into or retrieving information in the quantum hologram.

The fact that limitless amounts of information might be enfolded into the structure of the universe is an idea that has gained a great deal of support from many scientists, such as Rupert Sheldrake. Sheldrake has described how this holographic sea of information-carrying energy waves works. Whenever one person (or a member of any species) learns a new behavior, like a runner who breaks the four-minute-mile barrier, the energy field for the species changes.

Since Roger Bannister broke the four-minute mile record, several others have followed suit. If the behavior is repeated for long enough, it assumes "morphic resonance," meaning, through repetition, the pattern of breaking the four-minute mile develops memory and a greater probability of repeating itself, i.e., having others resonate with it. Through repetition, the patterns become increasingly probable,

---

281 Paul Reber. "What Is the Memory Capacity of the Human Brain?" Mind and Brain. Scientific American. May/June 2010. www.scientificamerican.com

increasingly available. They reside there, in the holographic field, available to the entire species.

Sheldrake calls this energetic pattern a "morphogenetic field," from *morph, form*, and *genesis* coming into being. The action of this field involves action at a distance in both space and time. Rather than form, or the material world we see, being determined by physical laws, the action of this information-carrying energy field depends on a particular energy frequency, a signature morphic resonance across time and space.

The implications of this are enormous. If morphic fields can propagate across space and time, current or past events can influence other events everywhere else. An example of this was demonstrated by Lyall Watson in what he calls the hundredth monkey principle.[282] Watson found that after a group of monkeys learned a new behavior, suddenly other monkeys on other islands with no possible "normal" means of communication learned that behavior too.

NEW ENERGY FOOTPRINTS IN HEALING

Healing works the same way. As more and more people learn to tap into their own power to heal, tap into new self-healing approaches, as more and more people break through the barrier of what is currently considered to be acceptable in the realm of medical treatments, new energetic "footprints" will pave the way to powerful self-healing. Just like the monkeys or Roger Bannister's breaking the four-minute mile barrier, many, many others will follow suit.

Carl Jung's earlier discoveries in relation to this field bear a striking resemblance to Sheldrake's in that both men observed the repetition of energy patterns in the unified field, even though Jung's observations led to his identification of archetypes in the field: accumulated "prototype" energy patterns representing humanity's well-known paths: the victim,

---

[282] Lyall Watson. *Lifetide: The Biology of the Unconscious.* Sceptre, 1987.

the martyr, the blessed one, and the hero, to name a few. Sheldrake's energy patterns were about newly tread groundbreaking signature paths.

Jung's "synchronicity" principle reveals his belief in the connections between the subjective and the material world, connections that can be explained in the context of a holographic universe. Jung coined the term "synchronicity", meaning a connection necessarily exists between the psyche and the physical world. Connecting or tuning in to this holographic sea of information, or to the "collective unconscious," as Jung called it, can be accomplished through centering thought, emotional releasing, meditation, or yoga, to name just a few. Dreams can also be tied to your unconscious and lead you to the lessons, the answers, and insights into the future that will make your healing path smoother.

THE UNIFIED FIELD: THE INTERRELATED NATURE OF PEOPLE AND THINGS

All these techniques, including experiences like premonitions, clairvoyance, and clairsentience, stand out as examples of ways in which we access—often unconsciously—the information in the hologram sea. The unified field seems to be an energetic repository of the conscious as well as unconscious behaviors of all of humankind, old and new. Why can we access it? Because we are part of the hologram; we are interconnected through this unified field, connected through the quantum hologram.

How many times have you thought about somebody you haven't seen for a long time and then in some sudden, unexpected manner, that person appears? Either she popped up on your e-mail, or she called you, or you ran into her in a "chance" meeting on the street or in a department store. How many times have you had a feeling come over you about a person or situation that gave you a deep knowing about what was happening?

Here's another example of how it works. A blindfolded woman is asked to pick out her painting out of a collection of six hundred paintings.[283] She pauses while she takes time to "center" herself. Then in a few minutes, she walks over to her painting.

What is actually happening? She is tapping into the quantum hologram, or the unified field, or what some call the source, this huge invisible database of invisible organizing energy fields, an invisible matrix that knows all. These energy fields serve as blueprints for form and behavior. The woman who picked out her painting likely had highly developed intuitive powers enabling her to resonate with it. She tuned into the energy frequencies carrying the information of her work.

The subtle organizing patterns of these vibrations reach across the time and space barriers we usually see. Their effects occur at a distance as well as at close range. These invisible energy fields are responsible for our intuitive knowledge, our surroundings, and even our patterns of behavior. And they can link the consciousness of one person to another.[284]

These energetic linkages tranmit information between individuals and even from their environments. One well documented event demonstrating this amazing phenomenon was the Asian tsunami of 2004. Everyone expected that the catastrophic deluge would take a heavy toll on the tribes living on the isolated island. They had no way of knowing it was coming—or so it seemed. But the tribespeople left for the Highlands just in time to escape the ferocious deadly waves. Some speculated that they knew the tsunami was coming by observing the behavior of animals, others by listening to signals of impending danger from nature itself.[285]

The higher the frequencies of your level of consciousness, the greater your ability to access the information in this field, the greater your intuitive understanding or your ability to "see" in the sense of an inner knowing. Vibrating energy, stored and transmitted in proteins, is

---

[283] The editors of Ode. *The Amazing Promises of the Zero Point Field.* Ode International Publishing Company, November 2003, 45.

[284] Erwin Laszlo, PhD. "Science and the Akashic Field." Inner Traditions. Rochester, Vermont, 2007, 150-151.

[285] Ibid.

many times more efficient in relaying information within your mind and body than physical signals such as hormones, neurotransmitters, other growth factors, and chemicals.[286]

Progress in quantum physics has brought to light that all phenomena in nature can be understood in terms of different underlying quantum energy fields that have the characteristics of a hologram. In particular, physicists have discovered that all the known dynamic interactions in nature can be described in terms of four separate fundamental energy force fields—the fields of the electromagnetic, weak, strong, and gravitational interactions. With progress in unified quantum field theories, however, it was also realized that all these different force fields are simply different aspects of one single unified field. They are all aspects of the pure energy, the *immense background of energy*, as Bohm referred to it, of the quantum hologram, the divine matrix, or the transcendental field underlying all phenomena found in nature. At a fundamental level, reality is not made of separate parts (particles) but one interconnected whole, the quantum holographic universe.

IN SUM: HEALING IN THE QUANTUM HOLOGRAM

To sum up, where healing is concerned, keep in mind the following important considerations:

- Healing one part heals the whole
- Capture the feeling of how you know you will feel when you are completely healed. Material things, including your body, only represent vibrations. Resonance attracts like energy frequencies—a violin

[286] L. Turin. *Journal of Biological Physics.* "Colin W. F. McClare: A Tribute." February 2009; 35 (i): 9–15.

string plucked here resonates with a string of the same note across the room. To heal, you must learn to tune into high-frequency energies.

- Thoughts are energy waves that are coherent and carry information that is stored in the quantum hologram as well as your cells; thoughts are the minds' energy that resonates with things—people, events, situations—of the same energy frequency.
- Regardless of separation in space and time, the consciousness of one individual can be linked to the consciousness of another. Healing energies can be transmitted from one to another. If our minds and the "consciousness" or energy frequencies that arise from them infuse our bodies, and in fact extend beyond them, which they have been shown to do, then our personal choices of what we think and feel—how we shape our mind's energy—is key in the creation of our reality in the holomovement.

Bohm speaks of the source as that which is beyond both the implicate, or sea of possibilities, and the explicate order, or the physical world which is expressed from it. We can imagine our source as the coherent light that illuminates and materializes the implicate realm giving rise to the explicate, or physical, realm[287].

And that brings us to the subject of our next chapter.

---

[287] Bohm posited that the implicate order consists of light waves everywhere present; and enfolds the entire universe in space and time. Furthermore, there is a continuous enfolding and unfolding occurring continuously. This is referred to as the holomovement.

XIII

YOU ARE THE LIGHT

Everything emanates from the light that is the Source of your being. This light is not separate from who you are but constitutes the very essence of your Being. In that light, there is infinite love and energy.

— Eckhart Tolle

The transitory scenes of our physical world are cast onto the screen of human consciousness by the infinite creative light. In need of a coherent light source to bring it forth, our holographic worlds are illuminated by the light source that is present everywhere and resides in the cells of our own bodies. As humans, we embody the light: one of the great discoveries of all time is that we emit a dynamic, coherent web of light.[288] Like the laser beam in the holographic plate that illuminates a picture and brings it to life, the light of our cells illuminates whatever we focus on in the world around us and brings it to life.

> When we're sick, the light in our cells becomes dimmer.

When we're sick, the light in our cells becomes dimmer. Because we are part of the holographic field, we receive vibrational feedback about areas where the light emitted by our cells isn't coherent. That's when disease is being created. When the light in our cells is thwarted, there is a loss of coherence. Because of the lack of coherent electromagnetic energy, the

---

[288] http://www.healingcancernaturally.com/healingwithlight8.html

repair and communication system between our cells gets damaged.[289] In effect, their light seems to be going out.

Since your body reflects a field of light energy, any shift in your energy field will be reflected in the body; and any shift in the body will be reflected by a shift in your energy field. These energy fields can then be altered when using any healing method. It can be bodywork, energy work like Reiki, or psychological work like cognitive behavior therapy.

The overarching goal in healing is to restore the healthy state of light coherence, which has been distorted by our inner conflicts, emotional traumas, upsetting beliefs, and thought forms. From an energy point of view, the aim is to come back to a true state of wholeness, or holiness, as in a state *full of light.* [290]

THE REVERENCE OF LIGHT

Holy visions are often surrounded by bright light. People throughout the ages have always talked about "light" in a holy sense. For centuries, devotees have shared experiences of "going to the light," "finding the light," being "embraced by the light," "dissolving into the light." In our seminars and discussions with him, Bill Bauman advised, "Let the light lead. The light will teach you and show you the way." When we know our partnership with the light, the ego doesn't need to take action. The light takes care of it. Then he said, "Pain of any kind occurs when light's attempt to create is frustrated." Before Bill's advice to let the light lead, spiritual life was little more than a concept to me. But then it became real because I saw firsthand that what he was saying.

---

[289] International Institute of Biophysics 2002 (formerly published at www. lifescientists.de/publication/pub2002-05.htm), edited for enhanced readability by Healing Cancer Naturally.

[290] Marco Bischof. *Biophotons – The Light in Our Cells.* German publisher: Zweitausendeins, Frankfurt. http://www.zweitausendeins.de/, publication date: March 1995.

YOU ARE THE LIGHT

Eventually he told us, "You are the light." Men and women who have had near-death experiences (NDEs) have vividly described being surrounded by a white light. Being *bathed* in white light seems to be common to all NDEs. But that's not what Bill was saying. Not all experiences of the light are related to dying. He was clear: we are made of light, light is who we are, and it comes from the soul.

> If you choose to forgive another instead of harboring anger, the frequency of your light shifts to a higher level. Any time you choose compassion, love, and kindness, the frequency of light increases.

The light of the soul is instantaneous. If you choose to forgive another instead of harboring anger, the frequency of your light shifts to a higher level. Any time you choose compassion, love, and kindness, the frequency of light increases. When you think loving thoughts about someone, you not only shift the light of your awareness to a higher level, but you also influence the energy field of the other person, whose light then grows stronger. As you act more from your soul, as distinct from your personality, the light of your awareness increases in frequency. When a person becomes fully aware and full of light, we say he is "enlightened."

> "We know today that man is essentially a being of light. Modern science has proven it. In terms of healing, the implications of this finding are immense." —Fritz Popp

Eastern sages and religious devotees have long taught that the essence of everything is light. Now science is telling us the same thing. In a great leap from mystics to modern science, physicist Fritz Popp declares, "We know today that man is essentially a being of light. Modern science has proven it. In matters of healing, the implications of this finding are immense. Healing our bodies with light beams may be a possibility that is closer than we think. We now know, for example, that light can initiate or arrest cascade-like reactions in the cells and that cellular damage can be virtually repaired, within hours, by faint beams of light."[291]

Fritz Popp's discovery echoes all the spiritual traditions that have spoken of the light within. Light is the language of the cells, and the cells of the body actually communicate with each other through particles of light. In other words, light is the activator, the means of communication, of our cells.

Miracles are the stock in trade of all those who have realized that the essence of creation is light."[292] They learn how to shape the rays of light, reflected from or originating from an object, passing through the eyes to the brain cells, converting it into thought impressions. In swirling vortexes, the light in our cells shifts into energy that moves through our chakras, or the energy centers in our bodies. Nothing is by accident. The energetic light journey has been elegantly mapped out in each of the energy centers (chakras) in our bodies as follows:

Root chakra: Generates the life force, creating our foundation and a feeling of being grounded. The energy of the root chakra relates to survival issues such as financial independence, money, and food.

Sacral chakra: Generates stability, safety, presence, and a sense of abundance and well-being. Pleasure and sexuality, as well as our connection and ability to accept others and new experiences, emanate from this chakra.

Solar plexus chakra: Generates a feeling of energy, relating to the ability to be in control of our lives and to issues related to our self-confidence, self-esteem, and self-worth; as well as empathy, patience and giving.

Heart chakra: Generates love, intimacy, passion, and a sense of bondedness; relates to feelings of joy and inner peace.

---

[291]   Fritz Popp interview with Supreme Master Television

[292]   Paramahansa Yogananda. *Autobiography of a Yogi*. Self-Realization Fellowship, Encinitas, California. 1993.

Throat chakra: Generates creativity, self-expression, communication, and the truth of who you are.

Third eye chakra: Creates conscious awareness; relates to intuition, insight, imagination, and wisdom.

Crown chakra: This is the gateway of universal energy which is referred to as light when it comes through the crown, because it has a spiritual quality to it. As light enters this chakra, it is dispersed to the lower chakras. This chakra relates to issues of higher awareness, spirituality.

Whirlpools of energy develop in these chakras based on how deeply we believe something. The extent of the belief or desire determines the relative force of these energy patterns. Accordingly, we condition our happiness. Stemming from our deeply held beliefs, a certain amount of energy—propensities and tendencies—is preconditioned, committed to these vortices. The Hindus call these tendencies *vrittis*. When enough energy in a particular chakra becomes tied up in *vrittis*, whether preconditioned or frustrated, the light in our cells diminishes. Because of unresolved issues related to beliefs that don't serve us, dis-ease results.

Fritz Popp, the brilliant scientist who risked his career when he became interested in light and its potential for healing, conducted pioneering research telling us that we are made of particles of light, or biophotons. These particles make up the electromagnetic frequency patterns that are found in all living things. Our bodies are like electrically charged batteries. Each of us vibrates at a characteristic electromagnetic frequency.

Popp's belief? That health is nothing more than well-ordered light. Every living organism continually communicates with the quantum hologram to tune into the collective blueprint of the health of their species.[293] Groundbreaking research has supported Popp's intuition, revealing that a healthy cell emits coherent light and an unhealthy cell

---

[293] The editors of *Ode*. *The Amazing Promises of the Zero Point Field*. Ode International Publishing Company, November 2003, 45.

emits chaotic light.[294] In this way, the light emitted from our cells can be used to tell whether we are healthy or not. We can tell the difference between cancer cells and healthy cells, for instance, by the difference in how they emit light and in differences in their degree of coherence.

Popp explains that the light living things emit is "ultra-weak," meaning it can't be seen by the naked eye and has a very high degree of coherence.[295] It's the high coherence that is the key to how light orchestrates the activity of our cells. When you consider that the coherence time[296] of the best laser is less than one-tenth of a second and the coherence time of light in a biological system is much longer, at least in the order of days or even weeks, it becomes apparent that we humans have a very, high degree of light coherence in our cells.[297] This allows a biological system plenty of time to communicate with the highest possible degree of clarity. This communication occurs at the speed of light or faster. For instance, there are one hundred thousand reactions in each cell per second, and these reactions are regulated by light, according to Popp.

Popp explains how it works: "The molecule takes up the photon (the particle of light) in a nanosecond. After this nanosecond, the cell is not transferred to heat;[298] it is given back to the light field and is available

---

[294]   Marco Bischof. "Biophotons: The Light in Our Cells." Part IV *Illness and Health*. German publisher, Zweitausendeins, Frankfurt. March 1995. www.// transpersonal.de/mbischof/english/webookeng.htm.

[295]   Fritz Albert Popp. "Macroscopic Quantum Coherence." Proceedings of an international conference at Boston University. Edited by Boston University and MIT, World Scientific, 1999.
        Note: Coherence means the degree to which all the subunits of something operate very efficiently in concert with the whole.

[296]   Coherence time is the time over which the field correlation function decays. So the longer the coherence time, the greater the time available for a biological system to cohere, to be correlated with necessary functions.

[297]   Physicsforum.com. What is coherent light? The greater the coherence, the longer its coherence time will be.

[298]   As the cell lives and grows, it converts energy. It releases heat energy as it synthesizes molecules and assembles them into cell structures. Heat is energy in its most disordered form—the random jostling of molecules. When the

for the next reaction. With one particle of light, you can trigger one hundred thousand reactions. It is an *autocatalytic* messenger for our cellular reactions,"[299] meaning light creates the reaction and is also a product of the reaction.

Further, information is created by the electromagnetic field; and the field is able to produce a pattern, not just a local pattern, a specially dynamic pattern, telling a cell what to do at what time and what place. The stability and the predictability of the pattern in our cells is governed by the coherence of light within us. Ultra-weak light or photon emission is the energy released through the changes in energy metabolism as our bodies directly and rhythmically emit light.

Popp's research shows the main condition that must be fulfilled for health: all the body's complex processes must occur in exquisitely orchestrated, timely synchrony, and they must occur at the speed of light. Any means of "information" transmission—other than light—including through biomolecules, chemical messengers, and so forth, would not be sufficient. They would be too slow to guarantee the integrity of the organism. Our bodies need light. An intimate cell-to-cell-communication must occur at the speed of light.

> Our bodies directly and rhythmically emit light.

Popp and one of his students, Bernard Ruth, found that we humans store light energy acquired from the sun and from plants consumed as food (photosynthesis) in our DNA. This stored light is released when we need it, as weak, extremely coherent biophotons. These ultra-weak photons regulate our bodily functions. At different frequencies, they perform different functions.[300]

---

cell releases heat to the field, it increases the intensity of molecular motions (thermal motion), thereby increasing the randomness, or disorder, of the field. *This same process does not occur with the energy of light.*

[299] Fritz Popp. "Living Light: Biophotons and the Human Body. Part 1." Supreme Master Television Interview with Fritz Popp.

[300] http://www.transpersonal.de/mbischof/englisch/webbookeng.htm

COHERENCE IN ILLNESS

Popp also discovered that when you're ill, not only is this inner communication disrupted but so is the communication with the quantum hologram. Sick people often emit too much light. Popp observed that the coherence of the light our bodies emit, the intensity, and the rhythmic patterns vary in people with different illnesses. Their light either "goes out" or is drawn out of them.[301] Tumors emit high quantities of light. But light emissions from cancer patients is very chaotic, lacking coherence and failing to follow normal rhythmic patterns.[302] People with multiple sclerosis, on the other hand, absorb too much light and their photon emissions display too much coherence.

> **Whether the light is from within a person, maybe that of a healer or from a man-made light system, light can be very effective in healing.**

Popp and colleagues at the International Institute of Biophysics have discovered that surface tumors and tumors excised during surgery respond to remedies with changes in the light they emit. Most possible treatments have no effect on the tumor's high emission rate. However, when the tumor responds to a remedy with decreased light emission, the remedy will likely improve the patient's condition and may even cure it.

LIGHT IN HEALING

The new research confirming that our bodies emit light bursts opens a new era in medicine. Popp's research stands in stark contrast to the

---

[301] The editors of *Ode*. "The Amazing Promises of the Zero Point Field." Ode Publishing Company, November 2003, 45.

[302] An average of 300 90 photons/cm per minute compared with normal tissue that emits an average of 22 6 photons/cm per minute.

current view of medical science, which sees our bodies as solid chemical objects. Not only does it give us a very new and different understanding about the energetic makeup of our bodies, but it also has obviously profound implications for how we treat and prevent diseases.

For healing, this information represents a huge breakthrough. Healing with light can actually be accomplished at the cellular level, given the right light frequencies and an understanding of how to administer it. Whether the light is from within a person, maybe that of a healer, or man-made light systems, light can be very effective in healing.

Certain FDA-approved commercially available sophisticated light systems have been shown to be effective in healing at the cellular level, specifically the mitochondria, responsible for producing energy in the cells.[303] In addition, friends and colleagues with conditions ranging from cardiovascular issues like swelling and wounds, arthritic joints, some cancers, and hip pain, to name a few, have been successfully healed with various forms of light. Preliminary research done by NASA, for instance, shows that red and infrared LEDs, or light-emitting diodes, can speed healing.

One study conducted by NASA found that LED therapy produced a 40 percent improvement in musculoskeletal training injuries in Navy SEALS, as well as a greatly reduced wound healing time. Similar studies have shown remarkable healing progress using light in treating chronic illnesses, cold sores, and acne.[304]

According to other scientists,[305] the fluctuations in how much light a person emits are related to fluctuations in the strength of relaxation and alpha waves in the brain. Some also suggest that the state of a person's light field is related to certain meditative states characterized by a high degree of coherence in their EEGs and accompanied by a high degree of coherence in their light fields.[306] Meditation helps in the healing

---

[303] In Light Wellness Systems, New Mexico.
[304] Jill Neimark. "Healing with Light." *Spirituality and Health.* January–February 2010.
[305] Van Wijk et al.
[306] Ibid.

of many illnesses, probably because it seems to influence the complex interactions of oxidative and anti-oxidative reactions that regulate how we emit light. Recording and analyzing the light emitted in, before, during, and after meditation supports the idea that meditation enhances our light. This is in keeping with the findings that various physiologic and biochemical shifts occur in meditators.[307]

Many scientists believe that light—the emission of biophotons—seems to be the mechanism through which the intention to heal, or focused thought patterns directed toward healing, can bring it about. When we intend to heal, we emit a constant current of light (or ultra-weak photons) as a means of directing light signals from one part of the body to another, as well as to other people or things in the outside world. Direct intention manifests itself as an electric and magnetic energy producing an ordered flux of light or photons. Our intentions seem to operate as highly coherent frequencies capable of changing the molecular structure of matter—in other words, capable of healing. Cases of spontaneous cures or cases of remote healing of extremely ill patients often represent instances of a great intention to heal the disease.

> Our intentions seem to operate as highly coherent frequencies capable of changing the molecular structure of matter—in other words, capable of healing.

The discovery that we emit light—biophotons—also lends scientific support to alternative methods of healing. The ch'i energy flowing through our bodies' energy channels, which, according to traditional Chinese medicine regulates our bodily functions, may be related to key nodes in our biophoton fields. In the same way, the prana of Indian yoga may be a similar regulating energy force that has a basis in weak, coherent electromagnetic biofields, energy fields of light.

Popp's work on light in us leads to many startling insights. It may well provide the foundation for a light-based science of medicine before long. The key to its therapeutic uses lies in different wavelengths and

---

[307] Herb Benson with Meg Stark. *Timeless Healing.* Scribner, 1997.

colors of light. Each affects our cells differently. The long wavelengths of infrared light, which penetrate deeply into the tissue, have been used to help repair cardiac tissue after a heart attack. Red light doesn't penetrate as deeply as infrared, for instance, but has been used on skin to help people look younger because it promotes collagen formation; moreover, its anti-inflammatory effect has been used to treat acne. Ultraviolet light is being used to treat viruses and bacterial infections, and blue light is being used as an antibacterial agent as well as helping people sleep. It resets the biological clock.[308]

In its healthy state, the human body literally glimmers. The intensity of the light emitted by the body is one thousand times lower than the sensitivity of our naked eyes. The light has different intensities for plant or animal cells, for different cell types, and it can vary from one moment to the next. It is not regular but comes often as "photon explosion" (spikes), especially when the cells are stimulated or excited by outside events.

Over the years, Popp and others have found that light, biophoton emissions, from healthy humans displays rhythmic patterns. Daily changes in photon emission patterns have been observed and seem to be linked to changes in energy metabolism.

SCIENCE IS CATCHING UP TO SPIRIT: WE ARE BEINGS OF LIGHT

What's fascinating is that these discoveries coincide with the Eastern notions of the light within and different states of awareness. We can live in darkness or in the light. At higher frequencies, you gravitate to interpretations and actions that reflect the light of your soul, your higher self, according to those scientists who have studied levels of consciousness. Like attracts like. As you awaken the light of your soul,

---

[308] Reed Karaim. "Light That Can Cure You." USA Weekend. February 2–4, 2007.

less harmonious energies are transmuted into lighter, more harmonious ones and the energy all around you vibrates at a higher frequency.

As you become lighter, you experience a stronger sense of personal power and a deepening sense of love and compassion. In addition, the people and situations that are exposed to your consciousness are affected. Many times they are healed, if the frequency of light is high enough.

As the light of your soul at these higher levels of awareness begins to operate like a spiritual laser in the holographic world around you, your life situation is transformed. Just as a laser transforms light waves, such as those radiating from a lightbulb, into a single beam of phase-coherent light, the light of the intentions you radiate as your awareness expands will have a transformative healing effect. It can work for you, yourself, or others. *It is this light that the stuff of miracles is made.*

> Just as a laser transforms light waves, such as those radiating from a lightbulb, into a single beam of phase-coherent light, the light you radiate as your awareness expands will have a transformative healing effect.

FIRSTHAND: HOW THE LIGHT WORKS

A vivid experience of how the light works was recounted by a young boy when he became blind at the age of eight: "I saw the whole world in light, existing through it and because of it. A light so continuous and so intense was so far beyond my comprehension that sometimes I doubted it, [supposed] it was not real, that I had only imagined it. Perhaps it would be enough to imagine the opposite, or just something different to make it go away. So I thought of testing it out and even resisting it. But light was still there and more serene than ever, looking like a lake at evening when the wind has dropped."[309]

---

[309] Jacques Lusseyran. *And There Was Light*. Parabola Books, July 1987.

The boy goes on to explain the amazing part: "Still, there were times when the light faded, almost to the point of disappearing. It happened every time I was afraid. If, instead of letting myself be carried along by confidence and throwing myself into things, I hesitated, calculated, thought about the half-open door, the key in the lock; if I said to myself that all these things were hostile and about to strike or scratch, then without exception I hit or wounded myself."

"The loss of my eyes had not done what fear had done. It was fear that made me blind. Anger and impatience had the same effect, throwing everything into confusion."
—Jacque Lusseyran

The lessons this young blind boy learned from the light serve as neon messages for us all. "The loss of my eyes had not done what fear had done. It was fear that made me blind. Anger and impatience had the same effect, throwing everything into confusion. The minute before, I knew just where everything in the room was, but if I got angry, things got angrier than I [did]. They went and hid in the most unlikely corners, mixed themselves up, turned turtle, muttered like crazy men, and turned wild. I no longer knew where to put my hand or foot. Everything hurt me. When I was playing with my small companions, if I suddenly grew anxious to win, to be first at all costs, then all at once I could see nothing. Literally I went into fog or smoke. But when I was happy and serene, approached people with confidence, and thought well of them, I was rewarded with light."[310]

Guided by the light described here, the young boy, Jacque Lusseyran, tells the story of his relationship with light and of how, with its help and guidance, he went on to become the leader of the French Resistance during World War II. Lusseyran had no need of an external moral code. He had only to look at the bright signal of light, which taught him how to live and in whom they could trust.

All the colors of the rainbow survived his blindness. Light threw its color on things and people, and all had characteristic colors that helped

---

[310]   Ibid.

257

him "see," in profound and penetrating ways, how life functions at its most fundamental level.

Lusseyran experienced his blindness as a great gift. Because of it, he entered a new world that we can all have access to, if we embrace it with the confidence and compassion of Lusseyran. Each of us functions at a different level of awareness. As our actions come more from the heart space, from the inspiration of the soul, from our confident, authentic selves, our level of awareness rises and we experience more light. The quantum hologram reflects it and sends it back to us to experience.

Our inner light increases when we act with assurance and compassion. Our energy fields resonate at a higher vibration and we attract people and experiences at that higher level. Our actions continually shape the light of our souls. While it may not be as visible as Lusseyran's light was to him, it works the same way and its effects are extremely apparent.

A persistent lack of light coherence in our bodies, fueled by a lack of integration of the mind and body and spirit reflected in negative thoughts, feelings, and actions, all lead to a breakdown in light's communication in our bodies' electromagnetic energy system and self-healing mechanisms.

What if you are ill and do not have many positive feelings? In fact, you're angry. "Why *me*? Why am *I* the one that had to get cancer?" The light in your cells has been compromised by your illness. But the healing response can be triggered by a high frequency of light (just as you experience in the presence of an enlightened person), by your intention to heal, or your faith that you will be healed, or in some cases even by being exposed to physical man-made light of the proper frequency and dosage. Light can activate your body's own healing powers, providing the means to restore healthy cellular functioning in the mitochondria.[311]

---

[311] Mitochondria are the powerhouses of the cell. They act like a digestive system, taking in nutrients, breaking them down, and creating energy for the cell.

AS YOU BECOME LIGHTER, ANYTHING HEALS

Science says when pure energy[312] slows down, lower dimensional matter is created. Everything in the physical world around us vibrates within certain ranges of frequency in order for human senses to perceive it. When the vibrational field speeds up and the frequency rate of vibration is outside the range of normal human perception, we enter higher dimensions of consciousness. And the higher our consciousness, the closer to our source, which is light, we become.

Your soul becomes more and more radiant with the awakening of the light of the universe within you. As your level of awareness expands and you become *lighter,* anything can be healed. How quickly you heal varies with your level of awareness, the frequency of your light. Expanded levels of awareness open doorways to the higher realms of light, revealing more and more light of the soul. At a high-enough level of awareness, healing is spontaneous. David Hawkins, who created a scale of levels of awareness,[313] says this happens at the six-hundred level. At that level of awareness, feelings of bliss and peacefulness arise naturally in response to life situations. Healing happens spontaneously.[314]

Light—given the proper frequency—will be able to heal much more quickly than chemicals, drugs, or chemotherapy. As science advances, medicine will be bound to expand its vision to include consciousness and healing with light. Just as Newtonian physics emerged as humans needed to learn to grasp the physical world through the intellect, and relativity came about as we began to understand the limits of individual perspectives in relation to the whole, quantum physics is now helping us learn about the relationship of consciousness to the physical world.[315]

---

[312] Light can be thought of as pure energy in that it has no mass but momentum, although scientists debate it.

[313] All of David Hawkins publications contain the scale of the various levels of awareness.

[314] David Hawkins. *Power vs Force.* Hay House, 2002, 75.

[315] Gary Zukav. *The Seat of the Soul,* Simon and Shuster, 1989.

We are moving into an age where our understanding is more about energy and spirit than it is about physical form.

Anyone in medicine has seen spontaneous remissions and recoveries that cannot be explained by medical science. That is because in medical science we are looking for explanations within a narrow linear framework. What we refer to as miracles are occurrences that create more light in the cells. Out of the realm of Newtonian science and into the realm of life-enhancing mind-sets—laughing, singing, dancing, meditating, praying—light can shine forth to do its healing work.

If light comes from your inner essence, from your soul, the key question is: What will bring you closer to the light of your soul? Your alignment with your source, your inner essence. When a person is fully aligned with their inner essence, fully aware of their source, they are "enlightened." Enlightenment, or awakening to the presence as the one-in-all and all-in-one source of all things, and then expressing that realization in every aspect of your life, is a process available to each one of us.

> As fields of light, the frequency of our light increases as we choose to forgive, to let go of resentment, to respond with compassion.

As fields of light, the frequency of our light increases as we choose to forgive, to let go of resentment, to respond with compassion. If you think it's your right to be angry, to harbor resentment because of what has been done to you, the frequency of your light will diminish—until you learn to feel differently. We can choose to learn through fear and doubt or through love and wisdom. As your light becomes more focused, and that happens when your thoughts and feelings are positive and aligned with your source, your ability to heal increases. Your light becomes like a laser beam or phase coherent light, a beam in which every wave precisely reinforces every other—light that, so to speak, doesn't struggle with itself.[316]

---

[316]   Gary Zukav. *The Seat of the Soul.* Simon and Shuster, 1989, 109.

Knowing the light's source, you can use it to guide your thoughts and feelings. You can begin to make choices intentionally designed to bring forth your highest consciousness to raise the vibration of your energy field. The mind-set that arises as your light body increases brings with it a strong faith that everything is meant to occur at a specific moment in time, whether you work toward earning it or not. Instead of trying to manifest outcomes at exactly the moment you think they're meant to exist, a highly activated light body inspires you to make choices in each moment to anchor higher frequencies of consciousness throughout your day-to-day life.

From a higher dimensional perspective, the people, places, and things that come your way are like neon signs created to help you practice bringing forth more conscious responses. Everything that happens is to help you expand your consciousness. Even—and perhaps especially—things that are stressful come to you as a good thing, to help you expand your awareness. The seemingly bad actions and behavior of others do not reflect something imbalanced in you ("Why did I attract *this?*") but were created as opportunities to match their unconsciousness[317] with a greater conscious response. When someone complains, try responding with a compliment. When someone judges you, try saying thank you. If someone is having a bad day, try offering encouragement. And throughout it all, if anything triggers you, take it as a reminder of the perfect moment in time to overlook it, let it go, and direct your self-talk to say something kind and calming to yourself. By learning to choose the higher road, you bring more light.

By learning to direct your thoughts and to go beyond them, by learning to manage your energy to choose the higher path, you can enjoy excellent health and conceivably bypass years of therapy, as well as drugs and invasive surgeries. Soon we may well be able to, in effect, do continuous genetic engineering on our own bodies![318]

---

[317] Sometimes seemingly negative things happen because you are part of the collective consciousness, not from any action on your part.

[318] Dawson Church. *The Genie in Your Genes: Epigenetic Medicine and the New Biology of Intention.* Elite Books, Santa Rosa California, 2007.

Developing your healing abilities by learning to enhance the light in your cells can give both immediate relief from long-standing anxieties and neuroses as well as miraculous healings of persistent physical conditions. The exciting discovery that we are light points to the future possibilities of a brand-new medicine that recognizes the soul as a vital source of light and the very source of our being.

As the essence of creation, pure light has been thought of as the light of God, the light of truth, the light of Buddha, the light of Jesus, cosmic light, an ocean of light, depending upon your persuasion. In the New Testament, John the Baptist, says, "He came as a witness to testify about the light that all might believe through him." Jesus himself said, "Put your trust in the light while there is still time so that you may become children of light …" He also said, "I am the light of the world; he who follows me will not walk in darkness but will have the light of life."

In the Jewish tradition, the sanctuary lamp in front of synagogues, in Hebrew, *ner tamid*, is translated as eternal light, symbolizing God's eternal light. British mystic George Fox, who founded the Quaker religion, used the term "inner light" to describe our ability to experience God within us personally.

In Buddhism, it is also believed that we all have an inner divine light. A spiritual search becomes a search for divine or sacred light. As we cultivate our inner essence in order to heal, what we are doing is searching for this light within—or searching for what some might call God.

XIV

ON GOD

Literature is full of examples of remarkable cures through the influence of the imagination, which is only an active phase of faith.

—Sir William Osler

The God most of us grew up with has a lot of baggage. That's why many don't want much to do with the God we learned about in Sunday school. But if you're paying attention, you get to a point in life where you see that the real power in our lives comes from a higher place—a power so much greater than what we can see—but we have to learn how to contact it. In *The Healing Light*, Sanford says it clearly:

"If we try turning on an electric iron and it doesn't work, we look to the wiring of the iron, the cord, or the house. We don't stand in dismay before the iron and cry, "Oh, electricity, please come into my iron and work!" We realize that while the whole world is full of that mysterious power we call electricity, only the amount that flows through the wiring of the iron will make the iron work for us.

The same principle is true of the creative energy of God. The whole universe is full of it, but only the amount that flows through our own beings will work for us."[319]

We are made in the image and likeness of God. As more and more of it is allowed to flow through us, that quote from Genesis becomes a

---

[319] Agnes Sanford. *The Healing Light.* First Ballantine Books, February 1991.

reality. "The kingdom of God is within you," said Jesus.[320] And it is the indwelling light, the secret place of high levels of consciousness, that brings the kingdom of heaven on earth. Living in the kingdom of heaven comes from learning to turn on the light of God within.

Made in God's image, we are creators. As Bill recently explained in one of his seminars, creation takes place at several levels of consciousness. At the physical level, it takes a lot of effort to create. At the mental and energetic levels, it gets easier. In our mastery seminars, he used to swirl his hands around in a deliberate way, in the space surrounding the person having the difficulty. The purpose was to shake up the energy around the person in a Reiki-like way to break up the energy and shift it up. Then, in a grand gesture, he made large, encompassing circular motions to create a space for a bigger vision, bigger than what the energetic space could hold in its smaller version. Then, reframing the problem, he would make new pronouncements, expanding the thought patterns behind the smaller constraining, painful vision and create a new more expansive space with new more expansive healing thought forms.

At this new energetic level, less effort is needed to create. At higher levels of consciousness, at the *light level*, creation happens like magic. It happens in an instant. As you make choices that bring you closer to the light of your soul and you clear up the emotional issues that pull and tug at you, the things that cause you discomfort, when very little can "push your buttons," your energy becomes lighter and more and more healing.

I have a close friend who has a deeply kind and forgiving soul. His wife, who was a Rockette[321], was murdered while she was walking their cocker spaniels in Central Park. In spite of the brutality of the act, he wasn't angry. His first response was compassion and forgiveness for the deranged man—suffering from schizophrenia--who did it. In fact, the entire family was forgiving and compassionate. How could human beings rise to such a high level of compassion when everything around

---

[320] See Deepak Chopra's *The Third Jesus*, where he explains how the teachings of Jesus lay out the path and the teachings that lead to enlightenment, a path accessible to all, ie finding the kingdom of heaven within us.

[321] Rockettes are dancers at Radio City in New York.

you wants to pull you down into rage and resentment? Chris transcended what would have been most people's worst nightmare. While he felt an overwhelming grief for his wife's death, he wasn't angry. In place of rage, he felt compassion. How could he do that? Because that's what was inside: compassion. He said, "I knew he couldn't help himself."

Most of us live from the outside in. Tapping your divine power means living from the inside out. Primary reality is within. Greater is He who is within me. Moving from your inner power to meet external circumstances, like Chris did, brings the strength to triumph over obstacles and to heal.

One spiritual teacher from India expressed it this way: people of different cultures have a certain characteristic energy. When they walk into a room, you can tell where they're from. You can sense it energetically. People from New York walk and talk with a different energy than people from the South or people from the West. Then there are others whose energy defies definition. Their energy is more clear and refined. You can't tell where they're from. That's because their power is rooted in their own souls, not in the outside world.

After I had been studying with Bill for a while and thought I understood that when you were cleared of all the energy tied up in issues related to repressed fear-based emotions, the rewards would be expanded consciousness, including healing. Once the energetic walls of repression and resistance we have built up in ourselves are lifted, we find ourselves closer to the light of our souls. If we want to heal, I reasoned, allowing our hearts and our minds to operate in the "now" from the light of present moment awareness, unencumbered, would lead to it.

Expanding our consciousness, we are transported to a level where healing and miracles occur. Because we are allowing the light, the infinite energy of creation to flow freely through us, allowing miracles becomes the natural order of things. In this way, a miracle is simply an event created by an undivided, unlimited consciousness, which our limited minds or the narrow nineteenth-century processes of the intellect cannot comprehend. That's what I learned and believed.

By this time I had seen Bill and the powerful light he emits heal people miraculously several times. I myself experienced it. But I also saw people heal where this *wasn't* the case. There was no process of clearing, not even much introspection or self-awareness. I was baffled by it. One day during one of his seminars, I mentioned this: "How is it that some people heal without going through any clearing process? People who still seem to harbor layers of repressed emotions, fears, and doubts, experience a spontaneous healing just the same. How does that happen?" I asked.

Bill quickly responded with a one-word answer: "Grace," he said.

Okay, I thought to myself *grraaaccce ... Really? What in the world is that?* After teaching us in many sessions and seminars over the years about how human energy and light work from a quantum perspective, now he was giving us a one-word answer that seemed to me to be laden with religious connotations (Bill didn't refer to God very much at all) and sort of coming out of left field. Clearly, it didn't seem to answer my question. It said nothing to me about *how* these healings where people still seemed to have much of the same baggage that created their illnesses occurred. *What is grace? What is he talking about?* It seemed to me, at the time, a lame response. I couldn't get my head around it.

> Once again, we see that belief is king where healing is concerned.

Eventually, I came to see it was far from lame. I learned what he meant by Grace. It is the magic energy that you have access to when you have faith, belief in a higher power. At higher states of consciousness, it is the energy that we refer to as God. Defined as "the free and unmerited favor of God,[322]" it's not something you have to earn. But it *is* something you have to be open to receiving. Once again, we see that belief is king. It's a receptive state we all have access to, a state where all good things come to us, if we believe they can. Healing can work this way too.

---

[322] We all have an instinct within that relates to a supreme power. Because we are taught to use the word *God* when we feel reverence, that's what we call it. But because to many the term means a punitive big white man in the sky with a beard, other terms like the universe, the source, or even just life are often used. Actually Bill taught that grace was a built in feature of the universe, available to all.

The main thing you really need is belief. You must be open to it, even to expect it. Christ said, "According to your belief it shall be done unto you." Christ wasn't preaching moral advice. He was telling us how things work, how our hearts and minds work. If you believe grace, God's favor, will assist you in your healing, then it will.

Grace can accomplish anything. It knows no conditions. It is pure positive energy of such power that it can create new circumstances and solutions in a flash and put to rest any problems you think you're having.

> The greatest healers of our time, from Florence Nightingale to Albert Schweitzer to Sir William Osler and Carolyn Myss, have been deeply steeped in grace.

Since that day I asked Bill the question, often when I'm in the midst of the most difficult circumstances, I unexpectedly feel a pervading, soothing energy overtake me, a reassurance that all is well, giving me the confidence that no matter the circumstances, I'll be up to the challenge and always protected. You might call it "the peace that passeth all understanding," as the apostle Paul referred to it in Philippians. Then, in some unexpected, often unforeseen way, the circumstances are resolved. But it can't be summoned at will. Once you experience it, you continue to search for it, to want to experience it repeatedly. You will if you learn to stay aligned with the energy of your soul, through meditation or studying with an enlightened teacher or in other grace-filled ways, like service to others.

> "Where shall I find God? In myself ... but then I myself must be in a state for him to come and dwell in me."
> —Florence Nightingale

The greatest healers of our time, from Florence Nightingale to Albert Schweitzer to Sir William Osler and Carolyn Myss, have been deeply steeped in Grace. Because of a deep faith and a belief in God, they all talked about having a mystical purpose, a calling with an unmistakably divine imprint. Further, they all believed that healing was divine, a thing of the soul.

As Nightingale put it in talking about mysticism:[323] "For what is mysticism? Is it not the attempt to draw near to God, not by rites or ceremonies, but by inward disposition? Is it not merely a hard word for 'The Kingdom of Heaven is Within'?" Heaven is neither a place nor a time. There might be a heaven not only here but now. "Where shall I find God? In myself. That is the true mystical doctrine. But then I myself must be in a state for him to come and dwell in me. This is the whole aim of the mystical life, and all mystical rules in all times and all countries have been laid down for putting the soul in such a state."[324]

In the same way, the great physician Albert Schweitzer's healing work was guided by his belief in the soul. Said Schweitzer, "What does the word 'soul' mean? No one can give a definition of the soul. But we know what it feels like. The soul is the sense of something higher than ourselves, something that stirs in us thoughts, hopes, and aspirations, which go out to the world of goodness, truth, and beauty. The soul is a burning desire to breathe in this world of light and never to lose it—to remain children of light." Schweitzer would say to his patients, "I didn't heal you; you healed yourself!" Because he understood that healing comes from the soul.[325]

Sir William Osler, a physician and one of the four founding professors of Johns Hopkins Hospital, said, "Faith is indeed one of the miracles of human nature which science is as ready to accept as it is to study its marvelous effects." Osler continued: "My experience has been that of the unconscious rather than the deliberate faith healer. Phenomenal, even what could be called miraculous, cures are not very uncommon. Like others, I have had cases any one of which, under

---

[323] Mysticism is the spiritual intuition of truths that transcend ordinary understanding.

[324] Barbara Dossey, PhD, RN, HNC, FAAN. *Florence Nightingale: Mystic, Visionary, Healer.* Washington National Cathedral. August 12, 2001. www.dosseydossey.com/barbara/florenceLecture.html

[325] Renate zum Tobel. *Physician of the Soul.*

suitable conditions, could have been worthy of a shrine or made the germ of a pilgrimage."[326]

Contemporary medical intuitive Dr. Carolyn Myss, talks about grace frequently in her seminars and publications. "Grace is the breath of God—an invisible essence beyond intellect that moves swiftly amongst us," teaches Myss. Is it possible to become a living conduit of this powerful force? "Not only is it possible," says Myss, a best-selling author on a variety of healing topics, "but grace is immediately accessible to you and the courage to follow divine guidance." Myss invites her audience into the "altitude of the mystics" to invoke this expansive energy of Grace in your life.[327]

In spite of the powerful progress of medical science, the only infallible path to healing is through the soul. Your soul always knows what to do to heal you. The soul, the divine light in each of us, gives hope and faith, and healing is accomplished not by might or by medical power but by grace. In other words, I am healed in spite of my shortcomings, in spite of medicine's limitations.

Grace is the language of the soul. As it's been said repeatedly throughout the previous chapters, alignment with your soul repatterns the mind, repatterns uncomfortable emotions, and transports you onto the path of healing. Just as the mind and body have become understood and accepted scientifically as integral in the healing process over the past few decades, the soul will grow to assume a more central role as its light and its power to heal and transform become more fully understood and realized by more and more people. As more and more souls become enlightened, the power of self-healing will become more accessible and more of a mainstay, a common practice in our lives.

Powerful souls like Bill Bauman, Matt Kahn, Christ, the Buddha, and others mentioned in this book, and many that are not, are showing

---

[326] Sir William Osler, MD. "The Faith That Heals." *The British Medical Journal.* June 18, 1910, 1, 471.

[327] Carolyn Myss, PhD. *Channeling Grace: Invoking the Power of the Divine.* www.Myss.com/catalogue/channeling-grace-invoking-the-power-of-the-divine.htm

us the way to connect with the lights of our souls and to the pure energy beyond. They are showing us how to get into the state that Nightingale referred to, a state that realizes the god that dwells within each of us.

Everyone and everything has a soul. As you develop the power of your soul by learning to listen to its messages, by nourishing its needs, by feeding it with the people, the places, the peace, the desires and the solitude it yearns for, your soul will be the healer within you. It will show you, it will guide you and lead you in profound and powerful ways, how to not only heal your mind and body but how to be happier than you could have ever imagined.

As you learn to listen to your soul by clearing away limiting beliefs, heeding your emotional guidance system, learning self-love and forgiveness, you allow its messages, its grace, to shine through and become the driver of your day-to-day life. Then, invariably, inevitably, you will discover the great light, the power of the divinity that lies within you. You will see that within you, within each of us, is a great, unlimited source of love, of inspiration, of creation, of joy, of the power to heal.

REFERENCES

Jonathan S. Abramowitz, PhD. "The Psychological Treatment of Obsessive-Compulsive Disorder." Canadian Journal of Psychiatry, 2006; 51: 407–416.

Agency for Healthcare Research and Quality. "Medical Expenditures Panel Survey. 2012." http://meps.ahrq.gov/mepsweb/data_files/publications/st382/stat382.pdf

David Agus MD, with Kristin Loberg. The End of Illness. Free Press, A Division of Simon and Shuster, 2011.

James W. Anderson MD. Science Daily. "Meditation Can Lower Blood Pressure." March 15, 2008. www.sciencedaily.com/releases/2008/03/080314130430.htm

The Anthropic Universe. Science Show, a radio interview, 18 February 2006.

J.A Astin. "Why Patients Use Alternative Medicine: Results of a National Study." Journal of the American Medical Association. 1998 May 20; 279 (19):1548–-53.

Michael J. Balick and Paul Allen Cox. Plants, People and Culture. Scientific American Library, 1996.

Mario Beauregard. The Spiritual Brain: A Neuroscientist's Case for The Existence of the Soul. Harper Collins, New York, 2007, www.harpercollins.com

Herb Benson. Timeless Healing. Simon Schuster, New York, 2009

Herbert Benson, MD, with Marg Stark. Timeless Healing. Schreibner, 1997.

Herbert Benson, MD. The Relaxation Response. pp. 162–-163.

Herbert Benson, MD. Harvard Weekly. 2013.

Biophotons – The Light in Our Cells. Marco Bischof. German publisher: Zweitausendeins, Frankfurt. http://www.zweitausendeins.de/, publication date: March 1995.

Marco Bischof. "Biophotons: The Light in Our Cells." Part IV Illness and Health. German publisher, Zweitausendeins, Frankfurt. March 1995. www.//transpersonal.de/mbischof/english/webookeng.htm.

S. Black, PhD, MPH. "Can Meditation Slow the Aging Process?" www.asa.org/blog/can-meditation-slow-aging-process, 3/4/14.

David Bohm, Wholeness and the Implicate Order, Routledge & Kegan Paul, London, Boston, 1980, p. 48.

Salynn Boyles. "Meditation May Reduce Pain." WebMD News, April 6, 2011.

William Braud. http://www.inclusivepsychology.com/uploads/HumanInterconnectedness.pdf

William Braud and Rosemarie Anderson. Transpersonal Research Methods for the Social Sciences: Honoring Human Experience. Sage Publications, Thousand Oaks, California, 1994.

Steven Brill. "Bitter Pill: Why medical Bills Are Killing Us." Time. February 20, 2013.

Malcolm Brown. "Far Apart, 2 Particles Respond Faster Than Light." New York Times, front page, Tuesday, July 22, 1997.

CERN home.web.cern.ch/about/physics

Thubten Chodron. Taming The Monkey Mind. Heian International, 1999.

Deepak Chopra. Quantum Healing. Bantam Books. June 1990.

Cohen et al. Multiple Personality Disorder from the Inside Out. 2009.

Complementary and Alternative Medicine in the United States. Institute of Medicine US Committee on the Use of Complementary and Alternative Medicine by the American Public. Washington DC National Academies Press, 2005.

Dawson Church. The Genie in Your Genes: Epigenetic Medicine and the New Biology of Intention. Elite Books, Santa Rosa California, 2007

Julie Corliss. Executive Editor. Harvard Health Letter. January 8, 2014. "Mindfulness Meditation May Ease Anxiety, Mental Stress." www. health.harvard.edu/blog/mindfulness-meditation-may-ease-anxiety-mental-stress-2014 10

Larry Dossey, MD. Healing Words. Harper Collins, New York, 1995.

Adam Dreamhealer. "Intention Heals: Truth Is Stranger Than Fiction," in Dan Brown's new novel, The Lost Symbol. Anchor Books, 2009.

Jeffrey A. Dusek, PhD. and Herbert Benson, MD. "Mind-Body Medicine." Minnesota Medicine. May 2009; 92(5): 47–50.

David M. Eisenberg et al. "Trends in Alternative Medicine Use in the United States." Journal of the American Medical Association. 1998 Nov 11;280 (18) : 1569–-75.

David Goldhill. "How American Health Care Killed My Father." The Atlantic. September 1, 2009.

Daniel Goleman. "Agreeableness vs Anger." New York Times Archives. April 16, 1989.

Malcolm Gladwell. Outliers: The Story of Success. Little Brown and Company. 2008

Daniel Goleman. "The Experience of Touch." NYT, Archives, February 2, 1988.

www.goodreads.com/author/quotes/35156.deanornish

Amit Goswami, Richard E. Reed, and Maggie Goswami: The Self-Aware Universe: How Consciousness Creates the Material World. Jeremy Tarcher/Putnam Books, New York, 1993.

Bruce Grierson. "What if Age Is Nothing but a Mind-Set?" New York Times Magazine, October 22, 2014.

Stephen S. Hall. "Revolution Postponed: Why the Genome Project Has Been Disappointing." Scientific American, October, 2010, Nature Publishing Group, New York.

David R. Hamilton, PhD. DrDavidHamilton.com, 170

Stephen Hawkins. A Brief History of Time. Random House Publising Group. 1998, 193.

Louise Hay. "My Story," in The Light Connection. December 2006.

David Hawkins. Power vs Force. Hay House, Carlsbad, California, 36–54.

Dan Hurley. "Breathing in vs. Spacing Out." NYT. January 14, 2014.

David R. Hamilton. "Further New Evidence for the Benefits of Meditation." Hay House, United Kingdom. www.hayhouse.co.uk/david-hamilton-newsletter-march2011

Valerie V. Hunt, PhD. Infinite Mind: The Science of Human Vibrations of Consciousness. Malibu Publishing Company, 1996.

In Light Wellness Systems, New Mexico

Institute of Heart Math. "Articles of the Heart." Heartmath.org

T. L. Jacobs et al. "Intensive Meditation Training, Immune Cell Telomerase Activity, and Psychological Mediators." Psychoneuroendocrinology. 2011 Jun; 36(5):664–81. doi: 10.1016/j.psyneuen.2010.09.010. Epub 2010 Oct 29

C. G. Jung, The Archetypes and the Collective Unconscious, 1996, London, 43.

Matt Kahn. "Anchoring a New Consciousness." YouTube.com.

Reed Karaim. Light That Can Cure You. USA Weekend. February 2–4, 2007.

www.KevinMD.com/blog/2012/patients-flock-alternative-medicine/providers.html

www.kevinmd.com/blog/2014/05/10-minutes-doctor.html

Thomas Kuhn. The Structure of Scientific Revolutions. University of Chicago Press, 1962.

Jeffrey Kluger. "Get Your Head in the Game." Time. February 23–March 2, 2015, 84.

JoEllen Koerner. Mother, Heal My Self: An Intergenerational Healing Journey Between Two Worlds. April 15, 2003.

Erwin Laszlo, PhD. "Science and the Akashic Field." Inner Traditions. Rochester, Vermont, 2007, 46–47.

Lester Levinson. Stillness Speaks. The Keys to Ultimate Freedom. Meditation with Quest. [PDF online].

Lester Levinson. No Attachments, No Aversions.

www.lifescientists.de/publication/pub2002-05.htm), edited for enhanced readability by Healing Cancer Naturally.

Bruce Lipton. The Biology of Belief. Hay House, www.hayhouse.com. June 2013.

www.Livescience.com/28808-spooky-quantum-entanglement-loophole-closed.html

Bernard Lown, MD. "Power to the People: Patient in Command." Blog Essay 32, November 3, 2012.

Jacques Lusseyran. And There Was Light. Parabola Books, July 1987.

Nisargadat Maharaj. I Am That. The Acorn Press, 1988.

Marty Makary, MD. Unaccountable: What Hospitals Won't Tell You and How Transparency Can Revolutionize Heallthcare. Marty Mackary, MD, 2012.

Stephen Hawley Martin. How to Master Life: The Science Behind the Secret. Oaklea Press, March 2007.

Sue McGreevey. "Mind-Body Genomics." Harvard Medical School News. May 1, 2013 (study published in the open access journal PLOS ONE, May 1, 2013).

Edgar Mitchell lecture. "The Quantum Hologram and ESP." March 29, 2005. Disclose. TV.

YouTube.com. "The Medicine-Less Hospital."

Arvind Modawal. MD, MPH. "Prescription Medication in the Elderly." NetWellness.org

Phillip Moffitt. Dancing With Life. Stage Three: Transparency. Dharmatown.org

Richard Moss, MD. The Black Butterfly: an Invitation to Radical Aliveness. 1986, Celestial Arts, Berkeley, California, p. 1.

Carolyn M. Myss, PhD. Anatomy of the Spirit. Three Rivers Press, 1996.

Carolyn Myss, PhD, and Norman Shealy, MD, PhD. The Creation of Health. Three Rivers, Random House, 1997, 154–192. John McClellan and Mary Clare King. "Genetic Heterogeneity in Human Disease." Cell. April 2010.

National Center for Complementary and Integrative Health. Nationwide survey reveals widespread use of mind and body practices, press release, February, 10, 2015.

Jill Neimark. "Healing with Light." Spirituality and Health. January–February 2010.

David E. Newman-Toker, MD, PhD. "BMJ Quality and Safety." Johns Hopkins Study of Diagnostic Error in Medicine. October 2013. vol. 22, Suppl. 2.

Maj-Britt Niemi. "Placebo Effect: A Cure in the Mind." Scientific American. February/March, 2009.

Dean Ornish. "Changing Lifestyle Changes Gene Expression." www.edge.org/conversation/changing lifestyle-changes-gene-expression.

Dean Ornish. "Reversing Heart Disease: A Formula." Annuals of Internal Medicine. 2003.

Paul Pearsall. The Heart's Code. Random House, New York, 1998.

Candace Pert, PhD. Molecules of Emotion. Touchstone, New York, 1997, 187.

Candace Pert. "Neuropeptides and Their Receptors. A Psychosomatic Network." Journal of Immunology. 1985, 135:820--826.

Max Planck. "Das wesen der Materie. [The Nature of Matter]." Speech in Florence, Italy, (1944,) (from archive zer Geschichte der Max Planck Gesellschaft, Abt. Va., Rep. 11 Planck, Nr. 1797).

Karl Pribam, MD. The Form Within: My Point of View. Prospecta Press, Westport, Connecticut, 2013.

www.physicsclassroom.com

Fritz Popp. "Living Light: Biophotons and the Human Body. Part 1." Supreme Master Television Interview with Fritz Popp

Roni Caryn Rabin. "Burnt Out Primary Care Docs Are Voting with Their Feet." Kaiser Health News, April 2014. Kaiserhealthnews.org

Ramachandran's TED Talk on YouTube.com

Paul Reber. "What Is the Memory Capacity of the Human Brain?" Mind and Brain. Scientific American. May/June 2010. www.scientificamerican.com

Bret R. Rutherford, MD, and Steven P. Roose, MD. A Model of Placebo Response. American Journal of Psychiatry. July 1, 2013; 170(7): 723–733.

Agnes Sanford. The Healing Light. First Ballantine Books, February 1991

John Sarno. Healing Back Pain: The Mind-Body Connection. Warner Books, A Time Warner Company, New York. 1999.

The Secret Life of Plants. Peter Tompkins and Christopher Bird. Harper & Row, New York, 1973, 3.

Semmelweis Society International. Semmelweis.org/

David Servan-Schreiber. Anticancer: A New Way of Life. Penguin Group, 2009, pp. 156–159.

Mona Lisa Shultz, MD, PhD. Awakening Intuition. Three Rivers Press, New York, 1998.

The Statistics Portal. Statista.com

Ester Sternberg, MD, interview "The Science of Healing Places." On Being with Krista Tippet. Onbeing.org/program/ the-science-of-healing-places/4856

Survey Sampling and The Research Intelligence Group. "Patients Around The World Are Not Happy with Their Physicians, Feeling Disrespected, Hurried Through Visits, and Shut out of Treatment Decisions."

Leonard Susskind, theoretical physicist at Stanford. "The Fabric of the Cosmos," with Brian Greene. NOVA.

Michael Talbot, The Holographic Universe, HarperCollins, New York, 1991, p. 271.

Sabrina Tavernise. Married Couples are No Longer a Majority, Census Finds. New York Times. May 26, 2011., New York, 1997, p. xiv.

Kelly Turner, PhD, Spontaneous Remission of Cancer: Theories from Healers, Physicians and Cancer Survivors. PhD dissertation. 2010.

http://www.prnewswire.com/news-releases/patients-around-the-world-are-not-happy-with-their-physicians-feeling-disrespected-hurried-through-visits-and-shut-out-of-treatment-decisions-125559353.html

Harold Varmus, M.D. "Ten Years On—The Human Genome and Medicine." NEJM 362; 21. May 27, 2010.

Nicholas Wade. "Disease Cause is Pinpointed with Genome." New York Times. Research. March 10, 2010. Ken Wilbur, editor. Quantum Questions: Mystical Writings of the World's Great Physicists,, 2001.

The Editors of Ode. "The Amazing Promises of the Zero Point Field." Ode Publishing Company, November, 2003, 45.

W. A. Tiller. Science and Human Transformation: Subtle Energies, Intentionality and Consciousness. Pavior Publishing, 1997.

Krista Tippett. "On Being. Ester Sternberg interview." The Science of Healing Places. www.onbeing.org/the-science-of-healing-places/4856

Eckhart Tolle. The Power of Now. New World Library. August 19th, 2004.

www.transpersonal.de/mbischof/englisch/webbookeng.htm

Jonathan Vespa, Jamie M. Lewis, and Rose M. Kreider. America's Families and Living Arrangements: 2012. Population Characteristics. https://www.census.gov/prod/2013pubs/p20-570.pdf

John A. Wheeler. "Information, Physics, Quantum: The Search for Links," in W. Zurek, Complexity, Entropy, and the Physics of Information, 1990, Redwood City, California: Addison-Wesley.

Paramahansa Yogananda. Autobiography of Aa Yogi. Self-Realization Fellowship, Los Angeles, California, 1998.

Gary Zukav. The Seat of the Soul, Simon and Shuster, 1989.

Made in the USA
Columbia, SC
05 October 2017